gateway to the world

B1

Teacher's Book
with Teacher's App

Welcome and Teacher support	
Welcome to *Gateway to the World*	p2
Course components	p4
Inclusion in the classroom	p6
Dave's top teaching tips	p8
Student's Book contents	p10
Teacher's notes	
Unit 1 Happy families	p12
Unit 2 Law and order	p22
Exam success units 1–2 and Collaborative project 1	p32
Unit 3 Plurilingual	p33
Unit 4 Take care!	p43
Exam success units 3–4 and Collaborative project 2	p53
Unit 5 Screen time	p54
Unit 6 Changing climates	p64
Exam success units 5–6 and Collaborative project 3	p74
Unit 7 Get to the top!	p75
Unit 8 Friendly advice	p85
Exam success units 7–8 and Collaborative project 4	p95
Unit 9 Facts about fiction	p96
Unit 10 Computer update	p106
Exam success units 9–10 and Collaborative project 5	p116
Reach higher	p117
Exam success (continuation)	
Units 1–2 and 3–4	p120
Units 5–6 and 7–8	p121
Units 9–10	p122
Audio and video scripts	
Class audio script	p123
Class video script	p139

Tim Foster

macmillan education

WELCOME TO *GATEWAY TO THE WORLD*

Gateway to the World retains many of the elements that have made *Gateway* so popular with teachers and students alike. It combines a balanced approach to grammar, vocabulary and skills with thorough exam preparation. The Student's Book has a clear, logical unit structure, which is easy to use for teachers and engaging for students. And, of course, *Gateway to the World* has been developed and written by best-selling author and teacher, David Spencer, who brings his knowledge and experience from years of teaching teenagers to the course.

Gateway to the World builds on the successful formula of the original course with new content and features, which not only help to motivate students and improve their language-learning potential, but also develop the skills and knowledge that they will need outside of the classroom in an ever more interconnected world.

What makes a great learner?

Great thinkers become great learners. The ability to think in different ways and deal with problems and challenges using a range of skills helps us to learn more effectively and achieve our goals and aspirations. What kinds of skills do your students need to become great thinkers … and great learners?

EMOTIONAL INTELLIGENCE

The ability to identify and manage your own emotions, as well as other people's.

CULTURAL AWARENESS

The ability to recognise and appreciate that there are both similarities and differences between cultures.

CRITICAL THINKING

The ability to think carefully about a subject or idea in a rational and open-minded way.

GLOBAL COMMUNICATION

The ability to interact successfully in the real world with people or through creating or understanding content such as videos or blog posts.

DIGITAL LITERACY

The ability to group together a range of computer-related competencies that enable us to find, evaluate, create and communicate information on digital platforms.

The material in *Gateway to the World* has been specially developed to give your students regular practice of these core great-thinker skills.

In the Student's Book …

Great Learners, Great Thinkers

This unique new section in each unit of the Student's Book combines a variety of beyond-the-classroom features which will help your students develop the skills they will need for life outside of the learning environment. The Great Learners, Great Thinkers pages have been specifically developed to help students improve their thinking skills and their understanding of their own emotional wellbeing. Thematically tied to the content of the unit, each double-page section features a **Visible Thinking Routine**. The routines help students develop alternative thinking strategies through scaffolded, step-by-step activities. Special **Social and Emotional Learning** SEL tasks encourage students to think about their own social and emotional wellbeing by exploring themes such as empathising, listening to others, and keeping an open mind. At the end of the lesson, students consider how well they think they apply the aspect of Social and Emotional Learning to their own lives by grading themselves in the **Learner profile** at the back of the Student's Book.

Documentary videos

Each Great Learners, Great Thinkers section begins with an impactful, engaging, real-world documentary video related to the topic of the lesson, which acts as a springboard to exploring the theme of the section. Each video is graded to the level and has a subtitles option. The videos are further exploited with a range of comprehension tasks.

Real-world content

The Student's Book is full of fascinating real-world content, which will resonate with teenage learners. Topics for texts and activities have been specifically selected with the interests of today's teenagers in mind. In particular, texts on the main Reading and Listening pages are always based on real people, places and events. This real-world content ensures that students are not only learning a language, they are also learning about the world outside the classroom.

Projects and Virtual Classroom Exchange

The Student's Book contains five **Collaborative projects**: one project after every two units which links back thematically to one of two **Culture exchange** activities in the preceding two units. The projects practise a range of skills, such as academic and digital skills, and give students the opportunity to work collaboratively in groups to research and create a project on a cultural topic from their own country. Not only can students present their project to the rest of their class, they can also take part in a **Virtual Classroom Exchange**. This unique feature allows students to connect online with other users of the course around the world, encouraging students to use English for a real communicative purpose in an authentic cultural exchange.

Flipped classroom video

The Flipped classroom refers to students learning new content outside of the classroom and then practising in class with the teacher. This allows the teacher to give more personalised help and attention during the practice stage. It also means students can work at their own pace during the presentation stage. All-new **flipped classroom grammar presentation videos** feature in every unit of *Gateway to the World*. The videos explain grammar using a variety of approaches and contexts. Depending on your students' needs, the videos can be 'flipped' and used before, during or after class for self-study.
There are four different types of flipped classroom video across the Student's Book.

The first features *Gateway to the World* author, David Spencer. He guides us through the grammar point, giving helpful examples and bringing his own unmistakable sense of humour to his explanations.

The second is a vlog presented by teenage '**Grammar Gurus**' Oli and Meg. The Grammar Gurus *love* grammar and, by using examples from their own everyday lives, they explain why, how and when to use it. Each vlog ends with a fun quiz for the whole class.

The third type of flipped classroom video uses engaging animation to present and explore each grammar point – spot the cat in each video!

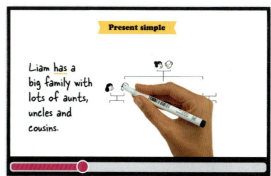

The fourth type of video uses a whiteboard animation approach, presenting each grammar point in a clear and logical way.
The variety of approaches in the flipped classroom videos help make learning grammar engaging and fun for teenage learners.

Exam success

After every two units, the Exam success pages give students further practice of the B1 Preliminary for Schools-style exam tasks they have seen in the preceding two units. As well as revising these task types, the pages also offer useful exam tips so students can maximise their potential in both school and official exams. There is also a full set of exam tips, which offer more in-depth help and exam strategies, in the Student's and Teacher's Resource Centres.

On-the-Go Practice

On-the-Go Practice provides students with gamified practice of the key grammar and vocabulary from the course for use on mobile devices.

In the Workbook ...

Exam trainer

The Exam trainer offers full practice of B1 Preliminary for Schools exam papers, plus a complete breakdown of the different parts of the exam, with information on assessment for each task and handy exam tips.

COURSE COMPONENTS

For students ...

Student's Book

The B1 *Gateway to the World* Student's Book contains ten units with grammar and vocabulary reference and revision in the **Check it** sections at the end of each unit. Exam-style activities appear throughout the Student's Book, with consolidation and practice after every two units on the **Exam success** pages.

Digital Student's Book

The B1 *Gateway to the World* Digital Student's Book offers a content-rich, interactive learning experience for your students. Enhanced Student's Book pages are easy to navigate, and contain embedded audio and video, as well as interactive activities.

Workbook

The Workbook provides consolidation of the core grammar and vocabulary from the Student's Book, with extra reading, listening, speaking and writing practice. **Cumulative review** pages after every two units offer further revision, whilst **Great students' tips** give advice on study and exam techniques.

Digital Workbook

The digital version of the Workbook features fully interactive activities, with audio and automated marking.

On-the-Go Practice

On-the-Go Practice offers fun practice of the vocabulary and grammar from the Student's Book. Students complete interactive activities and collect rewards in Challenge Mode through course-aligned, bite-sized activities, all designed for use on mobile devices.

Student's App

The Student's App gives students access to a selection of digital components, such as the Digital Student's Book, Digital Workbook, Student's Resource Centre and On-the-Go Practice. The app can be downloaded or opened online in a browser.

Student's Resource Centre (SRC)

The Student's Resource Centre contains materials accessible by your students, including **Tips for exam success** and audio for the Workbook.

Reader

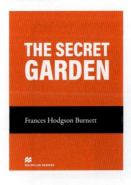

The digital version of the Graded Macmillan Reader, *The Secret Garden*, can be downloaded or viewed online by students.

For teachers ...

A flexible approach to lesson delivery is more important than ever in today's world where every teaching context is different, with its own advantages and challenges. *Gateway to the World* offers simple solutions to challenging classroom conditions by catering to a range of learning environments through its array of digital components. From in-person teaching to hybrid learning, the digital offer in *Gateway to the World* is designed to make preparation and delivery of classes straightforward and stress-free.

Classroom Presentation Kit

The Classroom Present Kit comprises the Digital Student's Book and Workbook with fully interactive activities. Enhanced Student's Book and Workbook pages are easy to navigate, and contain embedded audio, video and answer keys: perfect for setting up and correcting activities in all classroom contexts.

eBook

The eBook for teachers is a digital version of the Teacher's Book, accessible via the Teacher's Resource Centre.

Test language and add an exciting and fast-paced competitive element to class revision with specially-designed *Kahoot!* quizzes.
Go to www.macmillanenglish.com/kahoot

Teacher's Resource Centre (TRC)

The Teacher's Resource Centre offers a wide range of easy-to-access supplementary resource materials and worksheets, including extra grammar and reading practice, end-of-unit, mid-year and end-of-year tests at two levels of challenge, and translated wordlists.

Test Generator

Use the Test Generator to create and tailor tests to the individual needs of your students. You can also download existing end-of-unit, mid-year and end-of-year tests at two levels of challenge.

Teacher's App

The dedicated Teacher's App contains all of the *Gateway to the World* digital components including the Student's Book and Workbook which can be projected onto an interactive whiteboard. Teachers can also access a **Learning Management System** where they can create classes, add students and track their progress. The Teacher's App can be downloaded or opened online in a browser.

Homework Manager

Assign homework and set helpful reminder notifications for students who are using the Digital Student's Book, Digital Workbook or On-the-Go Practice to complete tasks in time for class. The Homework Manager is also a very useful channel of communication with your class when working remotely: you can send links to sharing platforms to all the class at once.

*Kahoot! and the K! logo are trademarks of Kahoot! AS

INCLUSION IN THE CLASSROOM

Diversity and inclusion

How the world is represented in educational materials is important. The content, wording, images and information students see on a regular basis shape their view of the world, which in turn helps to form their beliefs and opinions. This affects their interactions and behaviour towards others both in and outside of the classroom. With this in mind, the content of Gateway to the World has been developed with the aim of portraying a range of diverse groups in order to reflect the world we live in, from an even balance of genders in non-stereotypical scenarios, to a range of people from a variety of cultures and backgrounds.

Photos and artwork

Care has been taken to promote diversity through the visual aspect of the course, with a wide range of people from different backgrounds and cultures in photos and illustrations. Effort has also been made to portray a good balance of genders in images throughout the Student's Book and Workbook.

Content and subject material

There is a strong international feel to the content of the course with human stories featuring protagonists from a variety of backgrounds, nationalities and ethnicities.

Anti-gender stereotyping

Stereotyping and assigning specific roles and characteristics based on gender can have negative consequences for both boys and girls. This can affect educational choices and future career aspirations, as well as self-esteem. These stereotypes can be subconsciously reinforced through the subtle messages communicated in the things young people see and read. In Gateway to the World, students are exposed to positive role models from both sexes in non-stereotypical roles and contexts.

Mixed-language-level classes

All classes contain students who require varying degrees of support, and mixed-language-level – more commonly known as mixed ability – classes present teachers with considerable challenges when preparing and delivering their classes. Aside from the materials we might use to cater to mixed-language-level classes, successful and inclusive mixed-language-level teaching is heavily dependent on teacher attitude and classroom culture. It's important to build a supportive classroom environment in which all learners are valued and treated as individuals. Ways in which this can be achieved might include:

- Having high expectations of all students in the classroom, and consciously and unconsciously communicating to students that you believe in them.
- Involving all students in all lessons, through interactive teaching, graded questioning and tasks, and personalisation of topics.
- Fostering within students a sense of responsibility, importance and trust from the teacher.
- Avoiding labels such as 'weaker' or 'stronger' students, or thinking of ability as a 'fixed', unmovable concept.
- Rotating groups regularly to avoid creating any 'fixed-ability' or 'fixed level' sub-groups within the class.

Below are some possible strategies and techniques that you can try in your mixed-language-level classes to ensure that every student, no matter their language level, gets the most out of the class.

Group dynamics

Begin the whole class together with a lead-in activity to provide a sense of community and a foundation for the levelled tasks that will follow. Lead-in activities preview, present and practise language in a way that lends itself perfectly to whole-class, multi-level instruction. At the end of a lesson, always bring the class back together and assign a whole-class activity.

Group, pair and individual work

- Vary the way students work in the class to address different levels and needs. Organise students to work in pairs, small groups and teams. It is less stressful for students who need more support to work with other classmates because they have more time to think about tasks, and students can help and learn from each other.
- Regardless of the level of a student's English, they all get better results through working collaboratively than they do by working on their own. Pairwork is usually successful in the mixed-language-level classroom because it is easy to control and there is greater student participation. Depending on the task, decide how to organise your students into pairs: students with a similar level can work together at their own pace, or a more confident student can pair with a student who needs more support. The latter option can be useful as the more confident student can help and support the other student in the pair. Remember to rotate pairs regularly so students get a chance to work with different partners.
- Individual work allows for variations in speed and level. By giving a time limit rather than a quantity-of-work limit (e.g. 'Do as much as you can in two minutes.' instead of, 'Do exercise 7.'), students are able to work at their own pace.

How to increase the level of challenge

- Ask students to try to work out the meaning of new words from the context and to elicit grammar rules by looking at the language in context.
- When doing listening comprehension tasks, ask students to summarise what they heard after listening to the audio the first time (as a whole class or in pairs). Encourage students to write their own comprehension questions to ask the class.
- For reading texts, students could write their own comprehension questions to ask the class, select six new words from the reading text to write definitions for and learn, or create their own sentences using new vocabulary from the reading text.
- Indicate where something could be said in a more interesting or more complex way, and set creative and open-ended tasks that can be accessed at and taken to a higher level.

How to increase the level of support

- Give clear instructions, ideally via more than one sense (e.g. spoken and visual), and check students have understood the task before they begin with concept-checking questions.
- Grade your questions in whole-class activities to ensure that all students are able to participate, and praise small successes.
- Simplify gap-fill tasks by introducing optional answers, so students can identify the correct answer rather than having to produce it.
- Be selective in your error correction and praise students for what they have managed to do, regardless of what others have produced.
- Pause the audio regularly to check understanding during listening activities and explain if anything remains unclear. For more difficult texts, provide audio scripts after the first two listenings.

How *Gateway to the World* caters to mixed-language-level classes

The mixed-language-level materials in *Gateway to the World* have been divided into the three categories in the table below so that teachers can clearly identify which materials are intended to cater to individual students' needs, which can be used for whole-class mixed-language-level teaching, and those materials aimed at supporting the teacher with their mixed-language-level teaching.

Personalised support	Whole-class engagement	Teacher resources and development
Differentiated materials or alternative tasks for activities where students will benefit from different levels of challenge and support.	Solutions for ensuring all students are involved and engaged in group work and whole-class teaching.	Simple and practical tips and tools to allow teachers to manage the class with confidence.
Flipped classroom videos give students the chance to 'pre-study' the grammar for the following lesson, allowing them to study at their own pace. **Reach higher** activities in the Student's Book cater to more confident students who are more likely to finish activities in the core units earlier. A **star-rating system** in the Workbook enables teachers to set suitable tasks according to the language level of their individual students. **Unit, mid- and end-of-year progress tests** offer grammar, vocabulary and skills revision at two levels. **Extra grammar practice** worksheets provide grammar revision at two levels of difficulty. The **Test Generator** allows teachers to custom-build their own tests according to their students' needs.	**Collaborative projects** offer the opportunity for students to work at their own pace within mixed-language-level groups. **Great Learners, Great Thinkers** pages move away from linguistic and comprehension skills practice to focus on elements such as Social and Emotional Learning, and creativity and critical thinking. This puts an emphasis on non-linguistic knowledge and personalisation. **Documentary videos** can be watched with the whole class and have a subtitles option for extra support for students who need more support. **Peer review, pair and group work** tasks appear throughout the Student's Book so students can work together in mixed-language-level or same-level pairs and groups.	**Mixed-ability teaching tips** appear throughout the Teacher's notes in the Teacher's Book, allowing teachers to easily adapt certain activities for their mixed-language-level classes. **Professional development videos** offer teachers helpful teaching tips including suggestions and ideas for mixed-language-level classes. **Extra activities** in the Teacher's Book offer suggestions for how teachers can extend or increase or lower the level of challenge of activities in the Student's Book. **Fast finisher** activities in the Teacher's Book provide extra activities teachers can use to occupy fast-finishing students while students who need more support complete the main activity.

Global citizenship and Sustainable Development Goals

Global citizenship refers to the development of the knowledge, attitudes and skills needed to be globally competent and to have a positive impact on the world in which we live. Understanding different cultures, identities and perspectives, as well as themes of global importance such as the environment, resources, health and well-being underpins the concept of global citizenship. The Sustainable Development Goals are a set of 17 interlinked objectives established to achieve a better and more sustainable future for everyone on the planet. *Gateway to the World* promotes global citizenship and the Sustainable Development Goals. The content of the Student's Book has been mapped to the Sustainable Development Goals and the innovative Macmillan Global Citizenship Education Framework. The course promotes and encourages many of the ideals of the Sustainable Development Goals, with a particular focus on good health and wellbeing, gender equality, sustainable cities and communities, and climate change.

DAVE'S TOP TEACHING TIPS

Applying certain key strategies can help you to establish good learning practices to get the most out of the time you spend with your students so that they can maximise their potential as effective language learners. The following teaching tips can be used on a regular basis with your students to improve key areas such as classroom management, lesson planning and student training.

Dave

Using English in class

At the beginning of the school year, students may not feel very confident about using English in class. Be a good model for your students by regularly making simple and natural comments in English, e.g. *Really? That's a good idea, Luke. What do you think, Nora?* Use a small range of comments and use them consistently. At first, you can use gestures alongside the comments (e.g. thumbs up when you are saying something positive) to reinforce the idea of what you are saying. In time, students will start to imitate you and you can establish an English-only environment.

It is also useful to teach expressions that students can use for pair and group work. Put these expressions on posters in the classroom, or save them somewhere so you can use them at relevant times and refer to them to remind students to always use English in the class.

Finally, teach a few expressions that students can use to ask for meaning, pronunciation, spelling, repetition or clarification: *Could you say that again, please? Can you speak more slowly, please? How do you say ... in English? How do you pronounce/say this word? What does ... mean? How do you spell ...?*

Checking answers

Using different ways to check answers makes the feedback stage more fun and changes the pace of the lesson. Some ideas include:

- Give the students an answer key or put the answer key on the wall or the board. Students can work in pairs: one student runs to the wall to check the answer and goes back to tell their partner.
- Put students in pairs and give half of the answers to one student and half of the answers to the other student. They share their information like an information gap activity.
- One student has the answer key and plays the teacher.
- Get students to write their answers on the board.
- Get one student to read out his/her answers – the rest of the class see if they have the same.
- Students nominate each other to say the answer.
- Do it as a competition and award points for correct answers.

Projects and presentations

Doing projects in class can be fun and provide a welcome break from classroom routine. Collaborative projects mean students of different levels work together and this can improve teamwork. The Student's Book contains five Collaborative projects which you can use to set up a project culminating in a poster, presentation, video message or information leaflet.

You could organise the projects into four stages with your students:
1. Students discuss how they will present their project and the resources they will need.
2. Students brainstorm ideas and pool their knowledge.
3. Students choose from their ideas and say who will write about what. Each student then researches information and images for their contribution.
4. They then organise their different texts and images, and check and correct their writing.

If students present their projects in class, set a time limit for each presentation of around five minutes. Ask other students in the class to give feedback at the end of each presentation.

Teaching online

In your first class take some time to familiarise your students with whatever platform you are using and any relevant tools that they will be required to use during the lesson. Highlight the chat box, the microphone and the mute button and any other tools they will need. Establish rules for students' participation and explain how you expect them to interact with you and the other students. Ask students to keep their microphones on mute while they are not speaking and encourage them to use the chat box if they have any questions or queries during the lesson. At the beginning of each lesson, set objectives using the chat box or presentation slides so students know what they will be doing during the session. Try to be lively and animated in your tone of voice and use gestures. Keep the class's attention by nominating students at regular intervals or ensuring whole-class participation by asking them to respond regularly using the chat feature.

Visible Thinking Routines

Visible Thinking Routines are scaffolded techniques for approaching analysis and problem solving. They can be useful because they help to direct the way students think and can guide discussions and analysis in the classroom. Each routine highlights a different approach to thinking and they can be divided into three categories: 'Introducing and exploring ideas', 'Synthesising and exploring ideas', and 'Routines for digging deeper'. Examples of the thinking routines can be found on the Great Learners, Great Thinkers pages in the Student's Book. The routines, though, can be adapted to a range of tasks in which students are practising discussion, critical thinking or problem solving. Try to introduce them into your lessons, so they become a regular part of your class. The more students use them, the better they will become at incorporating the routines into their thinking. Make sure that the particular routine fits with the type of task students are doing, for example, 'Think, Question, Explore' on page 74 of the Student's Book works well with pre-reading or listening tasks, and 'Headlines' on page 37 lends itself to the comprehension of texts. Encourage students to use their imagination and think creatively when practising the routines, this will help them to generate more expansive and interesting answers and solutions. For longer, more complex routines with various stages, go through each stage, giving an example so students gain a clearer idea of what's expected of them. Have a feedback session afterwards so students can reflect on how well they did the routines and whether they were helpful in carrying out the tasks.

Error correction

Before pointing out errors, encourage students to recognise and correct their own mistakes. You can do this by asking a student to repeat what they have said, or by echoing what the student said and placing emphasis on the error. You can also reformulate the sentence and repeat it correctly. Students could create an 'Errors' list in their notebooks to remind themselves of the errors they should try to avoid. Unlike accuracy activities, fluency-based activities require less error correction. Correcting individual errors on the spot may discourage students and make them feel inhibited, so it is preferable for correction to take place at the end of the activity. Be on hand during the activity to help with any language difficulties and note down both good use of language and problem areas. Go through the errors at the end of the activity, without mentioning who made each one. Praise students who made good use of language.

Flipped classroom

The flipped classroom can be a useful tool for making students responsible for their own learning and avoiding lengthy grammar explanations in class. The flipped classroom videos in *Gateway to the World* can be used in a variety of ways. Ask students to watch the videos for homework in preparation for the next lesson. Make it clear to students *why* they are watching the video for homework and point out the benefits of the flipped classroom approach: they can watch the video in their own time and at their own pace and as many times as they like, and there will be more time in class for practice. Encourage them to make a note of any queries they have while watching the videos and to bring them to the class. At the beginning of the class, address any questions students have and elicit answers in open class. Check students have a good understanding of the grammar and continue on to practice of the language point. If students seem to be struggling with the concept of the grammar, go through the grammar explanation in the Check it section in the Student's Book before students do the practice activities. Alternatively, show the flipped classroom video again in class, stopping at intervals to check understanding or to give further examples. The video could also be used solely as a presentation tool in class. Students watch the video and do the task as a whole class before asking any questions. Students can also be given the video as homework after the class for revision.

Video in class

Video can be a great way to change the focus of a class, but try to make it an integral part of a lesson, rather than a one-off treat, as it works best when it forms part of a sequence of activities. Short video clips of between three to five minutes are advisable: longer excerpts can take up too much class time and students' attention may start to wander. Set pre-watching tasks so students have a reason to watch. Pause the video at regular intervals to ask questions or elicit clarifications. Give students activities to do whilst watching, such as note taking or comprehension questions. They should be questions that can be quickly and easily answered so students can write answers without missing what's on screen. You can also pause the video at intervals and ask students to predict what will happen or what someone will say next. Alternatively, play the clip without the sound and ask students to imagine what is happening or being said. Give students post watching tasks, such as questions, or elicit a discussion based on the content of the video.

Fast finishers

If you have students who always finish before everyone else, look at their answers and tell them how many they have got wrong, but not which ones. This is a good way to keep a fast finisher busy for a little while longer while the others catch up. It's also a good way to get students to look at their answers again, which is a useful exam strategy. You can also make use of the Reach higher tasks in the Student's Book to keep fast finishers occupied while the rest of the class finishes the main class activity.

Contents

		Vocabulary	Grammar	Reading	Listening
1	**Happy families** p6	Ages and stages of life The family Words connected with the family Noun suffixes -ment, -ion, -ence	1 Present simple and present continuous, State and action verbs 2 Articles **Culture exchange:** Family dinners	Sharing images on social media A newspaper article	Arguments between teenagers and parents A radio programme
2	**Law and order** p18	Crimes Detective work Phrasal verbs connected with investigating and finding	1 Past simple 2 Past continuous Used to	Surprising true crimes An online article	An actor involved in a crime A conversation
3	**Plurilingual** p32	Languages, countries and nationalities Learning languages Negative prefixes un-, in-, im-, ir-, il-	1 Countable and uncountable nouns Quantifiers 2 Defining and non-defining relative clauses **Culture exchange:** International English	English: The language that never sleeps A newspaper article	Toki Pona: an artificial language A podcast
4	**Take care!** p44	Parts of the body Health problems Compound nouns connected with health and healthcare	1 Present perfect with ever, never, for, since 2 Present perfect with just, yet, already	Is technology bad for your health? A magazine article	BASE jumping An interview
5	**Screen time** p58	TV programmes and series Words connected with TV and online video Adjectives describing TV programmes Adjectives ending in -ing and -ed	1 Comparatives and superlatives 2 so and such, too and (not) enough **Culture exchange:** TV in the UK	Reality TV An online blog	Binge-watching A radio programme
6	**Changing climates** p70	Geographical features The environment Different uses of get	1 will, be going to, and present continuous for future will, may, might 2 Zero conditional First conditional	Understanding climate change An article	Plogging A podcast interview
7	**Get to the top!** p84	Jobs and words connected with work Personal qualities Compound adjectives	1 Modal verbs of obligation, prohibition and advice 2 Second conditional, unless	Alan Geaam, chef and Ami Vitale, photographer A magazine article	Unusual jobs A conversation
8	**Friendly advice** p96	Feelings Friendships Noun suffixes -ness, -ship, -dom **Culture exchange:** Positive messages	1 Past perfect 2 Gerunds and infinitives	My best friend is a robot An information text	Friendship A conversation
9	**Facts about fiction** p110	Things we read Genres Book reviews Phrasal verbs connected with reading and writing	1 Reported speech – statements 2 Reported speech – questions **Culture exchange:** Three great British writers	Books on the move An online article	Using a pen name A literature podcast
10	**Computer update** p122	Computers and accessories Using a computer and the Internet Collocations with email and document	1 The passive – present simple 2 The passive – other tenses have something done **Culture exchange:** The Science Museum, London	Switching off the Internet An information text	The Museum Failure A podcast

Reach higher p136   Writing checklist p141   Learner profile p142   Exam success p144

Speaking	Writing	GREAT LEARNERS GREAT THINKERS	Exam success / Collaborative projects
Asking for personal information A role-play	**Introducing yourself** An informal email 1	**Attitudes to the young and old** ▶ Video: How does it feel to be old? *SEL: Keeping an open mind * Social and Emotional Learning	**Exam success 1–2** Reading: 4-option multiple choice p30 Listening: Gap fill p144 Speaking: Questions p144 Writing: An article p144
Apologising A dialogue Culture exchange: Saying sorry	**Helping someone in an unusual situation** A blog post	**Right and wrong actions** ▶ Video: Hacked! SEL: Being considerate	**Collaborative project 1** Family life in your country p31 Virtual Classroom Exchange
Asking for information A role-play	**Language learning experiences** An article 1	**Non-verbal communication** ▶ Video: Animal communication SEL: Having confident body language	**Exam success 3–4** Reading: Matching p56 Reading: 4-option multiple choice cloze p145 Speaking: Extended turn p145 Writing: An email p145
Describing photos Describing photos and giving feedback	**Replying to an email from a friend** An informal email 2 Culture exchange: Using abbreviations	**Your health, your responsibility** ▶ Video: Allergies all around us SEL: Looking after yourself	**Collaborative project 2** International words p57 Virtual Classroom Exchange
Negotiating A discussion	**Edutainment** An article 2	**The influence of TV and online video** ▶ Video: The popularity of online video SEL: Questioning your attitudes	**Exam success 5–6** Listening: 3-option multiple choice p82 Speaking: Discussion p82 Reading: Open cloze p146 Writing: An article p146
Making arrangements A role-play	**Spending time outdoors** An opinion essay Culture exchange: Kids and outdoor activities	**Plastic and the environment** ▶ Video: The plastic sea SEL: Being curious	**Collaborative project 3** TV and online video in your country p83 Virtual Classroom Exchange
Giving detailed personal information An interview	**Applying for a summer job** A job application Culture exchange: Jobs for American teenagers	**Attitudes to work** ▶ Video: Working in the great outdoors SEL: Listening to others	**Exam success 7–8** Reading: 3-option multiple choice p108 Listening: 3-option multiple choice p108 Speaking: General conversation p147 Writing: An email p147
Reporting a past event Talking about a past event	**Giving advice** An email of advice	**Making friends** ▶ Video: Buddy Benches SEL: Empathising	**Collaborative project 4** Jobs for teenagers in your country p109 Virtual Classroom Exchange
A presentation A book review	**Writing from a given first sentence** A story	**Books and their covers** ▶ Video: Books ... or art objects? SEL: Thinking creatively	**Exam success 9–10** Reading: Gapped text p134 Reading: Open cloze p148 Speaking: Extended turn p148 Listening: Gap fill p148
Comparing and contrasting photos Describing photos and talking about similarities and differences	**Messaging a friend** Messaging	**Human–computer interaction** ▶ Video: Can computers understand or display feelings? SEL: Justifying your opinion	**Collaborative project 5** A famous writer from your country p135 Virtual Classroom Exchange

Communication activities p149   Irregular verbs p151

1 HAPPY FAMILIES

Vocabulary in context p6
Using a range of lexis to talk about ages and stages of life and the family

> **Warmer**
> Ask what ideas and themes connected to the family students think they might study in this unit.
> Elicit ideas from around the class and write vocabulary that students suggest on the board.

1 SPEAKING 01
- There is an audio recording of every vocabulary set in the Student's Book. If you wish, play it before or after the related exercises, and ask students to listen and repeat each word/phrase.
- Check students understand the meaning of *stage*.
- After checking answers, elicit the spelling and drill the pronunciation of the irregular plurals: *child* /tʃaɪld/ – *children* /ˈtʃɪldrən/; *man* /mæn/ – *men* /men/; *woman* /ˈwʊmən/ – *women* /ˈwɪmɪn/.
- Follow up by asking: *Which stage of life is exact not approximate? Why?* (teenager, 13 to 19 years old, because these are the only numbers which end in '-teen')

> **Possible answers**
> 2 toddler, 2 to 3 years old   3 child, 4 to 12 years old
> 4 teenager, 13 to 19 years old   5 young adult, 20 to 39 years old
> 6 middle-aged (man/woman), 40 to 64 years old   7 senior citizen, 65+ years old

2 02
- After checking answers, if you feel your students need more support with the meaning of the vocabulary, draw your own family tree on the board (inventing family members if necessary), and briefly talk your students through who is who, contextualising vocabulary as appropriate.

> **Answers**
> **Male:** brother-in-law, father-in-law, grandfather, grandson, great-grandfather, husband, nephew, son, son-in-law, stepfather, uncle
> **Female:** aunt, sister-in-law, daughter, mother-in-law, grandmother, granddaughter, great-grandmother, niece, daughter-in-law, stepmother, wife
> **Male or female:** cousin, grandchild, grandparent

3a Before students do the task, point out that they need to change the form of some items. For less confident classes, clarify that this means they need to use plurals.

Culture notes
Chrissy Teigen (1985–) was born in Utah, US. Alongside her modelling career, she has found great success publishing recipe books; launching her own recipes website, *Cravings by Chrissy Teigen*; and selling a range of kitchenware.
John Legend (1978–) was born in Ohio, US. He started his professional music career playing nightclubs in New York where he developed his personal style, a mix of rhythm and blues and soul. He is one of only a few people to win the EGOT, all four major awards in the US: the Emmy, the Grammy, the Oscar and the Tony.

3b 03
- After checking answers, highlight the unusual plural, *brothers-in-law*, which takes the plural 's' in the middle rather than at the end. Ask students to look at the box in exercise 2 and guess which other words form the plural in the same way (*sisters-in-law*, *fathers-in-law/mothers-in-law*, *sons-in-law/daughters-in-law*).

> **Answers**
> a husband   b daughter   c son   d aunt   e uncles
> f sister-in-law   g brothers-in-law

3c SPEAKING
- Before students do the task, make clear that the definitions can be very simple, e.g. *My aunt and uncle's children are my ... My brother's daughter is my ...*
- Tell students to cross out the words in exercise 2 that they used in exercise 3a and to concentrate on giving definitions for all the others. Make clear that they can use the crossed-out words in their definitions, but they don't need to define these.

4 04
- Be sensitive when addressing the area of family, and make sure you do not subconsciously label some types of family as 'normal', e.g. husband and wife with two or three children. Your students may come from a wide range of backgrounds, including *divorced* parents, *one-parent* families and unmarried *partners*.

> **Answers**
> 1 single, divorced   2 only child   3 partner   4 One-parent
> 5 immediate, extended   6 twin   7 relative

Use it ... don't lose it!

5 SPEAKING
- Extend to a class discussion by asking: *How important is family in your country? How important is family to you? Which is more important to you, family or friends?* and allowing students to share their opinions with the class. Encourage turn-taking and make sure students listen to each other and agree or disagree using suitable phrases.

+ Extra activity
Ask students to draw their family tree and write a short paragraph underneath explaining how they are related to each person, e.g. *Sara is my mother's sister so she's my aunt.*

Homework Workbook page 4

HAPPY FAMILIES 1

Reading p7
Reading for gist and detail

> **Warmer**
> Write *social media* on the board. Introduce the topic and establish the link to the unit theme by discussing the following questions: *Which social networks do you use regularly? Which social networks do your parents use regularly? How can social media be useful for families?*

2 Before students do the task, make clear that they do not need to understand every word. They only need to read for gist and will read again for more detail in the next exercise.

> **Answers**
> Title 2 is the most appropriate. The article suggests that it is acceptable and legal for parents to post photos of children online but only if they check with their children first.

3
- The reading texts are recorded so students can listen to them as they read. This recorded material provides exposure to correct pronunciation, stress, and sentence rhythm. With less confident classes, use the audio to help support students as they read the text. With more confident classes, use the audio to check answers to comprehension questions, asking students to raise their hands when they hear the part with the answer.
- The best approach to this type of exam task is for students to first read the text quickly to get a general understanding, as they did in exercise 2.
- Students should then read all the answers carefully and note how the options are different. They should then find the section of the text where they think each answer comes and read it again in more detail.
- ✓ **Exam tip** To answer the question in the Exam tip box, students should eliminate answers which they know are not correct and then make a choice from the options remaining.
- When they finish, students should check they have an answer for each question. Point out that students should never leave answers blank in an exam.
- Pre-teach any words students may have problems with, not including the underlined words, e.g. *post (put writing or images online where other people can see them), phenomenon (an event or situation that we can see happens or exists)* and *force (make someone do something that they don't want to do).*

> **Answers**
> 1 a **incorrect** – There is no mention of the teenager being angry.
>   b **correct** – The parents of both the toddler and the teenager post videos of them online without asking their permission.
>   c **incorrect** – The toddler and the teenager are not doing anything wrong; it's what their parents are doing that people could consider wrong.
> 2 a **incorrect** – Parents may share *all sorts of photos*, not just those of their children doing bad things.
>   b **incorrect** – Parents may share *by accident*.
>   c **correct** – Some parents *don't check their privacy settings*.
> 3 a **correct** – Parents pay fines or can go to prison for a year if they share photos without their children's permission.
>   b **incorrect** – It's obviously possible for parents to post photos or there would be no fines.
>   c **incorrect** – The fines are *of up to €45,000*.
> 4 a **incorrect** – The last paragraph focuses on the solution rather than the problem.
>   b **correct** – *Let* them *say what they are happy to share, and who with*.
>   c **incorrect** – The last paragraph stresses the importance of communication.

Fast finishers »
Ask students to look at the text again and see how many words from the Vocabulary in context section they can find.

4 When checking answers, make sure students understand that in English *sensible* is not connected with emotions. If necessary, elicit or teach the word *sensitive (becomes angry or upset easily).*

> **Answers**
> *adolescents* – boys/girls who are becoming adults
> *sorts* – types
> *naughty* – badly-behaved
> *far away* – a long distance from here
> *privacy settings* – where you control what other people can see online
> *by accident* – not planned
> *fine* – money you have to pay for breaking the law
> *sensible* – reasonable

5 🧠 **Critical thinkers**
- Before students do the task, remind them that the objective is to justify their opinion and give suitable examples.

> **Possible answers**
> Speaking personally, I believe that 'sharenting' is a bad thing. My parents posted a lot of photos and videos of me when I was little. My grandparents really liked it because they lived far away and didn't see me very often, so they could see me grow up. But my parents didn't check their privacy settings. Years later, the day before I finished primary school, someone at my school found the photos and videos and shared them with everyone in my class. It was really embarrassing.

▶ **Flipped classroom**
You may want to ask students to watch the Flipped classroom video for Unit 1 as homework, in preparation for the grammar lesson.

🏠 Homework › Workbook page 5

1 HAPPY FAMILIES

Grammar in context 1 p8
Using the present simple and the present continuous; using state and action verbs

Warmer
Write the following sentences on the board:
1 We study English on _____ , _____ and _____ .*
2 We're studying English _____ _____ _____ .
Ask students to guess what the missing words are (*1 Mondays, Wednesdays, Fridays*; 2 at the moment*). Then circle the two verb forms, elicit the names of the tenses and explain that students are going to look at these in more detail.
*Change the days here to match your timetable or use *every day*.

1a If you didn't set the Flipped classroom video for homework, watch the video in class before working through the activities.

> **Answers**
> a present continuous b present simple c present simple

1b **Answers**
1 c 2 b 3 a

1c **Answers**
Present simple Negative: doesn't study; Question form: Does, study
Present continuous Affirmative: 's/is studying; Negative: isn't/is not studying; Question form: Is, studying

2a **Answers**
at the moment = present continuous; *usually* = present simple; *right now* = present continuous; *normally* = present simple

2b With less confident classes, work through the questions together one at a time, e.g. look at item 2 and ask: What tense do you need to use? (present continuous, as confirmed in exercise 2a); Do you need to include the words in bold in the question? (yes); What is shopping – an action, a place, a time, a quantity? (an action); What question word do we need for an action? (what); Do you need to include the underlined words in the question? (no); then give students time to write the question and check it with them before moving on to the next item.

> **Answers**
> 2 What are your grandparents doing at the moment?
> 3 Where do your cousins live?
> 4 Where does/do your family usually go in the summer holidays?
> 5 Is your best friend studying English right now?
> 6 How many languages does your dad speak?
> 7 Do you normally study on Friday evenings?

2c SPEAKING
• Before students do the task, tell them that they are free to say as much as they want in answer to the questions. However, if they are less confident, they can give simple answers using the sentences in exercise 2a, changing the information as necessary.

Fast finishers
Ask students to continue interviewing their partner by slightly varying the questions in exercise 2b, e.g. *What do you do on Sunday mornings?*, *What are your parents doing at the moment?*, *Where does your best friend live?*

3a Point out that the sentences are based on sentences from the reading on page 7.

3b Check students understand the meaning of *state*.

> **Answers**
> 1 1 to 3 describe states/situations; 4 describes an action.
> 2 yes (think)
> 3 present simple

3c Suggest students try using their instinct for what 'sounds right' by making sentences with some of the verbs in both the simple and continuous form, e.g. *I love video games. I'm loving video games. I believe you. I'm believing you.* If students establish that these verbs are generally not used in the present continuous, they should be able to work out that they are state verbs.

> **Answers**
> They usually describe states/situations.

Language notes
A small number of common verbs can be used as both state verbs and action verbs. For example, in exercise 3a, sentence 3 uses *think* to mean *have an opinion* (state), while sentence 4 uses it to describe *a mental process* (action).
Other common verbs that can describe actions or states include:
be: *I'm being silly.* (action) *I'm French.* (state)
have: *He's having a shower.* (action) *He has two sisters.* (state)
see: *I'm seeing Tom tomorrow.* (action) *I see what you mean.* (state)

4 Follow up by discussing the questions within the text as a class: *What do you think life is like as the son or daughter of a celebrity? Is it possible that some famous parents care about money but not about their children's privacy?*

> **Answers**
> a hate b post c do you think d want e are playing f know
> g are watching h understand i need j sell k believe l care

 Homework Workbook page 6

14

HAPPY FAMILIES 1

5 When checking answers, check the spelling of the -ing forms.
- Follow up by asking: *What things stop you studying at home? What do you do to avoid them?*

> **Answers**
> b 'm/am doing c are, studying d come e visit f make
> g know h 's/is i 's/is crying j think k 're/are taking
> l don't believe

Use it ... don't lose it!

6 SPEAKING
- Point out that the verb form students hear in the question is probably the one they will need to use first in their answer, e.g. *What are your parents doing at the moment? They're both working.* However, if students then give more information, they may need to use other verb forms to do this, e.g. *My mum works in an office, but my dad is working at home today.*

Developing vocabulary p9

Using noun suffixes -ment, -ion and -ence

> **Warmer**
> Books closed. Dictate the following questions:
> *What does that teacher teach you? What is that student studying?*
> Write the questions on the board for students to check. Circle the words *teacher teach* and *student studying*. Ask students which word in each pair is the verb and which is the noun. Underline the *-er* on *teacher* and the *-ent* on *student*, and ask if students know what this part of the word is called. Elicit or teach *suffix* and explain that suffixes are added to words to change the type of word.

1 After students have looked at the words and read the explanation, ask them what words they know connected with the words in the box, e.g. *argue, permit, different*.

Language notes

Like many points of English language learning, the rules for which suffix to use to form nouns are extremely complicated, difficult to remember and full of irregularities and exceptions. Therefore, it is far easier for students to learn the words on a case-by-case basis and consult a good dictionary where necessary. Tell students that many native English speakers have very little knowledge of how their own language works as it is so unpredictable and complicated – native speakers are drilled from an early age to memorise spelling and word formations rather than try to memorise the rules behind them.

2a Pre-teach any words students may have problems with, e.g. *idealised* (thinking something is better than it really is), *stay away* (not go near) and *low-tech* (technologically simple and old-fashioned).

> **Answers**
> **Verbs:** explain, embarrass, solve, enjoy, improve, connect
> **Adjectives:** confident, adolescent, independent

2b Make sure students understand that, although the words in bold in exercise 2a are a mix of verbs and adjectives, the only words that fit in the gaps grammatically are nouns.
- If you wish, allow students to use dictionaries and tell them to check the spelling of each word carefully.
- Follow up by asking: *Do you agree that social media can make young people unhappy? Do you think it's a good idea for parents to limit how much time their children spend online? Why/Why not?*

> **Answers**
> a explanation b confidence c adolescence d embarrassment
> e solution f enjoyment g improvement h independence
> i Connection

3 When checking answers, ask students to tell you the part of speech for each item, i.e. **1** verb; **2** adjective; **3** noun, verb; **4** noun.

> **Answers**
> 1 improve 2 independent 3 confidence, embarrass 4 differences

+ Extra activity

Ask students to write more sentences using nouns, verbs and adjectives from exercise 2a. They then read them out to the class without saying the noun, verb or adjective. The other students guess the missing word.

Use it ... don't lose it!

4 SPEAKING
- Remind students that one of the objectives of this exercise is to practise the noun forms, so although item 1 uses the verb *improve* in the question, if possible, students should try to use *improvement* in their answer.
- Point out that one way to show you have a good level of English is to use a variety of word forms to avoid repetition. In a speaking exam, for example, saying *There are lots of things that are different in English and Portuguese. One of the biggest differences is ...* allows students to show the examiner that they know two words, rather than just one.

Homework Workbook page 7

15

1 HAPPY FAMILIES

GREAT LEARNERS GREAT THINKERS p10

Thinking about the challenges and opportunities at different life stages

Warmer

Write *Being a teenager* at the top of the board, and under it draw two columns, headed *positives* and *negatives*. Brainstorm with students the positive and negative aspects of being a teenager.

Then ask *Has anyone ever treated you badly because you were a teenager?* and elicit examples, e.g. *Some people in the park last summer got angry with me and my friends.* and *Was it fair?*, e.g. *No, I don't think so. We were just listening to some music and chatting.*

1 SPEAKING

- If you used the Warmer, erase the brainstorm ideas and change the heading to *Being a senior citizen*. Students brainstorm in pairs before sharing their ideas with the class and discussing the second question together.

Possible answers
2 losing a job because of your age; not receiving the correct health care; people talking slowly and loudly to senior citizens; thinking all older people can't use technology

2 VIDEO

- After checking answers, ask students if they are surprised by how positive Chris feels about getting old. Extend the discussion by asking: *Do you think Chris would feel the same if he really were old?* You can also ask if there are any examples of ageism towards Chris in the video. Only people not paying attention to him is, possibly, a negative form of behaviour, while the others show respect and consideration.

Answers
1 People generally react to him in a positive way, they let him go up the stairs easily, bus drivers let him cross the street, he can always find a seat on public transport. However, not everybody pays attention to him.
2 generally happy

3 VIDEO

Answers
1 doctor 2 36, 80 3 dad 4 positive, seven 5 Bus drivers
6 public transport

4

Check students understand the meaning of *fundamentally* (*in a very important or basic way*).

- After checking answers, highlight the statistic *A quarter of millennials believe it's normal for older people to be unhappy* and ask students if they think it's true for their country.

Answers
1 They think old people are lonely and unhappy.
2 They stop us thinking of old age as an opportunity for new experiences, lead to increased memory loss, a worse ability to recover from illness and a negative body image.
3 People think older people are no different from people of other ages.

GREAT THINKERS

5 SPEAKING

- The *Sentence-Phrase-Word* thinking routine helps students to engage meaningfully with a text and then to structure a discussion about it. (Note that this routine may sometimes change order to *Word-Phrase-Sentence*.)
- Before students do the task, make clear that once they have selected their *sentence* (step 1), they can choose their *phrase* (step 2) from any part of the text. The phrase does not have to be part of the sentence they have chosen. Similarly, the *word* (step 3) does not have to be part of the phrase, or the sentence.
- Students work individually in steps 1–3 and then in small groups in step 4.
- In the groupwork stage, students should all first share the *sentences* they have chosen and discuss these one at a time; then share the *phrases* and discuss these; then share the *words*.
- If you wish, ask each group to report back to the class at the end. Encourage students to summarise the key ideas and themes they talked about.

6 SPEAKING

- If you used the Warmer, make sure students understand that in this exercise they are not thinking about the positive and negative aspects of being a teenager. They are thinking about the positive and negative attitudes other people have **towards** teenagers.

GREAT LEARNERS SEL

- During the discussion, encourage students to think of cases both of when they felt someone treated them unfairly, simply because they were a teenager, and examples of when they treated someone unfairly because of their age.
- In the first case, ask them to consider why the other person acted in that way, not whether it was fair or unfair. In the second case, ask them to question why they reacted as they did.

LEARNER PROFILE

- Ask students to read the statement and the question in the Learner profile on page 142, and then grade themselves from 1 to 5. Explain that here 1 means 'I'm not very open-minded or positive towards others', and 5 means 'I'm very open-minded and positive towards others'.
- If appropriate for your class, get students to share their grades with a partner or small group and, if they wish, to give their reasons. Encourage students to share suggestions for becoming more open-minded and positive towards others. Alternatively, ask students individually to think of ways to become more open-minded and positive towards others.

HAPPY FAMILIES   1

Listening p12
Listening for gist and detail

Warmer
Books closed. Write the following on the board: *1 Put your _____ down!, 2 Tidy your _____ !, 3 Go and do your _____ !, 4 Turn the _____ down!, 5 Switch the _____ off!*
Students work in pairs and think what words could complete each one.
After students share their ideas with the class, ask them who they think might be speaking, and elicit 'parents'.

Possible answers
1 mobile/phone/tablet   2 (bed)room   3 homework   4 music/radio/volume   5 TV

1 SPEAKING
- With less confident classes, collate ideas from this stage on the board.

2 06
- Before students do the task, make clear that they do not need to understand every word. They only need to listen for gist and will listen again for more detail in the next exercise.
- With less confident classes, pause after each speaker and discuss as a class what ideas they mentioned before moving on.

3 06

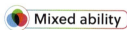 **Mixed ability**
To simplify the activity, give less confident students these names as the answers before they listen: *A Oliver, B Emma, C Charlotte, D Harry, E Oliver, F Emma*. As they listen, tell them to confirm whether these are the correct answers or not.

Answers
A Harry – *When I'm not studying or doing homework … my dad says, 'Hey, why aren't you working? Haven't you got anything to do?' But … when I'm doing homework or revising at home, my dad says, 'Hey, why are you spending all your time studying?! You need to relax and enjoy yourself!'. I never win!*
B Poppy – *I know my bedroom is a mess, but I just don't care. I have other things to do.*
C Charlotte – *She doesn't realise that it's my life and I need to decide for myself what I study and do afterwards.*
D not needed
E Oliver – *The only thing we really argue about is video games. My dad hates it when I play them; he says they're a waste of time, … I don't think it's fair …*
F Emma – *… my problem is my little sister …*

4 06

Answers
1 His parents give him a lot of independence.
2 because she is only ten
3 He is the headmaster at Harry's school.
4 She is a doctor.
5 Teenagers have arguments with parents because they see things differently.

5  Critical thinkers
- Before students do the task, remind them that the objective is to justify their opinion and give suitable examples.
- If you feel your students need more support, write these prompts on the board:
I'm certain/not sure (that) … because …
I (really) believe/feel/think (that) … because …
In my opinion, …
Speaking personally, …
I would say …

🏠 **Homework** > Workbook page 7

Grammar in context 2 p12
Using articles

Warmer
Write the following gapped sentences on the board:
1 I can't find _____ book I bought last week.
2 I can't find _____ good book to read.
Ask which sentence requires *a* and which *the*, and elicit the reason (sentence 1 refers to a specific book, whereas sentence 2 doesn't).
Ask students when *an* is used instead of *a* (before a vowel sound – note that a few common words, e.g. *university* and *uniform*, start with vowels but the first sound is /j/, like *yacht*, so they take the article *a*).

Answers
1 the   2 a

1a Point out that the sentences are based on sentences from the listening in the previous section.

Answers
2 the   3 a/an   4 the   5 a/an

Language notes
There are two pronunciations for each article. The stressed forms are rarely used except in the case of *the* before vowel sounds.
a   /ə/ (unstressed); /eɪ/ (stressed)
an   /ən/ (unstressed); /æn/ (stressed)
the   /ðə/ (unstressed); /ðiː/ (stressed; and before vowel sounds, e.g. *the arguments*)

2   **Answers**
1 the, –   2 –, –   3 the   4 the   5 –   6 the   7 the   8 –

3 Before students do the task, point out that there are three kinds of mistakes in the exercise: some items have the wrong article; some items have an article but don't need one; and – probably hardest for students – some items don't have an article but need one.

17

1 HAPPY FAMILIES

Answers
1 I have a ~~the~~ sister and two brothers.
2 My dad is a ~~the~~ doctor in a big hospital.
3 Can you send me the photos you took yesterday?
4 We had an argument yesterday but the ~~an~~ argument wasn't serious.
5 That man is a teacher at my cousin's school.
6 I'm reading a report from the University of Michigan.
7 Let me help you if you have a ~~the~~ problem.
8 ~~The~~ Concentration is really important when you study.

Culture exchange

4  Culture notes

Dolmio® was founded in Australia in 1985 before extending to the UK and Ireland the following year. It is a well-recognised brand in Australia, New Zealand, western Europe and North America.

A video of the experiment mentioned is available on the Internet. In the video, various children are featured and a range of more and more bizarre events take place. The children are oblivious to everything, including their parents swapping around pictures on the walls, their parents being swapped for total strangers, people wearing Viking helmets and walking in with rubber trees, a brother being swapped for a sister in the same clothes and a brother being swapped for a completely different brother twice the age and height of the original. In all cases the children are so involved with their tablets that they are shocked when the Internet is suddenly cut off at the end and they look up to see everything that has changed around them.

Answers
a an b – c – d – e – f a g – h – i a j a k a l a
m the n The

5 When checking answers, discuss items where a number of students have made the same mistake. Article use is an area where students' own language can interfere strongly and this may result in students using the wrong article, using articles where they are not needed or not using articles where they are needed.

Answers
1 – 2 –, – 3 –, an 4 – 5 a 6 the 7 –

6 SPEAKING

• If students query the answer to item a, make clear that rule 5 is also partially true, but it is more simplistic and applies to cases such as *My mum is a judge and my dad is a primary school teacher*. In the case of item a, *a doctor of neuroscience* is identifying Dean Burnett as one of many doctors of neuroscience.

Answers
a rule 3 b rule 4 c rule 3 d rule 2 e rule 1 f rule 1
g rule 1 h rule 1 i rule 4 j rule 1 k rule 1 l rule 4
m rule 4 n rule 3 o rule 3

Use it ... don't lose it!

7 SPEAKING

• When students interview each other, encourage the 'interviewer' to elicit as much information as possible from their partner and not just accept 'yes' or 'no' as an answer, e.g. *Really? Why? Why not? What sorts of things do you talk about at dinner? What other activities do you together with your family?*

+ Extra activity

Ask the questions in exercise 5 to the whole class and get students to vote *Yes* or *No* for each one.
Write the results on the board, e.g. Question 1: Yes – 16 students; No – 18 students.
Ask students to copy the results into their notebooks, and write them up for homework with full sentences to summarise what they found, e.g. *18 students think family dinners are a good idea*. Ask them to also include some visual representation of the results such as bar charts.

Homework > Workbook page 8

HAPPY FAMILIES 1

Developing speaking p14
Asking for personal information

Warmer

Show students a picture of a teenager (male or female). Invent a name and present him/her to the class. Explain that he/she is a new student. Brainstorm questions with students for making friends with a new classmate. Point out any errors and encourage students to self-correct.

1 SPEAKING

- Before students do the task, point out the use of *like* to express similarity. Tell students that using *as* in this context is not correct.

2 🔊 07

Answers
Holly's brother is 15 and he's at school, not at university. Dylan doesn't really like sport. Dylan doesn't play football at the weekends. Holly hates video games.

3 🔊 07

- When checking answers, highlight *What about you?* Explain that this is a very useful question as it allows the person who has just answered to 'return' the question so their partner answers as well.

Answers
any, about, at, often, Do, favourite

4a PRONUNCIATION 🔊 08

- Check students understand that the arrows show the movement of the voice at the end of each question, not the movement in the complete question.
- When checking answers, ask students what the difference is between the questions that go with diagram a and the ones that go with diagram b (a Yes/No questions; b Wh- questions).
- If students have problems relating the voice movement to the questions, write one question of each type on the board, and draw the rising/falling arrow over the last word to make it clearer visually:

Have you got any brothers or sisters? ↗

What about you? ↘

Answers

a
Have you got any brothers or sisters?
Do you like basketball?
b
What about you?
What do you do at the weekend/in the evenings/on Wednesdays?
How often do you play?
What's your favourite school subject?

4b 🔊 08

- In students' own languages, the intonation range may be narrower, so encourage them to exaggerate even if this feels very strange to them.

5 SPEAKING

- Before students do the task, if necessary, confirm which questions should have rising intonation (1, 5, 6) and which should have falling intonation (2, 3, 4, 7, 8).

Answers
1 any 2 How 3 do 4 at 5 Do 6 Do
7 favourite 8 often

6a-b SPEAKING

🔵 **Mixed ability**

To make the activity more challenging, tell the more confident students that they need to memorise their role, and give them time to do this before they start. Students note how much information their partner remembers correctly and feed back at the end on any incorrect details.

7 Tell students that the information they use here doesn't have to be true. The key thing is that it should be different to the information about Holly and Dylan.

Practice makes perfect

8a SPEAKING

- For this Test-Teach-Test type activity (exercise 8a – Exam tip – exercise 8b), it is important to let students tackle the task without any further support. The aim is for them to realise for themselves when they read the Exam tip that some of their answers could have been fuller and make that adjustment when they repeat the task in exercise 8b.

8b In speaking exams, the only time when students should answer with just *Yes* or *No* is if the examiner asks them to confirm simple personal details, e.g. *So, are you José Sánchez? Yes, I am.* Even in this situation, students should answer with a short answer, as this is a way of showing that they know how to formulate short answers correctly.

- ✅ **Exam tip** To answer the question in the Exam tip box, students should always try to give more information because the examiner wants to hear them speaking English.
- Tell students that in speaking exams, they are being tested on general fluency. This does not mean always being correct about everything, and marks are given for being in control of the situation. So if they don't understand, there is no problem using questions like *Sorry, can you say that again?* or *Sorry, could you speak more slowly?* as these show that students know how to interact and are fluent even in challenging circumstances.

Homework Workbook page 9

1 HAPPY FAMILIES

Developing writing p15
Writing an informal email 1

Warmer

Books closed. Write the following phrases on the board:
Dear Sir/Madam,
I look forward to hearing from you.
Yours sincerely,
Ask students *Where would you expect to find phrases like these?*, and elicit that they are commonly used phrases in formal letters.
Elicit some informal equivalents, e.g. *Hi (Robert), Hey (Robert); Write soon; All the best, Take care.*
Discuss as a class when students last – if ever – wrote a formal letter. Explain that even though this is not something they need to do often in modern life, developing a sense of formal vs informal is important for exams.

1 Before students read the email, ask them to look at the photo and brainstorm what sort of person they think Maya is, e.g. *fun, friendly*, and what she might enjoy doing, e.g. *having parties, going to the beach*.

- Ask students if any of them know where Brighton is, or if they have been there. Elicit or explain that it is a large town on the south coast of the UK and is a very popular destination for people doing English language courses.

Culture notes

Wolf Alice is a four-piece indie rock band from London. They released their first single in 2013. Their second album, released in 2017, won the Mercury Prize. This prize is for the best album by British or Irish performers. They have also won several NME awards.
Frida Kahlo® (1907–1954) is one of the most famous female artists of the 20th century. Many of her works are colourful, surreal, slightly disturbing self-portraits. The trauma of her personal life is as well-known as her work. Born in Mexico, she had polio as a child and as a teenager was involved in a bus accident which left her in agony for much of her life. She is also famous because of her turbulent relationship with, and two marriages to, painter Diego Rivera.

Extra activity

Check comprehension of the email by asking the following questions:
Is Maya's immediate family big or small? (quite big, five people in total)
There are three men and two women in Maya's immediate family. True or false? (false, two men and three women)
What is Maya doing at the same time as she is writing the email? (listening to music/a song by Wolf Alice)
Would Maya prefer running and swimming or volleyball and hockey? Why? (volleyball and hockey, because she especially likes team sports)
Which school subject does Maya enjoy the most? How do you know? (art, because she has special art classes on Saturdays and she's reading a book about Frida Kahlo)

2
Answers
Paragraph 2 = family
Paragraph 3 = hobbies
Paragraph 4 = favourite subjects at school
Paragraph 5 = asking for a reply

3 When checking answers, look at the contractions in the email and confirm what the full expression is in each case (*I'm = I am; I've = I have; father's = father is; that's = that is; you'd = you would*).

- Make sure students remember that *have* is only contracted when it is part of *have got* or part of the present perfect; when *have* is the main verb, it needs to be written out in full, as in paragraph 4: *I have special art classes; I have a lot of homework.*

Possible answers
I've, ☺, Anyway, all, back, wishes

4 Before students think about what they are going to say, check they understand that they are writing a <u>reply</u> to Maya, so their email will not have exactly the same format as the one in exercise 1. They will need to make reference to Maya's email at the start and have phrases to do this in the fifth bullet in exercise 3.

- Check students understand what the notes at the sides of the email are prompting, i.e. *Explain* = give information about your family; *Say two things you really like ...* = talk about two hobbies; *I like* = say what your favourite subjects at school are; *Ask about ...* = show interest in Maya and ask her more about herself.

Homework > Workbook page 10

20

HAPPY FAMILIES 1

Test yourself p17

Grammar test

1 Answers
1 watches, watching
2 lies, lying
3 writes, writing
4 cries, crying
5 gets, getting

Note
Answers in 1 are worth five points in total – one for each verb, i.e. half a point for the third person singular and half a point for the -*ing* form.

2 Answers
1 c 2 c 3 d 4 c 5 d 6 b

3 Answers
1 Do, understand 2 hate 3 'm/am thinking 4 need 5 knows

4 Answers
1 a, the 2 A, The 3 –, a 4 a, –

Vocabulary test

1 Answers
1 toddler 2 father-in-law 3 stepfather 4 single 5 one-parent
6 only child 7 senior citizen 8 immediate family 9 cousin

2 Answers
-ment: argument, enjoyment
-ion: explanation, permission, solution
-ence: adolescence, confidence

2 LAW AND ORDER

Vocabulary in context p18
Using a range of lexis to talk about crimes, criminals and detective work

> **Warmer**
> Books closed. Draw the following crossword on the board:
>
>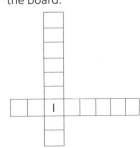
>
> Explain that these are two words for people and that each box contains a letter. As a class, students try to guess the words, letter by letter. Tell them to put their hands up when they have worked it out, not call out the solution. Once one student puts his/her hand up, ask him/her to say what letters he/she thinks are in the words, but <u>not</u> the answer, e.g. *I think there is a C in the horizontal word.* Confirm if this is right or wrong and keep asking for letters until the whole class has the two words.
> Follow up by asking: *What's the word for the place where a detective goes to investigate what a criminal has done?* Elicit *crime scene* or ask students to open their books and look at the photo and unit title at the top of the page.
>
> **Answers**
> Horizontal: CRIMINAL   Vertical: DETECTIVE

1 Before students do the task, check they have understood fully by asking: *Do you need to answer the clues in this exercise?* (No, the objective is only to check the meaning of the words in bold.)

> **Answers**
> *steals* – takes something that belongs to someone else without permission
> *breaks into* – enters a place using force and without permission
> *damages* – causes physical harm to something so that it is no longer in good condition
> *kills* – makes a person or living thing die
> *illegal* – not allowed by the law
> *violence* – using physical force towards other people
> *burns* – damages or destroys something with fire

2 09

> **Answers**
> 1 robbery/theft   2 burglary   3 vandalism   4 murder
> 5 shoplifting   6 cybercrime   7 mugging   8 kidnapping
> 9 smuggling   10 arson

3a Encourage students to guess if they are not sure of the answer.

3b 10

> **Answers**
> 1 arsonist   2 burglar   3 cybercriminal/hacker   4 kidnapper
> 5 mugger   6 murderer   7 robber/thief   8 shoplifter
> 9 smuggler   10 vandal

4 11

- Before students do the task, make sure they understand there is no 'right' answer.
- Pre-teach any words students may have problems with, e.g. the nouns *suspect* (*someone who the police believe may have committed a crime*), *evidence* (*facts or physical details that help show something is true*) and *witness* (*someone who sees a crime or something connected with a crime happen*) and the verbs *arrest* (*take a person to a police station because they have committed a crime*), *charge* (*say formally that someone has committed a crime*) and *prove* (*show something is true*).

> **Possible answers**
> **Beginning:** analyse evidence, arrest a suspect, investigate a case, question a witness, search for evidence
> **End:** accuse a suspect, charge a suspect, prove something

5b 12

- After checking answers, point out that the phrases in exercise 4 are slightly flexible, for example, **a** is *investigate the* case, not *investigate a case* (because it is unique, see page 12); **c** is *analyse it* (because *evidence* is used earlier in the sentence so there is no reason to repeat it).

> **Answers**
> a investigate   b search   c analyse   d witness   e prove
> f accuse   g arrest   h charge

6 Before students do the task, write *permit* (v) → *permi___* (n) and *explain* (v) → *explan___* (n) on the board, and elicit the ending of each word (*permi**ssion**, explan**ation***). Remind them of the work they did in Developing vocabulary on page 9 as the *-ion* suffix will help with some of the answers in this exercise.

- When checking answers, highlight the shifting word stress in ac<u>cuse</u> – accu<u>sa</u>tion; <u>a</u>nalyse – a<u>na</u>lysis; in<u>ves</u>tigate – investi<u>ga</u>tion and the pronunciation of *prove* (/pruːv/) and *proof* (/pruːf/).

> **Answers**
> accuse → accusation, analyse → analysis, arrest → arrest,
> charge → charge, investigate → investigation, prove → proof,
> question → question, search → search

Fast finishers »
Ask students to make sentences combining a noun from exercise 6 with a crime from exercise 2 or a criminal from exercise 3a, e.g. *After the <u>search</u> the police said there was no evidence of <u>arson</u>. The <u>mugger</u> used the old lady's credit card later – that was the <u>proof</u>!*

Use it ... don't lose it!

7 SPEAKING

- After students do the task in pairs, extend to a class discussion by asking: *Do you know anyone who does detective or police work? Who? What do they say about their job? What would be the worst parts of detective work do you think?*

LAW AND ORDER 2

Reading p19
Predicting content, reading for gist and detail

> **Warmer**
> Write these crimes on the board:
> *A rich woman stole from a department store.*
> *A driver hit someone crossing the street.*
> *A vandal drew graffiti on a shop.*
> Divide the class into groups and assign each group one of the crimes. Students work in pairs within their group to agree on what a detective should do in each situation, e.g. question witnesses, analyse the graffiti style, search for the owner of the car. Nominate one student from each group to feed back to the class.

1a
> **Answers**
> 1 b 2 a 3 c

1b SPEAKING

- Tell students that looking at titles and pictures first can often help them understand a text.
- Elicit some ideas for each story from the class, but don't confirm if they are correct or not.

2 Pre-teach any words students may have problems with, not including the underlined words, e.g. *witness report* (document written by a police officer which contains the information a witness gives about a crime), *overhead* (in the sky above you) and *suspected* (of a crime that the police still have to prove).

- **Note:** the stories contextualise the phrasal verbs covered in Developing vocabulary on page 21. If students ask about these, explain that they will be studying them in more detail later.
- Remind students that once they have the general idea of the whole text, they may find they can guess the meaning of new words more easily.

> **Answers**
> Story A: title: 1 Eating the evidence
> Story B: title: 3 Where did the criminals go?!
> Story C: title: 2 A criminal pastime

Culture notes

All three stories were in the news in 2016.
Story A took place about 2 km from the White House in Washington DC, US, at an Italian Pizza Kitchen restaurant.
Story B took place in Capel, Surrey, UK. A group of children were on a traditional *Easter egg hunt* (*a game in which children have to find hidden chocolate eggs*) when they helped police catch the criminals. Afterwards, the helicopter landed, and the children and their families shared some of their chocolate with the crew.
Story C had a further surprise. The 91-year-old woman, possibly prompted by her lawyer, later tried to claim a share of the copyright of the 'new' artwork. She said that her additions had added to the value of the piece by Koepcke. However, the museum by that point had removed her answers on the crossword and restored it.

3 🔊 13

- Before students do the task, make clear they now have time to read the text more carefully and understand it more fully.

> **Answers**
> 1 in Washington DC on Wednesday night
> 2 He asked her to stop.
> 3 to guide the police helicopter to the suspects
> 4 The police caught the criminals and they thanked the children and adults.
> 5 It cost almost $90,000. It is by the artist Arthur Koepcke.
> 6 She said she was following the artist's instructions.
> 7 They think she was confused by the interactive art.

4
> **Answers**
> *pay (any) attention* – listen or watch someone or something carefully
> *sufficient* – enough
> *realised* – suddenly knew
> *in search of* – looking for
> *got on the ground* – lay down
> *in fact* – in reality
> *Insert* – put something into something
> *misunderstanding* – not understanding something correctly

Fast finishers »

Ask students to write example sentences using some of the underlined words and phrases from the text. When checking answers to exercise 4, ask students to give additional example sentences as you discuss the meanings.

5 🧠 Critical thinkers

- Before students do the task, remind them that the objective is to justify their opinion and give suitable examples.
- Encourage them to think about victims, whether people are hurt, whether people lose business, etc.
- Give more confident students additional vocabulary such as *consequences*, *implications* and *punishment*.

> **Possible answers**
> I would say that the woman in Story A is a criminal, but she's not a criminal like an arsonist or a murderer. Nobody was hurt, the restaurant didn't lose money, and the police officer only lost three of his chips! I really believe that the police should investigate more important crimes than the theft of three chips. And anyway, if a normal person lost three chips, I don't think the police would do anything. Go to the police station here and accuse someone of stealing three of your French fries and the police would laugh at you!

▶ Flipped classroom

You may want to ask students to watch the Flipped classroom video for Unit 2 as homework, in preparation for the grammar lesson.

🏠 Homework Workbook page 13

2 LAW AND ORDER

Grammar in context 1 p20
Using the past simple

Warmer

Write the following sentences on the board:
a The police searched the house for evidence.
b The police started to investigate the burglary.
c The police arrested and charged a suspect.
Students put them in the most logical order. Circle the past simple verbs in the sentences (*searched*, *started*, *arrested*, *charged*), and ask students what they notice about them (they are all in the past simple).

Answers
1 b   2 a   3 c

1a If you didn't set the Flipped classroom video for homework, watch the video in class before working through the activities.
- Point out that the sentences are based on sentences from the reading on page 19.

Answers
2 f   3 a   4 d   5 b   6 e

1b Follow up by asking: *When do we use the auxiliary verb did?* (in negatives and question forms of most verbs); *What form of the verb do we use with did?* (the infinitive); *What's the order of words in a question with did?* (*did* + subject + infinitive); *Which verb do we not use did with?* (*be*); *How do we make negatives with be?* (using *wasn't/weren't*); *How do we make question forms with be?* (*be* + subject, e.g. *Was he ...? Were you ...?*)

Answers
b wasn't/didn't walk/didn't go
c Was/Did/Did
d –/walk/go

2a PRONUNCIATION

Language notes

Past simple verb endings demonstrate clearly the difference between voiced and voiceless sounds. Students can feel the difference by putting their hand on their throat. If they feel a vibration when they say a consonant sound, it is voiced; if they do not, it is voiceless.
Voiced: If the verb stem ends with a vowel sound or a voiced consonant (/b/, /g/, /l/, /m/, /n/, /ð/, /v/ or /z/), the pronunciation of the -ed is /d/.
Voiceless: If the verb stem ends with a voiceless consonant (/f/, /p/, /k/, /s/, /θ/, /ʃ/, /tʃ/ or /h/), the pronunciation of the -ed is /t/.
The e in the -ed ending in both cases is silent and the difference between /d/ and /t/ is very small. The main problem for many students is adding an extra syllable to the verb stem to make the past simple. This only happens in the case of verb stems ending in /t/ or /d/, which add the syllable /ɪd/.

2b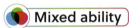
- When checking answers, make sure students are not adding an extra syllable to any of the verbs in the first two columns.

Answers
/t/: finished, liked, passed, watched
/d/: discovered, planned, stayed
/ɪd/: needed, painted, started, wanted

2c Students answer the question in pairs or as a class.

Answers
t and *d*

Mixed ability

Put less confident students into pairs, and ask them to take turns testing each other on the past simple form of the irregular verbs from the irregular verbs list on page 159.
Put more confident students into pairs, and ask them to brainstorm all the irregular verbs they can remember, focusing only on the past simple form, not the past participle.

3 Follow up by asking: *Do you think a police officer would respond in the same way to a game in the street where you live? Why/Why not?*

Answers
a called   b wasn't   c went   d found   e didn't stop   f started
g came   h didn't believe   i played   j left   k told   l saw
m became   n met   o helped

4

Answers
1 did, investigate   2 did, find   3 Did, stop   4 did, do   5 Were
6 did, become

5 SPEAKING
- Remind students not to use the -ed ending for past simple questions and not to use *did* with the verb *be*.

24

LAW AND ORDER 2

6 SPEAKING
- If your class is less confident, put Student As together into pairs or small groups to prepare the questions together, and Student Bs together to do the same.
- Discretely check the questions for each group before students move on to exercise 7.

> **Possible answers**
> **Student A**
> b Where did Edgar Allan Poe come from?
> c Who was the murderer in the story?
> d What did Conan Doyle work as?
> e What did Liu Yongbiao do in 1995?
> f When did Lindsey Davis write her first Roman crime novel?
> g What did McCall Smith write a story about in 2003?
> **Student B**
> a How many crime and thriller books did British people buy in 2017?
> b When did Conan Doyle create Sherlock Holmes?
> c When did Poe write the story?
> d What did Poe do?/What was Poe?
> e What did Colin Dexter teach?
> f What did Lindsey Davis write about?
> g What did the BBC® do in 2008?

Use it ... don't lose it!

7 SPEAKING
- Follow up by asking: *Do you enjoy reading crime fiction? Why/Why not? If you do, what do you think about the authors in the text? Can you recommend any good crime books?*

Developing vocabulary p21
Using phrasal verbs connected with investigating and finding

> **Warmer**
> Write the following gapped sentences on the board:
> He _____ the piece of paper from the floor.
> He _____ English very quickly.
> Explain that the same two words fill both gaps. Tell students to put their hands up when they have worked it out, not call out the answer.
> Write the answer, *picked up*, on the board and remind students what phrasal verbs are. Elicit that they are made up of a verb followed by a particle and/or preposition. Point out that they can be literal, as in the first example, or idiomatic, as in the second.

1
Point out that the phrasal verbs come from the reading on page 19. Ask students to find them there and circle them to see them in context.

> **Answers**
> 1 look into 2 come across 3 work out 4 look for 5 find out
> 6 turn up 7 look up 8 come up with

Language notes
Associating phrasal verbs with a topic, e.g. investigating and finding, can help students remember them more easily. This section is designed to focus on the meaning of the phrasal verbs without focusing on the complicated grammar.
When phrasal verbs take an object, they can either be separable (*look up, work out*) or non-separable (*come across, come up with, find out*, look for, look into, turn up**). A separable phrasal verb can have the object between the verb and the particle (*look **the word** up*) or after the particle (*look up **the word***), if the object is a noun. However, it must have the object between the verb and the particle if it is a pronoun (*look **it** up* not ~~*look up it*~~). A non-separable phrasal verb will always have the object after the particle.
*find out and *turn up* can also be used without an object.

2 SPEAKING

> **Possible answers**
> I looked for the key/the answer.
> I looked up the answer/the identity of the criminal.
> I found out the answer/the identity of the criminal.
> I came across the key/the answer/the identity of the criminal.
> I worked out the answer/the identity of the criminal.

➕ Extra activity
Write the following sentence beginnings on the left of the board:
1 The detective turned up
2 The shoplifter came up with
3 The police looked into
and the following sentence endings on the right of the board:
a the cybercrime, but didn't catch the hacker.
b at the crime scene two hours after the robbery.
c a crazy excuse, so the police didn't believe him.
Ask students to match the sentence halves. Then ask students about each situation, e.g. *Why did the detective not get to the crime scene for two hours? What excuse do you think the shoplifter invented? Why did the police not catch the hacker?*

> **Answers**
> 1 b 2 c 3 a

3a
> **Answers**
> 1 across 2 out 3 up 4 out 5 for 6 into 7 up 8 up

Use it ... don't lose it!

4 SPEAKING
- After students do the task, ask some students who have given interesting answers to tell the class. Encourage discussion by allowing students to ask each other follow-up questions where appropriate.

Homework Workbook page 15

25

2 LAW AND ORDER

GREAT LEARNERS GREAT THINKERS p22

Thinking about right and wrong actions and how they affect us and others

Warmer

Tell students you are going to write a series of numbers and letters on the board and they have to guess what the connection between them is. Tell them to put their hands up when they have worked it out, not call out the solution. Write *111111*, *iloveyou*, *qwerty*, *123456*, *abc123* and *password* on the board, one at a time. Once one student puts his/her hand up, ask him/her to say what he/she thinks the connection is between the items. (They are the most frequently used, and easiest to guess, passwords.)

1 SPEAKING

- After students discuss the questions, briefly discuss what they can do to make their passwords more secure, e.g. don't use the same password on more than one website.

2 VIDEO

- Pre-teach *switch on* (*make something electric or electronic start working*), *charge* (*put electricity into the battery of something, e.g. a phone, a laptop*), *value* (*something, not money, which is important to the way we live our lives*), *account* (*a private area online, e.g. for email, on a shopping website*) and *respect* (*treating someone in a polite and kind way*).

Answers
The hackers stole his complete digital life.

3 VIDEO

- After checking answers, ask students if they can remember the three adjectives Mat used to describe how he felt (*angry*, *scared*, *concerned*). Ask if they have ever had problems online and how they felt about it. If not, ask them how they would feel in Mat's position.

Answers
1 e 2 f 3 c 4 h 5 a 6 b 7 i 8 g 9 d

4 SEL

- When discussing the answer to item 2, elicit from students what would be a better way to help software/IT companies protect people, i.e. contacting software designers/computer manufacturers with a 'bug report'.

Answers
1 to help companies to learn how to protect people's digital lives
3 The hackers deleted Mat's only photos of his daughter when she was young.
4 respecting people's property; thinking about others

GREAT THINKERS

5 SPEAKING

- The *Circle of viewpoints* thinking routine encourages students to consider the same situation from more than one perspective. It can show how each participant in an event may see it, and feel about it, in a very different way. It's particularly useful to help address controversial issues.
- Before students do the task, make clear that the role-play should not become a confrontation. It should be three people meeting to calmly discuss the events from their respective points of view. In step 1, the idea is that they consider the situation only from the point of view of their character, not the situation in general terms. If your class does not divide neatly into groups of three, double up the role of the hacker and make groups of four as necessary.
- Students then 'meet' and discuss the crime in step 2 in their groups. If you feel your students need more support, write these prompts on the board:

  I was thinking about the hack from the perspective of …
  As Mat / Mat's teenage daughter / the hacker, I think …
  One question I have from Mat's / Mat's daughter's / the hacker's point of view is …

6 SPEAKING

- Before students do the task, point out that the situations may have grey areas. For example, in situation 1, you could take the €20 ('black'), or you could run immediately to the secretary's office to hand the €20 in ('white'). Alternatively, you might wait outside the classroom and, if no one comes back in 15 minutes, go back in and take the money ('grey'). Encourage students to think about the range of possibilities in each case.

GREAT LEARNERS

- Guide the discussion by first asking students to think of some of the consequences of taking the easy option in the situations in exercise 6. Use students' ideas to help show that this is often not the best idea.

LEARNER PROFILE

- Ask students to read the statement and the question in the Learner profile on page 142, and then grade themselves from 1 to 5. Explain that here 1 means 'I don't always act with integrity and honesty', and 5 means 'I always act with integrity and honesty'.
- If appropriate for your class, get students to share their grades with a partner or small group and, if they wish, to give their reasons. Encourage students to share suggestions for acting with more integrity and honesty. Alternatively, ask students individually to think of ways to act with more integrity and honesty.

LAW AND ORDER 2

Listening p24
Listening for gist and specific information

Warmer

Books closed. Draw a circle with a '?' in it on the board and six lines running off it. Tell students they have to guess the name and to put their hands up when they have worked it out.

Write the following clues around the circle: *London*, *Robert Downey Jr.*, *strange hat*, *Moriarty*, *detective*, *Watson*.

Elicit the answer (*Sherlock Holmes*) and then ask students the connection with the photo on page 24.

1

Benedict Cumberbatch (1976–) is a British actor. He has performed on stage and television and in film. He is probably most famous for his role as Sherlock Holmes in the TV series *Sherlock*, but he also appears in various Marvel® superhero films, including *Doctor Strange*.

2 🔊 15

- ✅ **Exam tip** To answer the question in the Exam tip box, the first thing to do is read the statements carefully. They can give ideas about the topic and the vocabulary students are likely to hear.
- Remind students that they will usually hear the recording twice so they should not panic if they do not understand the information the first time. If they don't hear the answer to one question, they should start listening immediately for the answer to the next question.
- Students should use the second listening to complete and check their answers.
- Remind students to never leave answers blank in an exam.

Answers
1 False 2 False 3 True 4 False 5 True 6 True
7 False 8 False

3 🔊 15

Possible answers
1 False – Detective series aren't Ava's favourite. She watched *Sherlock* because she likes Benedict Cumberbatch.
2 False – Benedict Cumberbatch was in a taxi when he saw the crime.
4 False – He pulled the muggers away from the cyclist.
7 False – The only person to speak about it was the taxi driver.
8 False – The taxi driver helped but Cumberbatch's wife did not.

4 Pre-teach *publicity* (information to help a company sell something or make people interested in something).

Answers
1 The taxi driver called Benedict Cumberbatch a *superhero*.
2 The cyclist didn't have to go to *hospital*.
3 The crime happened close to *Baker Street*, where Sherlock Holmes used to live.
4 Ava thought the incident was *publicity for a new TV series*.
5 *Sophie Hunter* is Benedict Cumberbatch's wife. She was also in the taxi.
6 Ava imagined how strange it would be for Sherlock Holmes (Benedict Cumberbatch) to show up at a *police station* with the muggers.

5 💭 **Critical thinkers**
- Before students do the task, remind them that the objective is to justify their opinion and give suitable examples.

🏠 Homework ▸ Workbook page 15

Grammar in context 2 p24
Using the past continuous; using *used to*

Warmer

Write the following sentence on the board:
When Cumberbatch saw the muggers, they were attacking a cyclist.
and the following timeline:

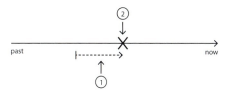

Ask students: *Which underlined verb matches 1 and which matches 2?*

Answers
1 were attacking 2 saw

1a Point out that the sentences are based on sentences from the listening in the previous section.

Answers
1 c 2 d 3 a 4 b

1b **Answers**
be

Language notes
Some verbs are not often used in the past continuous because they describe states/situations, e.g. *believe*, *love*, *want*.

2 Remind students that the spelling rules for *-ing* endings are the same as for the present continuous.

Answers
2 Logan wasn't swimming.
3 Evelyn and Ivy were studying.
4 Alfie was watching TV.
5 Becky and Adam weren't cooking.
6 Jamie and Steph were talking on the phone.

3 After checking answers, use item 4 to show students how the pronunciation of *was* changes according to whether it is stressed or not. In questions we generally use the weak form, i.e. *Was* /wəz/ *ALFIE WATCHing TV?* In affirmative short answers, we use the strong form, i.e. *YES, he WAS* /wɒz/. We generally also use the weak form in affirmative sentences, e.g. *LOGAN was* /wəz/ *SWIMming*.

27

2 LAW AND ORDER

Answers
1 What was Mia doing?
  She was running.
2 Was Logan swimming?
  No, he wasn't.
3 Were Evelyn and Ivy studying?
  Yes, they were.
4 Was Alfie watching TV?
  Yes, he was.
5 Were Becky and Adam cooking?
  No, they weren't.
6 What were Jamie and Steph doing?
  They were talking on the phone.

+ Extra activity

Put students into pairs, and ask them to take turns to draw pictures of members of their family yesterday at 6.30 pm. Their partner then makes past continuous sentences about the pictures, e.g. *Your sister was playing tennis*.

4 With less confident classes, look at the picture together first and identify the six differences as a class.

Answers
In the listening,
they were mugging a young cyclist of about 20, not an elderly man.
the muggers were trying to steal his bike, not his bag.
it happened in London, not in New York.
the taxi driver got out to help, he wasn't texting.
police officers did not run to help.

5 SPEAKING
- Check students understand that in this exercise they can write about anything in the picture, they don't need to focus only on the differences between the listening text and the picture.

7 Point out that the sentences are based on sentences from the listening in the previous section.
- When checking answers, model the pronunciation of the affirmative and negative forms of *used to*, i.e. *used to watch …* (/ˌjuːstəˈwɒtʃ/), … *didn't use to happen* (/ˌdɪdnjuːstəˈhæpən/).

Answers
a use b don't use c the infinitive d use to

Language notes

Used to is used to talk about past habits and repeated actions that don't happen now, and also to talk about permanent longer states and situations in the past which don't continue now.
There are three key things which students should remember about *used to* in order not to make typical learner mistakes:
1 We never use *used to* to talk about a single action.
2 Only the affirmative form has -*d* at the end, both negatives and questions are formed with *use*. *Used to* is therefore a regular structure because it forms the past with -*d*, negatives with *didn't* and questions with *did*.
3 We can only use the structure in the past. Students' own language may include a verb which seems similar to *used to* but can also be used in the present. If it does, make sure students understand that this is not the case with *used to* and that this idea can be expressed in the present with the adverb *usually*.

8 Pre-teach any words students may have problems with (by showing students a photo/video online or using mime if necessary), e.g. *rattle* (*a wooden object, shaped like a flag, that you can spin to make a loud clicking noise*), *whistle* (*a metal or plastic object you put in your mouth and blow through to make a loud noise*) and *assistance* (*help*).

Answers
a used to be b used to call c Did, use to have d used to carry e didn't use to have f used to make g used to need

+ Extra activity

Write *My granny is an arsonist!* on the board. Quickly tell students the story of your 'granny': that she lived near you in a quiet little village and that two years ago the police arrested her, charged her with arson and sent her to prison. She burned seven buildings before they caught her!
Ask students: *How do you think Granny* (your surname here)'s *life has changed?* And elicit a sentence with *used to* and another with *didn't use to*, e.g. *She used to have barbecues in the summer – she can't have them in prison of course! She didn't use to do exercise but now she does 30 minutes every day.*
Put students into pairs to invent more sentences with *used to* about how they think life is different for your granny. Then ask students to share some of their ideas with the class.

9 Before students do the task, check they have understood fully by asking: *Should the false sentences be very obvious?* (No, they should be believable.) Explain that if they make the sentences very clearly false, then the next exercise will be too easy.

Use it … don't lose it!

10 SPEAKING
- Before students do the task, allow them to ask you some of the questions from exercise 9. Give a mix of true and false answers and see if they can identify your lies.
- If you wish, when students are doing the task, allow them to ask their partner additional questions using the past simple and/or *used to* to try and find out if the answers are true or false.

28

LAW AND ORDER 2

Developing speaking p26
Apologising

Warmer

Books closed. Elicit the word *sorry* by saying the following: *I forgot your birthday. I'm ...* and asking students to complete the sentence.

In pairs, give students one minute to think of as many situations as they can when you might say sorry.

Nominate a few pairs to give their suggestions. Then ask if students know the word for the action of saying sorry. Elicit or teach the verb *to apologise*, and tell them they are going to look at ways of apologising and accepting apologies in the lesson.

1 SPEAKING

- Before students do the task, make sure they understand that they should not just describe what they can see but should also use the text on each photo to imagine how the people are feeling. Explain that using your imagination is an important part of many speaking exams.

    Possible answers
    a There is a teenager sitting outside. She is sending a message to her friend, who is 20 minutes late. She is angry because her friend is late.
    b There are two teenagers talking to each other. One of the teenagers feels upset because the other teenager told a secret. The other teenager feels sorry.

Culture exchange

3a After students do the task, collate ideas on the board but don't confirm if they are correct or not. However, make sure students are clear that items a–d need to be completed with numbers and items e and f with words.

Mixed ability

For less confident students, instead of having them guess the missing numbers and words in exercise 3a, tell them to circle all the numbers already in the text and check they know how to say them.

3b

- Follow up by asking: *Do you think people in your country are generally more or less polite than English speakers? Why?*

    Answers
    a eight b 20 c 84 d 73 e hits f polite

4

- Tell students you can either *accept* or *reject* an apology.

    Answers
    Dialogue 1: He apologises for taking her water. She accepts it.
    Dialogue 2: He apologises for leaving the boy's book at home. He doesn't accept it.

5

    Answers
    1 so 2 doesn't 3 only 4 Let 5 make 6 last 7 feel

6 After checking answers, highlight the expressions *It's only (water).* and *That's the last time (I lend you anything).* Warn students that they need to be careful with these two expressions, particularly with the intonation, as they can sound rude in certain contexts.

Answers
Making apologies
I'm so sorry.
Let me (get you a new bottle in the break).
I'll make it up to you.
I feel terrible.
Responding to apologies
It doesn't matter.
It's only (water).
That's the last time (I lend you anything).

7 Make sure students understand that they don't need to plan out all the details of the situations at this point, just come up with general ideas. Remind them that they may be able to develop some of their ideas from the Warmer here.

8 SPEAKING

- Point out that as students have a range of situations here to work with, they should accept some apologies and politely reject others.

Practice makes perfect

9a SPEAKING

- Tell students they need to alternate roles so they can practise both making and responding to apologies.

9b SPEAKING

- Ask the students listening to note down the following:
    - if the person accepts or rejects the apology
    - which expressions from the Speaking bank they hear

Homework > Workbook page 17

2 LAW AND ORDER

Developing writing p27
Writing a blog post

> **Warmer**
> Write *blogs, blogs, blogs* on the board and discuss the topic with the class, using questions like: *Which blogs do you read? Do you and your friends read the same blogs? Which ones? Have you or has one of your friends got a blog? Have you ever written a blog post? What do you think makes a blog popular?*

1 SPEAKING

- Before students do the task, check they know the words for what they can see in the photos. Encourage them to use the gender-neutral term *police officer*, rather than *policewoman*. Use c to pre-teach *gardening equipment* and tell students to treat this as a set of items, rather than worrying about the specific word for each tool.

2 Extra activity

Tell students to highlight the phrase 'one of them' in the third line of paragraph 2. Then tell students to look at the questions in 4 and answer them as if they were the person referred to in the blog post.

> **Answers**
> 1 I helped a police officer.
> 2 I threw a ball at the person she was chasing.
> 3 I was in the park.
> 4 I was with my friends and we were playing basketball.
> 5 I threw the ball at the suspect and he fell off his bike.
> 6 Yes. The police thanked me and my friends on social media.
> 7 The police arrested the burglar.

3 When checking answers, ask students: *What do you notice about the order of the words and expressions in the box?* Elicit that they appear in approximately the order you would expect them to be used in a text.

> **Answers**
> It all started when …; Then; Meanwhile; Suddenly; Finally; A few minutes/hours/days later; The next day

4 With less confident classes, allow students to do this stage in pairs or small groups. If students write variations on the same story in exercise 5a, then they can also compare their stories later to see how similar or different they are.

Practice makes perfect

5a Before students do the task, draw attention to the paragraph structure of the *Kids doing good!* article. Elicit that there are two paragraphs in this case because there are two separate sets of events happening, i.e. paragraph 1: details of the crime and the events before the arrest of the burglar; paragraph 2: details of the 'hero' of the story and how he was involved in catching the burglar.

- Explain that blog posts and stories have a very flexible paragraph structure. Students can therefore organise their stories in any logical way.

5b Remind students that in exams it is important to know how many marks there are for different sections and to know what the examiners want.

- **Exam tip** To answer the question in the Exam tip box, in an exercise of this type, examiners usually want to see if students answer the question and include the information it asks for, write clearly, organise their ideas logically, use accurate and varied grammar and vocabulary and use punctuation and capital letters correctly.

Homework › Workbook page 18

LAW AND ORDER 2

Test yourself p28

Grammar test

1 Answers
1 Richard and I were students at this school.
2 We left school at five o'clock.
3 She caught the bus at that stop.
4 What time did you finish work?
5 She didn't teach English.
6 They had (got) a problem.

2 Answers
1 was reading 2 were, listening 3 wasn't writing 4 weren't waiting 5 were, sitting

3 Answers
1 was travelling, rang 2 stole, was looking 3 was driving, remembered 4 broke, ran

4 Answers
1 Did you use ~~used~~ to have long hair?
2 He used to visit ~~visits~~ his grandparents every weekend.
3 One day last year she caught ~~used to catch~~ a criminal.
4 correct

Vocabulary test

1 Answers
1 mug 2 steal 3 Thief 4 Burglary 5 kidnapper 6 Smuggling 7 vandal

2 Answers
1 accusation 2 proof 3 analyse 4 questioned

3 Answers
1 a for b up c across
2 d into e out f with

Exam success Units 1–2 p30

Reading

2 **Answers**

1 **A** incorrect – Paragraph 1 states that *Zeki … lived in a tent for almost a year*, but doesn't talk about advantages/disadvantages.
B incorrect – Two locations are mentioned (*the island of Skye in Scotland* and *the mountains in the Highlands*), but these are not the focus.
C incorrect – Zeki's family and the reason for him moving are both mentioned (*to learn how to live away from the city*), but these are not the focus.
D correct – Various reasons are given for why this was natural for Zeki: *It can seem unusual … but it wasn't for him.*; *some of his best memories were of growing up in the mountains*; *They used to live far away from any towns …*

2 **A** incorrect – Paragraph 2 says they *travelled to lots of places abroad*, but doesn't say how Zeki felt about this.
B correct – *He saw how people were able to use the land and natural products, and he also wanted to do that one day.* (paragraph 2)
C incorrect – Paragraphs 1 and 2 contain information about the family home, but don't say how Zeki felt about it.
D incorrect – not stated in the text

3 **A** correct – *he knew to stay calm and not panic*; *Some people were extremely tired and anxious … , but it wasn't a problem for him.*
B incorrect – The <u>situations</u> were difficult, but Zeki reacted positively.
C incorrect – Zeki's reaction described in paragraph 3 is positive, but *impatient* and *angry* in the question are negative.
D incorrect – Zeki reacted confidently, the people with him didn't.

4 **A** incorrect – Important abilities are mentioned (*to use the land and natural products* (paragraph 2); *to stay calm and not panic* (paragraph 3)), but these aren't the reason people should try living in the wild.
B incorrect – Learning to live in a tent is not the main objective.
C incorrect – Living apart from your family is not the main objective.
D correct – *if people connect more with nature, they will understand and enjoy it* (paragraph 4)

5 **A** incorrect – not stated in the text
B incorrect – The text talks about difficulties, but it doesn't say that Zeki thought it was <u>too</u> difficult.
C correct – *some of his best memories were of growing up in the mountains* (paragraph 1); *Zeki was comfortable playing and exploring in nature* (paragraph 2); *Zeki continues to enjoy the outdoors … as a young adult.* (paragraph 4)
D incorrect – The end of Paragraph 4 makes clear Zeki still has lots of contact with nature.

- If you wish, go to page 144 to continue working through the Exam success section for these two units.
- See the Exam trainer, Workbook page 96, for more information and practice on this Preliminary for Schools task.

Collaborative project 1 p31

Family life in your country

1 **SPEAKING**
- Students work in groups of three to four.
- Follow up by asking: *Could the same thing happen in your family? Why/Why not?*

2 **SPEAKING**
- Students continue to work in their groups from exercise 1.
- After reading the *Research areas*, ask students to consider which ones they may be able to find concrete data for (possibly *typical size of …* and *time spent with …*) and which they are more likely to find opinions about (the other three). Point out that if they can find concrete data, one 'official' source will be enough for this project, but if they find opinions, they should look for various sources to make sure the opinions are roughly the same.

3
- Ask individuals to read aloud the tips and discuss them with the class.
- In the *Collaboration* section, make sure students understand that the *Useful language* contains phrases to help them work together and complete the task in English, not phrases that they should use in their finished project.

4 **SPEAKING**
- Outline a timeframe for the project, starting with the deadline for presenting it. Include key interim dates and make sure students are clear about which stages of the project they need to do at home and which they will have time to do in future classes.
- Point out that, when working on the project, as much discussion as possible should be in English, both in and out of class.

5 Explain that Presentation here means the way a project has been created and done, e.g. the quality and general attractiveness of the layout and design of a poster or leaflet, or the clarity and coherence of a spoken presentation or video message.

Virtual Classroom Exchange

- Connect with teachers and students in other countries and encourage students to present their projects to each other.

PLURILINGUAL 3

Vocabulary in context p32
Using a range of lexis to talk about languages, countries and nationalities and learning languages

Warmer
In pairs, students discuss the meaning of the unit title *Plurilingual* and what they think the unit is going to be about. Elicit ideas from the class.

Possible answers
The word 'plurilingual' suggests something about a range of different languages. The unit could look at various important world languages and where they are spoken and by whom. It may also look at certain people who speak various different languages.

1a SPEAKING
- Before students do the task, if you have students of any of these nationalities in your class, ask them to tell the class which one is 'Hello' in their language and to teach the correct pronunciation.

1b 18

Answers
1 Spanish 2 French 3 Arabic 4 Russian 5 German
6 Polish 7 Turkish 8 Portuguese 9 Bulgarian 10 Thai
11 Japanese 12 Italian

2 19
- Before students do the task, if possible, project a world map on the board and ask them to point out the countries on it.
- German is the language spoken by the largest proportion of the Swiss population, but there are four official languages, German, French, Italian and Romansh.
- In Turkey, the official language is Turkish, spoken by 90% of the population. Other languages include Kurdish and Arabic but these are not official languages.

Answers
Argentina: Spanish; **Austria:** German; **Brazil:** Portuguese; **Bulgaria:** Bulgarian; **Egypt:** Arabic; **Japan:** Japanese; **Mexico:** Spanish; **Poland:** Polish; **Russia:** Russian; **Switzerland:** French, German, Italian; **Thailand:** Thai; **Turkey:** Turkish, Arabic

3 Remind students that, in English, languages, countries and nationalities always begin with a capital letter.

Answers
Austria/Austrian; Brazil/Brazilian; Bulgaria/Bulgarian; Egypt/Egyptian; Japan/Japanese; Mexico/Mexican; Poland/Polish; Russia/Russian; Switzerland/Swiss; Thailand/Thai; Turkey/Turkish

Language notes
Most languages and nationalities end in *-(i)an*, and the stress usually comes before the *-(i)an* sound, e.g. Argen<u>tin</u>ian, Bra<u>zil</u>ian, Bul<u>gar</u>ian, E<u>gypt</u>ian, <u>Ger</u>man, I<u>tal</u>ian, <u>Rus</u>sian.
Many of the other languages and nationalities end in *-ish*. These are generally two-syllable words, and the stress is on the first syllable, e.g. <u>Pol</u>ish, <u>Span</u>ish, <u>Turk</u>ish.

A few languages and nationalities end in *-ese*, and the stress is always on the *-ese* sound, e.g. Japan<u>ese</u>, Portug<u>uese</u>. There are also a few exceptions, e.g. <u>Austr</u>ian and <u>Mex</u>ican (which have the stress on the first syllable) and the 'irregular' <u>Ar</u>abic (from many Arabic countries), <u>French</u> (from France), <u>Swiss</u> (from Switzerland) and <u>Thai</u> (from Thailand).

Fast finishers
Students think of a famous person from each country in exercise 2. They then read out the names for the other students to say where they come from, their nationality and which language(s) they speak.

4 SPEAKING
- After students do the task, extend to a class discussion by asking some students to say which countries they would like to visit and which languages they would like to speak and to explain their answers in each case.

5a 20
- Highlight that the word stress shifts in *memori<u>sa</u>tion* (n.) and *<u>mem</u>orise* (v.), that the noun *practice* and the verb *practise* have different spellings but identical pronunciation; and that the pronunciation of 'i' changes in *revise* (v.) (/rɪˈvaɪz/) and *revision* (n.) (/rɪˈvɪʒən/).
- Before students do the task, point out that they need to be careful with the form of some items. With less confident classes, check students understand that there are different forms for some items in the box, e.g. *accuracy* (n.) and *accurate* (adj.), so students need to think exactly which word form they need in each gap and that they may need to make nouns plural.

5b 21

Answers
a mistakes b practise c revision d memorise e Translation
f accuracy g fluent

6 The following general rules can be given, but there are many exceptions:
- *do* is used when someone performs an action, activity or some kind of work.
- *make* is used when someone is constructing, building or creating something or preparing food.

Possible answers
do an exam, take an exam, pass an exam, fail an exam
do an exercise, check an exercise, correct an exercise
make a mistake, correct a mistake
do English, study English, learn English
do homework, check homework

7 Answer
1 study 2 revise 3 make

Use it ... don't lose it!
8 SPEAKING
- Follow up by brainstorming with the class different ways to study English outside the classroom. Students could give their own ideas or favourite English websites. Suggest all students try a new idea or website before the next class.

 Homework > Workbook page 22

33

3 PLURILINGUAL

Reading p33
Predicting content, reading for gist and detail

> **Warmer**
> Write these words on the board: *chicken finger, fashionable, lonely, manager, YouTuber* and *vlog*.
> Ask students which words they think were added to the dictionary during their lives and which are older.
> Elicit that *chicken finger*, *YouTuber* and *vlog* are all relatively new words.
> Then ask them: *When do you think fashionable, lonely and manager were first used in English?*
> Discuss as a class before telling them that the first recorded use of all three words was actually by Shakespeare about 400 years ago.

1 SPEAKING
- Ask students how we say # in English and elicit the word *hashtag*. Discuss where we usually use hashtags (on social media, particularly Twitter®) and if students have ever seen the hashtags #FOMO and #SNACCIDENT.

> **Possible answer**
> English is a language that is always changing.

2 Pre-teach any words students may have problems with, not including the underlined words and not including the blended words or acronyms as these are all explained within the text itself, e.g. *innovation* (*a new idea or way of doing something*).
- Check students understand that in this context a *language academy* is not a school but is an official organisation which controls what is considered 'correct' language use.

> **Answer**
> 2 No

3 🔊 22

> **Answer**
> a 7 b 2 c 6 d 1 e 8 f 4 g 3

> ➕ **Extra activity**
> Ask students to look in detail at sentences 1–8 in the correct places a–g and think about how they relate to the text immediately before and after them. Discuss each item as a class to help students develop an awareness of referencing within a text and how this can help them complete this exercise type.

> **Answers**
> a 7 *Is that why* (= the fact that there aren't any official organisations which watch over the development of English) *English continues to change …?*
> b 2 *A lot of them* (= the new words and expressions) *are blends.*
> c 6 *These are young people* (= teen**ag**ers) *who spend a lot of time in front of a screen.*
> d 1 *That's the fear of missing out* (= FOMO), …
> e 8 *These words are made with the first letters of a phrase or expression* (= acronyms, e.g. FOMO, POTUS, FLOTUS) …
> f 4 *All languages change and evolve.* (That's because *the world changes*, too.)
> g 3 *But there were many changes in England in the 16th century, too.* (This innovation of language has been happening for a long time, even since *Shakespeare*.)

4
> **Answers**
> 1 *blending*: the name for the process of two words coming together to make a new word
> 2 *POTUS*: an example of an acronym (President of the United States)
> 3 *snaccident*: an example of a blend ('snack' and 'accident')
> 4 *acronyms*: the name of abbreviations consisting of letters that form a word
> 5 *social media*: it is responsible for a lot of new language
> 6 *technology*: a possible reason for why language is changing quickly
> 7 *FOMO*: an example of an acronym (Fear Of Missing Out)
> 8 *Shakespeare*: language has been changing since Shakespeare's time

5 Before students do the task, point out that two of the sentences in exercise 3 also contain underlined words and phrases.

> **Answers**
> *development* – change, growth or improvement over time
> *blending* – mixing two or more things together
> *posts* – a piece of writing on social media
> *First Lady* – the wife of the President of the United States
> *missing out* – losing an opportunity to do something
> *evolve* – grow and change

6 💡 **Critical thinkers**
- Before students do the task, remind them that the objective is to justify their opinion and give suitable examples.

> **Possible answers**
> I would say that it's important for a dictionary to include the words people really use, not just the words that academics want us to use! I'm not sure that they should add every new word to the dictionary, as some words quickly disappear. But when people have used a word for a few years, then I really feel that it should go into the dictionary. It's also important so that people who don't know the new words can check them when they hear them. For example, there are lots of older people who don't know words connected with technology, and I'm certain that they would want new technology words to be in the dictionary so they can look up the meaning.

▶️ **Flipped classroom**
You may want to ask students to watch the Flipped classroom video for Unit 3 as homework, in preparation for the grammar lesson.

# PLURILINGUAL 3

Grammar in context 1 p34
Using countable and uncountable nouns; using *some, any, much, many, a lot of, a few, a little*

Warmer
Write these words on the board: *biscuit, cake, carrot, coffee, egg, milk* and *rice*.
Put students into pairs to discuss if they are *countable, uncountable* or *it depends*.
Discuss as a class, making sure students understand the different implied meanings of *cake, coffee* and *sugar* and eliciting words that can be used to make the uncountable nouns countable.

Answers
Countable: biscuit
Depends: cake (a whole item is 'a cake', countable; a piece from a larger whole is uncountable but can be made countable with 'a slice/piece of'); carrot and egg (whole items are countable; the ingredient is uncountable); coffee (in a café we can ask for 'a coffee' [= a cup of], countable; the ingredient is uncountable).
Uncountable: milk ('a bottle/litre of' = countable); rice ('a packet/kilo of' = countable)

1 If you didn't set the Flipped classroom video for homework, watch the video in class before working through the activities.
- Before students do the task, tell them to also look at the sentences in exercise 3 on page 33 and that there is more than one example of some of the words. They first decide if the words are countable or uncountable as presented in the text.
- When checking answers, make sure students understand that *language* and *time* are used as both countable and uncountable nouns in the text and discuss why (see answers).
- When discussing whether the same word can be countable or uncountable depending on the context, use the information in the Warmer to discuss *chocolate* (countable in the text but also uncountable) and *yoghurt* (uncountable in the text but also countable [= a pot of yoghurt]). Make sure that students realise that some nouns can only be countable, like *example* and *word*.
- Both *imagination* and *innovation* are uncountable nouns in the text but can both be countable when a specific instance of the general thing is referred to, e.g. *a vivid imagination, recent innovations*. A similar example which students may find easier to understand is *change*.

Answers
1 in title, 'their language' (paragraph 1) and 'languages' (sentence 4): countable – referring to the particular grammar and vocabulary used by a group, e.g. English, can be counted; in paragraphs 3 and 4: uncountable – referring to types of words used generally, can't be counted
2 'for a long time' (paragraph 4) and 'a lot of time' (sentence 6): uncountable – it can't be counted but there can be more or less of it; 'a good time' (sentence 1): countable – means 'an experience', can be counted
3 uncountable   4 countable   5 countable   6 uncountable
7 countable   8 uncountable
Some words can be countable or uncountable depending on the context.

2 When checking answers, contrast the meaning of the word *time* in items 1 and 6. Elicit that in item 1 *time* is uncountable, but in item 6 it means 'how often something happens' and is countable. Point out that *yoghurt* in item 4 is countable.

Answers
1 time   2 imagination   3 language   4 a yoghurt   5 an example
6 times

3 Point out that the sentences are based on sentences from the reading on page 33.
- When checking answers, elicit that both *countries* and *problems* are countable.

Answers
b some, any, many, a lot of, a few
c any, many, much, a lot of
d many, a lot of
e a few, a little

4 Pre-teach *knowledge* (*everything you know about a particular subject*).
- When checking answers, elicit which words are countable in the context (*words, friends, hour*) and which are uncountable (*knowledge, ice cream, orange juice*). Point out that *ice cream* can also be countable (a single 'individual' ice cream from a kiosk) and that *orange juice* can also be countable (= a glass of).

Answers
1 some   2 any   3 some   4 any   5 an   6 some

 Culture exchange

5 When checking answers, elicit the key words/expressions connected with each item, and highlight whether each one is countable or uncountable, i.e. (a) and (b) *words* [C]; (c) *names, words or expressions* [C]; (d) *expressions* [C]; (e) *sense* [U]; (f) *adverts and posters* [C]; (g) *companies* [C]; (h) *need* [U]; (i) *experts* [C]; (j) and (k) *products* [C]; (l) *time* [U]; (m) *words* [C].

Answers
a many   b a lot   c many   d some   e any   f a few   g a lot of
h any   i Many   j lots of   k a few   l a little   m many

+ Extra activity
Students write sentences to practise the phrases for quantity in exercise 3 using nouns from exercises 1–5. They should not repeat either phrases for quantity or nouns in their sentences. Ask some students to share their sentences with the class.

Homework › Workbook page 24

35

3 PLURILINGUAL

7 After students do the task, extend to a class discussion by asking some students to share their sentences with the class.

8 When checking answers, highlight the difference in meaning with and without the article *a/an*. Ask students if there are expressions in their language which have a similar change in meaning.

- If helpful, extend each sentence to show more clearly the positive/negative meaning, e.g. *1 But there are lots more.*, *2 These are the only ones I can think of.*, *3 It's a real problem for them.*, *4 It's not difficult.*

> **Answers**
> a negative
> b countable = (a) few; uncountable = (a) little

9 Make sure students understand that the exercise is testing two areas: whether the word after each phrase for quantity is countable (*[a] few*) or uncountable (*[a] little*) and whether it is positive (*a few/little*) or negative (*few/little*). Remind them that *a lot of/lots of* can be used with both countable and uncountable nouns.

> **Answers**
> 1 lots of 2 little 3 A few 4 a lot of

10 Before students do the task, check which words are countable and which are uncountable. Highlight possible problem areas, e.g. *food* and *fruit* are both uncountable, but many specific foods and fruits are countable (*biscuits*, *bananas*); *people* is countable, but is an irregular plural, (*one person*, *two people*). Pre-teach *tourism* (the business of people going on holiday) and elicit that it is uncountable.

- With less confident classes, have students work in pairs to make their notes. They can then either work with a new partner in exercise 11 or work in groups of four.

Use it ... don't lose it!

11 SPEAKING

- Before students do the task, elicit two blocks of questions on the board to show where they should use the phrases for quantity, i.e.
  Is there   any ...   Are there   any ...
  *   much ... ?   many ... ?*
  *   (a) little ...   (a) few ...*
- Elicit the four possible short answers, i.e. *Yes, there is.*; *No, there isn't.*; *Yes, there are.*; *No, there aren't.*
- After students do the task, nominate some students who chose unusual countries for the class to try and guess.

Developing vocabulary p35

Using negative prefixes *un-*, *in-*, *im-*, *ir-*, *il-*

> **Warmer**
> Books closed. Write the following gapped sentences on the board:
> 1 If the law says you can do something, it is _____.
> 2 I smile when I feel _____.
> 3 My teacher writes a ✓ when the answer is _____.
> Put students into pairs to complete the sentences. Check the answers and elicit that these are all positive words. Tell students that they are going to look at ways they can make these words negative.

> **Answers**
> 1 legal 2 happy 3 correct

1

> **Language notes**
> *Un-* is the most common negative prefix, but there are few rules for which prefix is used with which word (except words that start with the letter *m*, which always take the prefix *im-*). The main stress is usually on the original word, e.g. un**com**fortable, but there is often a secondary stress on the prefix. Prefixes can be also be added to verbs and nouns.

2a 🔊 23

- When checking answers, check the spelling of each item as it can be quite hard to hear the difference between the prefixes *in-*, *im-*, *ir-* and *il-* in some cases.

> **Answers**
> uncomfortable, incorrect, informal, unhappy, illegal, illogical, unofficial, impolite, impossible, irregular, irresponsible, unusual, invisible

2c 🔊 23

> **Answers**
> un**com**fortable, in**cor**rect, in**for**mal, un**hap**py, il**le**gal, il**log**ical, un**offi**cial, im**po**lite, im**pos**sible, ir**reg**ular, ir**res**ponsible, un**u**sual, in**vis**ible
> No, we don't stress the prefix.

3 Make sure students understand that all the sentences should be completed with negatives from the box in 1. None of the sentences use positive adjectives.

> **Answers**
> 1 irregular 2 irresponsible 3 impolite 4 illegal 5 incorrect
> 6 informal 7 unusual 8 impossible

Use it ... don't lose it!

5 SPEAKING

- After students do the task, ask them to share any sentences they had which were the same with the class and see if any other pairs also had those sentences.

36

PLURILINGUAL 3

GREAT LEARNERS GREAT THINKERS p36

Investigating how animals and humans communicate with signs and body language

- **Warmer**
  Model various adjectives and ask students to try and guess how you are feeling just by looking at your face and body language, e.g. *tired, frightened, unhappy, excited* and *uncomfortable*.

1 SPEAKING

- Before students do the task, write the following two definitions on the board for them to match to *language* and *communication*:

  the process of giving information or of making emotions or ideas known to someone (communication)

  signs, symbols, sounds, and other methods of communicating information, emotions, or ideas (language)

- Make sure students understand that there is a very fine line between the two areas and even specialists argue over what is considered *language*. In this exercise there are no 'correct' answers as the examples have been chosen to make students think about a range of difficult cases.

2a VIDEO

- After students watch the video, elicit some of the things they saw, e.g. *chimpanzees, a country house/zoo, a presenter* (students may recognise Stephen Fry, the actor, comedian and writer), various species of *monkeys, birds, meerkats, a lion, an elephant, dolphins* and *an expert/zoologist*. Discuss as a class what they think they will hear.

2b VIDEO

- Pre-teach *click* (*a short sound made with your tongue which sounds like the sound when you press a switch*) and *muscle* /ˈmʌsəl/ (*a piece of flesh that is used for moving a particular part of your body*).

  Answers
  someone being interviewed; apes/monkeys/gorillas in their habitat; apes gesturing/making hand signals; apes communicating and throwing fruit

3 VIDEO

  Answers
  1 meerkats – danger; dolphins – food
  2 fear, joy, love
  3 language separates humans and other animals
  4 primate communication is more limited and inflexible; primates don't have the necessary muscles in their faces to make sounds like humans do

4 SPEAKING

- Before students do the task, check the meaning of each example of non-verbal communication by asking pairs of students to demonstrate them, e.g. *Judit and Julio, can you both sit up straight, please? Fran and Teo, can you both fold your arms?* etc.

5 After checking answers, ask students: *In what other situations can body language be particularly important?* and elicit students' ideas, e.g. *in an oral exam, when presenting something to the class*.

  Answers
  2 … interviewers often base their decisions on non-verbal factors.
  3 We can appear insecure, uncomfortable and informal.

GREAT THINKERS

6 SPEAKING

- The *Headlines* thinking routine helps students to identify and focus on the central issue in a text. It also requires them to have understood the main message(s) of a text and to find a way to express their understanding clearly.
- Students work individually in the first instance. However, if your class is less confident, ask them to share their headline with a partner before sharing one or both with a larger group or the class. Ask students to note the headlines which they think reflect the main message(s) of the text particularly well.

7 Collate students' ideas on the board and give them the chance to share the tips and advice they found before they move on to the Great learners exercise.

GREAT LEARNERS SEL

- Be particularly sensitive when discussing body language with students. Some may be quite self-conscious, so consider keeping this as a time for personal reflection, and do not push students to share with the class.

LEARNER PROFILE

- Ask students to read the statement and the question in the Learner profile on page 142, and then grade themselves from 1 to 5. Explain that here 1 means 'I don't have very confident body language', and 5 means 'I have very confident body language'.
- If appropriate for your class, get students to share their grades with a partner or small group and, if they wish, to give their reasons. Encourage students to share suggestions for showing more confident body language. Alternatively, ask students individually to think of ways to show more confident body language.

3 PLURILINGUAL

Listening p38
Listening for specific information

> **Warmer**
> Write on the board: *Spanish*, *Esperanto*, *French*, *Japanese* and *Klingon*. Students work in pairs or small groups noting down briefly what they know about each one. Take feedback as a class.

> **Possible answers**
> Spanish is a European language spoken in Spain and many countries in South America. It's quite difficult.
> Esperanto is an invented language. It was supposed to become a universal language.
> French is a European language spoken in France and some other parts of the world. It's quite difficult.
> Japanese is a very difficult language. It uses symbols not words. It's spoken in Japan and is a little bit like Korean.
> Klingon is an invented language spoken by the Klingons from the *Star Trek*™ series.

1 SPEAKING
- After students do the task, collate ideas from this preparation stage on the board.

3 🔊 24
- Before students do the task, ask them to look at the incomplete notes and guess which gaps they expect to be filled with words and which with numbers. Ask students to be more precise where possible, e.g. *(a) word – job*; *(b)–(d) words*; *(e) number – year*; *(f) word*; *(g) number*; etc.

> **Answers**
> **a** translator **b** good **c** language **d** simple **e** 2001 **f** letters **g** 120 **h** few **i** blue **j** many **k** body language **l** 30 **m** New Zealand **n** Argentina

🌐 **Culture notes**
Toki Pona was originally created in 2001 but really started to grow after Sonja Lang published *Toki Pona: The Language of Good* in 2014. The book was also published in French in 2016. There is now a Facebook® group and various forums and chat sites where people can practise the language.
The Klingons have appeared in the *Star Trek* series and films since the 1960s. According to the Guinness World Records, their language is the most widely spoken fictional language in the world. There is also a Klingon Dictionary and even a translation in Klingon of *Hamlet*.
Esperanto was originally created in 1887 by Ludwik Lejzer Zamenhof, and the first details of its form and structure were published in 1905 in his *Fundamento de Esperanto*. It was designed to be an easy-to-learn, regular language, but its use never spread as its inventor hoped.

4 ➕ **Extra activity**
Students imagine they have the opportunity to interview Sonja Lang. Put them into pairs to use the questions they wrote in 1 to form the basis of the interview, adapting them as necessary. They should write a script, including suitable phrases to welcome Sonja and thank her for agreeing to be interviewed and her answers. They should use the Internet to find the answers to the questions not answered in the recording. They can then practise their script and act it out for another pair, a small group or the class.

5 ✳ **Critical thinkers**
- Before students do the task, remind them that the objective is to justify their opinion and give suitable examples.

 Homework Workbook page 25

Grammar in context 2 p38
Using defining and non-defining relative clauses

> **Warmer**
> Write the following sentences on the board:
> 1 *This is the thing which you can use to look up new words.*
> 2 *This is the person who helps you learn something new.*
> 3 *This is the place where you go to study until you are 18.*
> Put students into pairs to identify the words. Check the answers and then circle 'the thing which', 'the person who' and 'the place where'. Tell students that they are going to look at phrases like these to give information about things they want to describe.

> **Answers**
> **1** dictionary **2** teacher **3** school

1a Point out that the sentences are based on sentences from the listening in the previous section.

1b Check students understand that *that* can be used instead of *who* and *which* but <u>not</u> instead of *whose*, *where* or *when*.

> **Answers**
> **a** that **b** which, that **c** whose **d** where **e** when

2a If necessary, give students more examples showing where relative pronouns can be omitted, e.g. *Klingon is a language (which/that) characters in* Star Trek *speak.*; *She's the teacher (who/that) I studied Spanish with last year.* Make sure students understand that to omit the pronoun, the second verb (i.e. 'speak'; 'studied') needs its own subject (i.e. 'characters in *Star Trek*'; 'I').

> **Answer**
> No, we can't.

2b > **Answer**
> They give essential information.

3 Make sure students understand that in various cases both alternatives are correct. They should focus on whether the second verb has its own subject or not to help them decide.

> **Answers**
> **1** who **2** both **3** which **4** both **5** both **6** who **7** both **8** which

PLURILINGUAL 3

4 ✓ Exam tip To answer the question in the Exam tip box on page 38, reading the complete text first, without thinking about the gaps, helps students get a general understanding of the text.
- Tell students that before they look at the answers they are given, they should think about the *type* of word they need in each gap (noun, verb, pronoun, article, etc.) and the general *meaning*.
- Students should then read the answers they are given and choose the one which they think is best. They should look very carefully at the words which come just before and after the gap to see if they help them identify the answer.
- Remind students that if they aren't sure which answer is right, they should take away any answers which they know are not correct.
- Students should then read the sentence again with their answer in the gap.
- Remind students that when they finish, they should check that they have an answer for each question. They should never leave answers blank in an exam.

Answers
1 a 2 c 3 a 4 d 5 b 6 a 7 d 8 a 9 b

🌐 Culture notes
Xhosa (/ˈkɔːsə/) is one of the 11 official languages of South Africa and is mainly spoken in the south east of the country along the coast. Approximately 8 million people speak it as a first language and 11 million as a second language. Its most characteristic features are its use of 'clicking' sounds and the use of high and low tones to distinguish different words which would otherwise sound the same.

Fast finishers ➤➤
Ask students to write a personal example sentence for each relative pronoun. Ask some students to write their sentences on the board, and discuss as a class if alternative relative pronouns can be used in each case or if the relative pronoun can be omitted.

5
a True b True c False d True

Language notes
Distinguishing between information which is essential and information which is extra and non-essential can be a challenge for some students. If necessary, give more examples, and ask questions to check students fully understand the difference, e.g.:

The teacher who taught me French last year was brilliant. – How many teachers do I have each year? (lots, one for each subject); How do we know which teacher was brilliant? (because the sentence tells us it's the French teacher); Does the sentence make sense if we say 'The teacher was brilliant'? (no, because we don't know which teacher it is talking about without more information); Is 'who taught me French' essential or extra information? (essential)

My English teacher, who goes to Brighton every summer, speaks English perfectly. – Does the sentence make sense if we say 'My English teacher speaks English perfectly.'? (Yes, we know which teacher it is talking about.); Is 'who goes to Brighton every summer' essential or extra information? (extra)

6a With less confident classes, give students one or two words for each gap to help them complete the sentences, e.g. 2 *blend*; 3 *wife*; 4 *Shakespeare*; 5 *changing*; 6 *people* or 2 *snack + accident*; 3 *wife + First Lady*; 4 *Shakespeare + alive*; 5 *always + changing*; 6 *speak + Spanish*.

6b SPEAKING 👥
- Before students do the task, show how the commas in the sentences signal short pauses in speech, e.g. *Shakespeare,* [pause] *who was born in England,* [pause] *invented a lot of new words.*

> **Possible answers**
> 2 is a blend of 'snack' and 'accident'
> 3 wife is called the First Lady
> 4 Shakespeare was alive
> 5 is always changing
> 6 people speak Spanish

Use it ... don't lose it!
8 SPEAKING 👥
- Before students do the task, point out that in sentences with defining relative clauses there are no short pauses in speech. Tell students to make sure they do not pause before or after the relative clauses when they say their sentences from exercise 7.

🏠 **Homework** ➤ Workbook page 26

39

3 PLURILINGUAL

Developing speaking p40
Asking for information

Warmer
Brainstorm some advantages and disadvantages of learning English at a summer school in an English-speaking country.

Possible answers
Advantages: You can hear the language all day; you can meet people from other countries; you won't just meet people who speak your language and make the same mistakes as you; you will be able to practise English with native speakers.
Disadvantages: You may be homesick; you may not have time to go sightseeing; it's expensive.

1 SPEAKING
- After students do the task, discuss the questions as a class. Find out which cities and countries are popular with your students, and collate all the factors students can think of on the board.

Possible answers
2 dates, cost, age of students, quality of teaching, other activities, size of school, distance to nearest town, food

2 🔊 25
- Before students do the task, make clear that they do not need to understand every word. They only need to listen for gist and will be able to listen again for more details in the next exercise.
- Pre-teach any words students may have problems with, e.g. *accommodation* (*a place for someone to stay or live in*), *excursions* (*short visits to interesting places, particularly for tourists*) and *registration form* (*a document you complete with information when you want to do an activity, join a class, etc.*).

Answer
The Language Centre is in Toronto.

3 🔊 25
- Follow up by asking: *Would you like to do the course in Toronto? Why/Why not?*

Answers
Name of centre: Toronto Easy English Centre
Course begins: 2nd July
Course lasts: two weeks
Price: $1,400 Canadian
Hours of class per day: four
Other activities: excursions, sports activities, e.g. tennis and hockey

4 SPEAKING

Answers
a 7 b 1 c 4 d 8 e 2 f 9 g 6 h 5 i 3

5
Answers
The language centre is in Toronto, not Vancouver.
The course starts on 2nd July, not 3rd July.
The price is $1,400, not $1,500.
There are four hours of classes each day, not five.
Activities include hockey, not rugby.

6 When checking answers, make sure students understand that *Pardon?* and *Could you repeat that?* have the same function, i.e. to get the other person to repeat what they have just said. Elicit possible ways to complete the other two expressions, e.g. *Sorry, did you say the 3rd July / $1,500 / rugby?*; *I'm not sure I understood what you said / that correctly / how long the course is*.

Answers
Sorry, say
sure, understood (what you said)

7 SPEAKING
- If you wish, allow students to practise the dialogue in exercise 4 again, substituting the different information from exercise 3 as necessary.

Mixed ability
To make the activity more challenging, tell more confident students that they need to practise the dialogue without looking at exercise 4 or the Speaking bank. Give them a few moments to memorise the useful expressions, then tell them to role-play the dialogue using only the notes in exercise 3. If students have problems, allow them to quickly refer to exercise 4 and the Speaking bank as they work, but encourage them to do as much as possible without referring to the Student's Book.

Practice makes perfect
8a-b SPEAKING
- Remind students that in exams it is important to know how many marks there are for different sections and to know what the examiners want.
- ✓ **Exam tip** To answer the question in the Exam tip box, students need to communicate successfully, speak fluently, use accurate and varied grammar and vocabulary and pronounce words clearly.

PLURILINGUAL 3

Developing writing p41
Writing an article 1

> **Warmer**
>
> Discuss one of the following sets of questions as a class.
> If your school has a website:
> - What's the address of the school website?
> - When was the last time you visited it? Why did you visit it?
> - What sections are there on the website?
> - Which sections do you find most useful?
> - Which sections do you find most interesting?
> - Are there any sections it doesn't have that you think the school should add?
> - Have you ever written anything that has been published on the school website? If so, what?
>
> If your school doesn't have a website:
> - Do you think it would be a good idea for the school to have a website? Why/Why not?
> - What sort of information would it be useful to have on a school website?
> - What would you be interested in reading on a school website?
> - Would you be interested in writing something for a school website? What?
> - Would you be interested in reading what your classmates and other students write?

1 SPEAKING

- After students do the task, brainstorm some tips for learning a language, e.g. *watch TV series and films in the original language with subtitles*; *use the view lyrics function on Spotify® for your favourite songs*; *try to learn chunks of language, not individual words*. Collate ideas on the board and tell students to make a note of these so they can use some of them in the final task.

2 Follow up by asking students to give some examples of *everyday conversations*, e.g. conversations about hobbies and interests, what they did at the weekend, where they are going on holiday, what they are studying at school at the moment, etc. Ask students how confident they feel having these sorts of conversations in English and if they can do this in any other languages. Then ask if they have tried any of Leah's tips for learning a language themselves.

- After students do the task, ask them what is wrong with the text and elicit that it doesn't have any paragraphs.

3 When checking answers, point out that the three paragraphs correspond to the three bullet points in the advert in exercise 1.

> **Answers**
> **Paragraph 1:** *Let me begin by giving you … I know a few words in French.* (about her and the languages she speaks)
> **Paragraph 2:** *At the moment, … that helps me to practise outside school, too.* (how she learns and practises speaking English)
> **Paragraph 3:** *Personally, … Try it!* (tips for learning English)

4 Check students understand that the topic of a paragraph should follow logically from the topic of the previous paragraph and should lead on to the topic of the next paragraph.

- Explain that, in general, the purpose of a paragraph is to express one main point, idea or opinion.

> **Answer**
> Paragraphs are important to help organise your ideas. This makes your writing clearer for the reader.

+ Extra activity

Tell students that you want them to look more closely at the content of the three paragraphs in exercise 2. Write or project the following items, or read them out one at a time. Students refer to the text by Leah and organise the items according to their position within the model text.

fun things to do to help you learn; how much contact you have with English/other languages; more serious things to do to help you learn; other things you study in English; the languages you study; where you were born; who you practise with; your age; your family; your level of different languages

> **Answers**
> **Paragraph 1:** your age; your family; where you were born; your level of different languages
> **Paragraph 2:** the languages you study; other things you study in English; how much contact you have with English/other languages; who you practise with
> **Paragraph 3:** fun things to do to help you learn; more serious things to do to help you learn

Practice makes perfect

5a-b Before students do the task, make sure they understand that there is a very clear objective for their article: it should contain three paragraphs, each one covering one of the bullet points from exercise 1.

- Remind students that they can use some of the tips they brainstormed in exercise 1 if they wish.

Homework › Workbook page 28

3 PLURILINGUAL

Test yourself p43

Grammar test

1 **Answers**
1 a few 2 any 3 a little 4 many/a lot of 5 much/a lot of 6 some/a little

2 **Answers**
1 little 2 few 3 a little 4 a few

3 **Answers**
2 John Kani is an actor who speaks Xhosa.
3 The park is a beautiful place where you can go at the weekend.
4 Last year was a special year when a lot of important things happened.
5 That's the teacher whose classes are brilliant.
6 This is a great book that/which they want to translate into English.

4 **Answers**
1 Pirahã, which ~~that~~ only about 200 people speak, is an unusual language.
2 Patrick Rothfuss, who wrote *The Name of the Wind*, is a great fantasy author.
3 French, which I learned ~~it~~ at school, is one of my favourite languages.
4 My grandfather, who is ~~whose~~ 80, runs every day.
5 Ellie, who I work with, is from Wales.
6 The necklace, which ~~who~~ I lost, was a present from my mum.

Vocabulary test

1 **Answers**
1 Thailand 2 Portuguese 3 Turkish 4 German 5 Egyptian 6 Switzerland

2 **Answers**
1 translation 2 Revision 3 fluent 4 make 5 do 6 exercise

3 **Answers**
1 illegal 2 impolite 3 informal 4 correct 5 irresponsible 6 unofficial 7 correct

TAKE CARE! 4

Vocabulary in context p44
Using a range of lexis to talk about parts of the body and health problems

Warmer

Books closed. Ask students if they think they are healthy at the moment. Elicit any minor health problems students have, avoiding any more serious problems you know students suffer from, and see if students know how to express these in English, e.g. *My nose is blocked. I have got a cold.; I fell off my bike yesterday – look at my hand!* Then focus attention on the unit title and opening photo, and elicit the meaning of *take care* (be careful in a dangerous situation).

1 SPEAKING 26

- Highlight the pronunciation of *stomach* (/ˈstʌmək/), and explain that the final 'ch' is pronounced with the same sound as the final 'ck' at the end of *neck* (/nek/).

2 27

- Before students do the task, make sure they understand that these are more advanced words than the set in exercise 1, so they are less likely to know them. If you wish, allow students to use dictionaries and/or work in pairs.

3 28

- After checking answers, highlight the silent 'k' at the beginning of *knee* (/niː/). Ask students *Which other words do you know* (/nəʊ/!) *with a silent 'k'?* to elicit *know*. Students may know some other words, e.g. *knock, knife*.

Answers
1 heel 2 ankle 3 calf 4 knee 5 thigh 6 elbow 7 thumb
8 chest 9 chin 10 cheek 11 forehead 12 jaw 13 throat
14 shoulder 15 back 16 wrist 17 hip

4a After students do the task, ask them to draw a picture to illustrate the two people not in the photos, i.e. Karen and Mike. Choose the best picture for each person, and ask the 'artist' to show the class to help clarify meaning.

Answers
a Luke b Liam

4b When checking answers, highlight the pronunciation of *cough* (/kɒf/ rhymes with *off*) and *temperature* (/ˈtemprɪtʃə(r)/). Point out that *stomach ache* contains two examples 'ch' pronounced as /k/ as seen earlier, i.e. /ˈstʌmək ˌeɪk/.

Answers
broken – damaged and in more than one piece
injured – hurt in an accident
hurts – causes pain in your body
pains – feelings you have in your body when hurt or injured
a bad cold – an illness that blocks your nose and makes you cough
flu – a common infectious disease that lasts a short time and makes you feel hot or cold, weak and tired
coughing – forcing air through your throat with a sudden noise
sore – painful/uncomfortable, often as a result of injury or infection
sprained – an injured joint from sudden stretching or turning
swollen – increased in size from injury or illness
cut – an injury caused by something sharp
scratches – small cuts on the surface of your skin
bruises – marks on your body from hitting or falling
a high temperature – when your body temperature is higher than normal
stomach ache – pain in your stomach
a virus – a small organism that can make you ill

5 SPEAKING

- Mime suddenly an ache or pain, e.g. grab the back of your jaw and wince (for *toothache*). Use this to elicit the question *What's the matter?* to ask what is wrong. With less confident classes, mime the various options in the exercise to elicit/teach the phrases.

Possible answers
1 toothache, headache 2 arm, ankle 3 thumb, back
4 wrist, elbow 5 lip, wrist

Language notes

There are various common compound nouns with *ache*. Most are written as one word, e.g. *toothache* and *headache*, but *stomach ache* is usually written as two. Students need to learn these on a case-by-case basis.
Headache is usually used with an article, but *toothache* and *stomach ache* are not.

6 With less confident classes, give students the first and last letter of each word to help them.

- When checking answers, nominate students to spell out the words as you write them on the board. Write up exactly the letters students say in order to highlight and correct any persistent mistakes with the alphabet, e.g. confusing *e* and *i*, mispronouncing *k*.
- Highlight that we add an extra syllable to the plurals *vi-rus, vi-rus-es; scratch, scratch-es;* and *bruise, bruis-es* but not *cuts*.

Answers
1 viruses 2 cuts, scratches, bruises 3 break, sprain

7 SPEAKING

Extra activity

In pairs, ask students to choose two or three words from the page. They write a short dialogue between a patient and a doctor including these words and including the question *What's the matter?* Ask a few pairs to perform their dialogues for the class.

4 TAKE CARE!

Reading p45
Predicting content, skimming and scanning for global and specific information

Warmer
Books closed. Point at parts of your body to elicit and revise the following words: *back*, *neck*, *head*, *hand*, *eye*, *arm* and *leg*, all of which appear in the article in exercise 2. Then put students into pairs to take turns pointing at other body parts and testing each other on the vocabulary from the previous section.

1 SPEAKING
- Elicit ideas for each photo from the class, but don't confirm if they are correct or not.

2
Before students do the task, make clear that they do not need to understand every word. They only need to read for gist and will be able to read again for more detail in the next exercise.

Answers
1 1 B 2 C 3 A

Culture notes
EyeForcer Smart Glasses™ were introduced in 2018. They come with non-prescription lenses, so anyone can wear them, but the lenses can be replaced with prescription lenses for people who usually wear glasses. As well as the app, which tells the wearer if he/she needs to change position, there is also a warning LED on the frames themselves which lights up whenever the glasses detect bad posture.

Various cities are experimenting with pavement traffic lights as well as traditional lights next to pedestrian crossings. These include Bodegraven in the Netherlands, Augsburg in Germany and Sydney in Australia. The lights flash red and only turn green when it is safe to cross the road.

3 🔊 29
- In this type of activity, students have to say which text or part of a text contains a piece of information.
- ✓ **Exam tip** To answer the question in the Exam tip box, the best approach to this type of exam task is for students to read the text quickly to get a general understanding, as they did in exercise 2.
- Students should then read the piece(s) of information that they need to find. They should look for key words that help them to find the text or part of the text which contains the information. They should then read that specific text or part of the text again in more detail.
- Tell students that if they are not sure that they have found the correct answer, they should read other sections again in more detail.
- When they finish, students should check they have an answer for each question. Point out that students should never leave answers blank in an exam.
- Pre-teach any words students may have problems with, not including the underlined words, e.g. *present* (existing somewhere), *a black eye* (a dark mark that forms on the skin around your eye as a result of being hit), *a first-aid kit* (a small box or bag with things you can use to help someone if they are suddenly sick or injured) and *fatal* (makes someone die).

Answers
1 B 2 A 3 C 4 A 5 C 6 B 7 A 8 C

Mixed ability
To simplify the activity, tell less confident students or the whole class to answer only questions 1–3, and tell them to use each paragraph (A–C) only once.

If students are able to complete this successfully, repeat the process with questions 4–6, again making clear they should use each paragraph only once. Students can then complete items 7 and 8, and in this case, there is one extra paragraph they don't need.

4
Answers
detect – notice
sit up straight – sit with your back upright
'home' button – the main button on a smartphone or tablet
lamppost – tall poles on streets with streetlights
lock – prevent you from using
pavement – the side of the street where you walk
miss – not notice

5 Critical thinkers
- Before students do the task, remind them that the objective is to justify their opinion and give suitable examples.
- If you feel your students need more support, write these prompts on the board:

    I'm certain / not sure (that) … because …
    I (really) believe/feel/think (that) … because …
    In my opinion, …
    Speaking personally, …
    I would say …

▶ Flipped classroom
You may want to ask students to watch the Flipped classroom video for Unit 4 as homework, in preparation for the grammar lesson.

Homework — Workbook page 31

TAKE CARE! 4

Grammar in context 1 p46
Using the present perfect with *ever*, *never*, *for* and *since*

Warmer

Write *Have you ever …?* on the board and ask specific students the following questions: *Have you ever broken an arm/a leg? Have you ever walked into a wall/lamppost? Have you ever sprained an ankle/elbow/knee/wrist? Have you ever had a sore neck/a headache from playing video games?*
Encourage students to answer with the short answers *Yes, I have./No, I haven't*. With more confident classes, ask follow-up questions in the past simple when students answer yes.

1a If you didn't set the Flipped classroom video for homework, watch the video in class before working through the activities.
- Point out that the sentences are based on sentences from the reading on page 45.

Answers
1 a 2 c 3 b

1b Answers
have, past participle

1c Answers
has seen/visited
hasn't seen/visited
Has, seen/visited

1d Follow up by asking: *Which word do we use in questions, ever or never?* (ever) *Which word has a negative meaning, ever or never?* (never) *Do we use an affirmative or a negative verb with* never? (affirmative, i.e. *I've never been …* not *I haven't never been …*)

Answers
1 Ever 2 Never 3 before

2 With less confident classes, remind students that there is a list of irregular verbs on page 159.

Answers
a Have, heard b 's/has happened c 's/has had d Has, broken e Have, told f haven't done

+ Extra activity

Put students into pairs to practise the dialogue and invent variations on it. Highlight the parts of the dialogue which can easily be changed, e.g. *Max* can be changed for any other name, male or female; the details of the accident *A car knocked him off his bike.* can be changed for *A bike hit him on a pedestrian crossing.*; the details of the injury *No, he was lucky.* can be changed for *Yes, he has. He's broken his ankle and sprained his wrist.*; etc.
Ask some pairs to perform their variations for the class.

3a Ask students *What's the usual position of* ever? and elicit that it is just before the past participle. Refer them back to rule 3 in exercise 1d if necessary.

Answers
1 has ever fallen 2 Has, ever stopped 3 has ever dived
4 Has, ever run 5 has ever swum 6 Has, ever broken

3b SPEAKING
- With more confident classes, elicit the words *odd numbers* for 1, 3 and 5 and *even numbers* for 2, 4 and 6.

3c 30

Answers
1 False – *Vesna Vulović (Serbia, 1950–2016) was a flight attendant who fell 10,160 metres after a bomb caused her plane to crash in Czechoslovakia (now the Czech Republic). She was in hospital for 16 months. She holds the Guinness World Record 'by accident'.*
2 Yes – *Aleix Segura Vendrell (Spain, 1986–) broke the Guinness World Record for holding his breath during the Mediterranean Dive Show in 2016.*
3 False – *Herbert Nitsch (Austria, 1970–) broke the Guinness World Record for diving 214 metres in Greece in 2007. He dived 253.2 metres in 2012 but severely injured himself in the process and has caused himself permanent health problems.*
4 No – *Eliud Kipchoge (Kenya, 1984–) currently holds the Guinness World Record for fastest marathon. He completed the Berlin Marathon in 2018 in 2 hours, 1 minute and 39 seconds.*
5 False – *Martin Strel (Slovenia, 1954–) holds the Guinness World Record for the longest distance open-water swim for swimming the whole of the Amazon River in 2007 in 66 days, breaking his 2001 record. He has also swum the whole of the Danube, the Mississippi and the Yangtze.*
6 Yes – *Evel Knievel (US, 1938–2007) was one of the most famous stunt performers of all time. He was given the Guinness World Record for most broken bones in 1975.*

4a Ask students *What's the usual position of* never? and elicit that it is the same as *ever*, i.e. just before the past participle. Refer them back to rule 3 in exercise 1d if necessary.

Answers
1 I have never worn ~~never~~ glasses or contact lenses.
2 I ~~never~~ have never taken medicine that tasted good.
3 correct
4 I have never had a broken arm ~~never~~.
5 correct
6 My best friend ~~never~~ has never had an accident while walking with a mobile phone.

4c SPEAKING
- When students feed back to the class, if necessary, remind them that we use the present perfect to introduce a topic, e.g. *Fran hasn't broken his arm, but he's broken his leg.* But then to give further details, we use the past simple and/or continuous, e.g. *He was skiing on holiday when he fell and …*

Homework > Workbook page 32

45

4 TAKE CARE!

5a Answers
a since b for

5b Point out that *for* and *since* always go just before the time expression.

Answers
1 M 2 P 3 P 4 M 5 M 6 M 7 P 8 P

5c Answers
We use *How long* to ask about duration.

6a Before students do the task, check they have understood fully by asking: *Are you going to complete the gaps?* (yes); *Are you going to choose from the two black underlined words?* (yes); *What are you going to do with the red numbers?* (nothing)
- Pre-teach any words students may have problems with, e.g. *active ingredient* (*the specific part of a drug or medicine that makes it work*).

Answers
1 have used, since, 2 has existed, since 3 have known, for
4 have studied, since 5 has been, for

6c 🔊 31
- After checking answers, ask students if any of the facts surprised them.

Answers
1 400 BC 2 1863 3 50 4 1600 5 120

🌐 Culture notes

The natural form of the active ingredient in aspirin is found in the leaves and bark of the willow tree. Its use is recorded in various ancient texts, including the work of Hippocrates (Greece, 460 BC–370 BC).

The International Red Cross and Red Crescent Movement was started to help those injured in wars, but its work now extends to helping in a much wider range of situations. It is commonly referred to as the Red Cross in Christian countries and the Red Crescent in Muslim countries.

The first human heart transplant was made in Cape Town, South Africa, on 3rd December 1967.

The first optical microscopes were invented in Europe in the early 1600s though no one person can specifically claim the invention as their own.

X-rays were discovered by Wilhelm Conrad Röntgen (Prussia [now Germany], 1845–1923). They are referred to as Röntgen rays in various languages. The first X-ray of a human body part was of his wife's hand.

7 Remind students that they should use contractions in all the sentences in this exercise.

Answers
1 've known 2 've had 3 haven't caught 4 've been

Use it ... don't lose it!

8 SPEAKING
- Before students do the task, demonstrate it yourself. Allow students to ask you one of the questions and give them a false answer. Encourage them to ask you additional questions using the past simple to try and find out if your answer is true or false.

Developing vocabulary p47
Using compound nouns connected with health and healthcare

Warmer

Write *ache*, *white*, *board* and *tooth* on the board, and ask students to match them to make words (*toothache*, *whiteboard*). Ask students what these types of words are called (compound nouns) and how they are made (noun + noun or adjective + noun). Explain that some compound nouns are written as one word and some as two.

1 When checking answers, point out that *black eye*, *heart disease* and *food poisoning* are written as two words, but *nosebleed* and *sunburn* are written as one.

Answers
1 black eye 2 heart disease 3 nosebleed 4 sunburn
5 food poisoning

Language notes

Students need to learn which compound nouns are written as one word and which as two on a case-by-case basis. The general trend is that as a compound becomes more common, it changes from being written as two words to being written as one. However, as there is no official language academy for English, there are often differences between dictionaries, and native speakers themselves often don't agree.

The word stress for compounds is equally irregular. The stress is usually on the first word, e.g. HEART disease, NOSEbleed, SUNburn, FOOD poisoning, but in some cases, it is on the second, e.g. black EYE. Again, students need to learn this on a case-by-case basis.

2 Answers
1 heart disease 2 sunburn 3 black eye 4 food poisoning
5 nosebleed

3 When checking answers, point out that *health centre*, *first-aid kit* and *waiting room* are written as two words, but *wheelchair* and *painkiller* are written as one.
- Model and drill the compound nouns to show the word stress, i.e. WHEELchair, HEALTH centre, first-AID kit, WAITing room and PAINkiller.

Answers
1 chair 2 centre 3 kit 4 room 5 killer

 Homework › Workbook page 33

46

TAKE CARE! 4

GREAT LEARNERS GREAT THINKERS p48

Thinking about the importance of taking responsibility for your own health

Warmer

Write _ _ _ _ _ _ _ _ _ on the board. Nominate a student to say a letter. If it is in the word (*allergies*), write the letter in all the places it appears. If not, draw the stem of a flower on the board. The turn then passes to another student. Repeat the process. If the student guesses correctly, write in the letter; if not, draw the centre of a flower at the top of the stem. Repeat, drawing a series of five petals around the flower. When it is nearly complete, mime being about to sneeze and give a student one final turn. If the student doesn't guess correctly, draw the last petal and pretend to sneeze!

1 SPEAKING

- Pre-teach *stings* (*when insects push a sharp part of their body into your skin*), *bites* (*when insects use their mouths to make a small hole in your skin*), *itchy* (*a feeling on your skin that makes you want to scratch it*) and *watery* (*filled with water*).

2a VIDEO

- Before students watch and listen for specific information, play the video first without sound. Ask students to look for the things they see in the video which could cause allergies (*animals* [*deer/dogs*], *grass* and *trees*).
- After the viewing without sound, ask students whether they would expect more allergies in towns and cities or in the country. Return to the question after students have watched the video with sound and after checking the answers to the exercise. (*People are more likely to develop allergies in a town/city than in the country.*)

> **Answers**
> 1 False 2 True 3 False 4 False 5 True

2b VIDEO

> **Answers**
> 1 False – About <u>1%</u> of children in the UK had asthma in the 1950s.
> 3 False – There is a big risk of allergies <u>in more developed countries</u>.
> 4 False – The problem today is that <u>modern life is separating us from microorganisms</u>.

GREAT THINKERS

3 SPEAKING

- *The four Cs: Connections, Challenges, Concepts, Changes* thinking routine helps students structure a discussion. It encourages students to connect a video/recording/text to their own life, ask questions about it, identify key concepts from it and consider how they might change as a result of it.
- Students work individually in steps 1–4 and then in small groups in step 5.
- If possible, share a copy of the video script with students. For this task it is ideal if students can highlight the *connections*, *challenges*, *concepts* and *changes* in different colours for reference in the final step.
- In the groupwork stage, students should all first share the *connections* they have made between the video and their lives / the lives of people they know and explain/discuss these one at a time; then share the *challenges* and discuss these; then share the *concepts*; and finally share the *changes*.

4 SEL

- Bear in mind that there are big differences in the way healthcare works in different countries. If possible, make sure you are fully informed about the system in your students' country so that you can highlight anything specific which is not covered in the quiz.

5 Unless all students answer 'Yes' to all the questions, make sure you set time aside in a future lesson to check students have done the necessary research and found the information they were missing.

GREAT LEARNERS

- Discuss as a class and elicit how in this particular case the information from the lesson, from the quiz in exercise 4 in particular, is extremely important in the world outside the classroom. Students aren't always with their parents or friends, so in the case of an accident or emergency they might need to answer questions from a healthcare professional themselves.

LEARNER PROFILE

- Ask students to read the statement and the question in the Learner profile on page 142, and then grade themselves from 1 to 5. Explain that here 1 means 'I don't often make connections between what I learn in class and the world outside', and 5 means 'I frequently make connections between what I learn in class and the world outside'.
- If appropriate for your class, get students to share their grades with a partner or small group and, if they wish, to give their reasons. Encourage students to share suggestions for making more connections between what they learn in class and the world outside. Alternatively, ask students to do this individually.

4 TAKE CARE!

Listening p50

Listening for gist and specific information

Warmer

Books closed. Ask students: *How far can you jump? And how high?* Elicit approximate distances, and find out if any students are particularly good at 'jumping' type sports, e.g. long jump, high jump, hurdles. Then ask: *What would you jump off?* And give examples of increasing height, e.g. *a chair, a table, a wall, a roof.* Find out which students seem most fearless.

2 🔊 32

- Pre-teach any words students may have problems with, e.g. *antenna* (*a long, thin piece of metal, often on a roof, to send and receive radio, TV signals, etc.*) and *span* (*in this case, the part of a bridge between two supporting points*).

Answers
They are talking about Karina Hollekim, a BASE jumper from Norway. She is special because she had a serious accident, but she is now able to walk again and even go skiing.

3 🔊 32

- Before students do the task, give them time to read all the answers carefully. Remind them that if they are not sure of the correct answer, they should eliminate answers which they know are not correct and then make a choice from the options remaining.

Answers
1 a **correct** – *B is for building, A is for antenna, S is for span (...) and E is for earth ...*
  b incorrect – There are four different types of base.
  c incorrect – BASE has a very specific meaning.
2 a incorrect – A sprained ankle, cuts and bruises are not serious accidents.
  b **correct** – *I've already sprained my right ankle and had a few cuts and bruises.*
  c incorrect – Karina had the bad accident, not Mike.
3 a incorrect – *I'm actually very careful in my day-to-day life.*
  b incorrect – Karina *gives talks to motivate others.*
  c **correct** – *It's more about controlling and beating your fears.*
4 a **correct** – *... when she touched the ground, she wasn't in a terrible position.*
  b incorrect – hit the ground at over 100 kilometres per hour
  c incorrect – an easy dive, a skydive, not a BASE jump
5 a incorrect – *The doctors told her it was impossible for her to walk again.*
  b incorrect – no indication of this
  c **correct** – *The doctors told her it was impossible for her to walk again.*
6 a **correct** – *She's already begun skiing again, which is something she's always loved.*
  b incorrect – Skiing is something she knew how to do before the accident.
  c incorrect – She hasn't done jumps since the accident.

Fast finishers »

If you repeat the recording, ask students who have already completed the task in exercise 3 to this time look at the incorrect options for each question and make notes about why these are incorrect. When checking answers, ask students to explain why certain options are incorrect, rather than explaining it yourself.

4 🧠 **Critical thinkers**

- Before students do the task, remind them that the objective is to justify their opinion and give suitable examples.

 Homework Workbook page 33

Grammar in context 2 p50

Using the present perfect with *just*, *yet*, *already*; using the present perfect and the past simple

Warmer

Individually, students write three sentences in the present perfect about things that they have done (two should be true and one false), e.g. *I have tried BASE jumping.* In pairs, they read each other's sentences and ask questions to guess which sentence is false, e.g. *When did you try base jumping?* They can lie in their answers to questions about the false sentences.

Alternatively, write three sentences on the board about yourself, and have students question you and try to identify the false sentence.

1a Point out that the sentences are based on sentences from the listening in the previous section.

Answers
1 just 2 yet 3 already

1b **Answers**
1 negative 2 before

Language notes

Yet and *already* may not be easy concepts for students to understand if the same word is used for both in their language. Both words add emphasis. There is not much difference between *I haven't done it.* and *I haven't done it yet.*, but *yet* emphasises the idea that you are going to do it in the future.

2a Before students do the task, make clear that the sentences are correct, but adding in *just*, *yet* and *already* gives a more precise meaning.

Answers
1 One of my friends has already decided they want to be a doctor.
2 I've just had a nosebleed.
3 We haven't studied robotics at our school yet.
4 They've just opened a big new health centre in my town/city.
5 We've already finished all our exams.
6 We've just started studying biology this year.
7 Have you decided if you want to go to university yet?
8 Have you decided on your future profession yet?

TAKE CARE! 4

3a With less confident classes, brainstorm a few ideas together as a class first, and write the key words on the board.
- Before students do the task, revise the meaning of the three key words by asking: *Which word do we use for something very recent?* (just); *Which word do we use for something that has happened, possibly before we expected?* (already); *Which word do we use for something that has not happened, but that we think is going to happen soon?* (yet).

3b SPEAKING
- After students do the task, ask them to share any sentences they had which were the same with the class, and see if any other pairs also had those sentences.

4 Point out that the dialogue extract is based on the dialogue in the listening in the previous section.
- Before students do the task, ask them to read the dialogue extract quickly and tell you who 'she' is (Karina).

> **Answers**
> 1 present perfect 2 general experience 3 past simple
> 4 a specific moment in the past

Language notes
The past simple is used to talk about actions in the past that have finished. It talks about then and <u>excludes now</u>.
The present perfect is used to look back on actions in the past which have a link to the present. It always <u>includes now</u>. The present perfect is often used to talk about someone's experiences or about something in the past which is relevant to the immediate present.

➕ Extra activity
Write another mini-dialogue on the board, based around *you* rather than third person, and go through questions 1–4 in the Grammar box a second time.
A: *Have you seen the new* Fantastic Beasts *film?*
B: *Yes, I have.*
A: *Oh, when did you see it?*
B: *I saw it on the plane while I was going on holiday.*

5 Before students do the task, point out that gaps (a) and (h) are both 'double' gaps and the verb is in brackets after the second gap. Point out also that (b) does not have a verb in brackets because it is a short answer.

> **Answers**
> a Has, had b has c crashed d broke e 's/has broken
> f did g got h Did, win i was j 's/has finished

🌐 Culture notes
Valentino Rossi (Italy, 1979–) is one of the most famous motorcycle riders in the world. He won nine Grands Prix between 1997 and 2009 and holds numerous other records. He broke his right leg in 2010 and then broke the same leg again in 2017. Both accidents happened while training in Italy.

6
> **Answers**
> 2 Have you ever won a competition or prize?
> 3 Have you ever ridden a banana boat?
> 4 Have you ever been on a big rollercoaster?
> 5 Have you ever broken a phone, tablet or laptop?
> 6 Have you ever visited another country?

Use it ... don't lose it!

7 SPEAKING
- Write the six question words on the board (*what*, *why*, *when*, *how*, *where* and *who*) to help students.
- Before students do the task, remind them that the follow-up questions can use the verb *be*, as in the examples, but can also use *did*, e.g. *Where did you eat tomato ice cream? What did it taste like? A real tomato or tomato ketchup?*
- After students do the task, extend to a class discussion by asking some students to share some of the stranger experiences with the class. Encourage discussion by allowing students to ask each other past simple follow-up questions where appropriate.

Homework Workbook page 34

49

4 TAKE CARE!

Developing speaking p52
Describing photos

Warmer

Books closed. Divide the class into small teams. Tell students you are going to give them a part of the body, e.g. *leg*. They then work together in their team to note down <u>all</u> the possible problems with that part of the body, e.g. *have a broken leg, injure your leg, your leg hurts, have a pain in your leg, your leg is swollen, have a cut/scratch/bruise on your leg*, etc. Ask each team in turn to give you <u>one</u> possible problem and award a point to each team that can offer an original idea. Also award teams a point if they can express an idea already used in a different form, e.g. *have a <u>cut</u> on your leg* (= noun) > <u>cut</u> *your leg* (= verb).

When none of the teams can think of anything new, give students another part of the body and continue.

1 SPEAKING

- After checking the answer, ask students *Have you ever had an accident like these?* If they answer yes, ask follow-up questions, or encourage other students in the class to ask follow-up questions, using the past simple. Take the opportunity to pre-teach any words students may have problems with, and encourage students to note these down to use in the final task, e.g. *snowboard, protective gloves, goggles, sports kit, helmet*.

Answers
All the photos are of injuries or accidents that have happened while people were doing sports.

2a 33

Answers
b

2b 33

- With less confident classes, give students time to read the questions and then discuss ideas for questions 1–7 as a class. Don't confirm if their ideas are correct or not, but elicit key vocabulary related to each question which students might expect to hear, e.g. *1 stadium, pitch; 2 football players, footballers, team; 3 football boots, long socks, blue shirts and shorts*; etc.

Answers
2, 3, 4, 5, 6, 8, 9

Mixed ability

To make the activity more challenging, tell the more confident students to cover the questions in 2b. As they listen, they make notes of all the key details they hear. They then look at the questions and, based on the notes they made, work out which questions the girl answered.
When checking answers, if the less confident students are unsure if the girl answered specific questions, ask the more confident students to refer to their notes to see what – if anything – she said related to each question.

3 33

- When checking answers, make sure students are clear that we use 'on' with *on the left/right*, but we use 'in' with *in the background/foreground* and *in the middle of the photo*.
- Check the meaning of *background* and *foreground* using photo c: *What is in the background?* (lots of trees); *What is in the foreground?* (two people, a bicycle and a helmet).

Answers
can see (four people), middle, not, look very

4 SPEAKING

- Before students do the task, make sure they understand that they should take turns to describe photo b. They should not describe photos a or c at this point.

Practice makes perfect

5a SPEAKING

- Remind students that they don't need to answer all the questions from exercise 2b. The girl on the recording, for example, didn't answer 1 or 7. However, students should answer both questions 8 and 9 which are repeated in the Practice makes perfect box.

50

TAKE CARE! 4

Developing writing p53
Writing an informal email 2

Warmer

Books closed. Write or project these sentences on the board:
a That's all for now.
b Write back soon.
c Thanks for your email.
d All the best.
e How are things?
f It was great to hear from you.

Ask students:
- *Where would you see sentences like these?* (in an informal email)
- *Which usually come at the beginning of an email and which at the end?* (beginning c, e, f; end: a, b, d)

Remind students that they saw all these expressions in Unit 1, page 15.

1 After checking answers, ask students to look at the photo, elicit what Ella is holding (a thermometer), and ask what the problem probably is (she has a high temperature).

> **Answers**
> 1 She's got terrible flu.
> 2 She wants to know if there are any exams next week. She needs the notes from this week to revise. She wants you to explain to Mr Scott that she is ill.

2
> **Answers**
> I'm really sorry to hear that …
> Get well soon!
> Take care!

3
> **Answers**
> 1 b 2 c 3 e 4 a 5 f 6 g 7 h 8 d

+ Extra activity

Put students into small groups to think of other abbreviations they have seen used online, on social media, in emails and in text/instant messages. Then discuss these as a class.
Students may suggest **days of the week** (*Mon, Tues, Weds, Thurs, Fri, Sat, Sun* [highlight that *Mon, Fri, Sat* and *Sun* are all three letters, but *Tues, Weds* and *Thurs* have more]): These could be useful in exercise 4a to talk about when the maths and biology tests are for next week and to talk about what they've done in class. Students may also suggest **other common abbreviations** like *LOL* (*laughing out loud*) and *BFF* (*best friends forever*). These could be useful to make the email in exercise 4a friendly and fun.
Students may also know the abbreviations for **months** (*Jan, Feb, Mar, Apr, May, June, July, Aug, Sept, Oct, Nov, Dec* [highlight that most months are three letters, but *June* and *July* are not usually shortened and *Sept* has four letters]), and for **common measurements** (*kg, g, km, m, cm, mm,* etc.)

Practice makes perfect

4a Check students understand that they are writing a reply to Ella, so their email will not have exactly the same format as the one in exercise 1. They will need to make reference to Ella's email at the start of theirs.

- Remind students that they have already seen some useful words and expressions for informal emails in Unit 1, page 15. They should try and use some of these in their reply here.
- Check students understand what each note on the email in exercise 1 is prompting, i.e. *Yes – maths and biology* = give information about the exams next week; *Yes! Me too.* = you want Ella to come back to school as well.

4b When students write letters, emails, messages and notes, it is essential to write in the correct style.

- ☑ **Exam tip** To answer the questions in the Exam tip box, if an exam writing task involves writing to a friend, students should use contractions and informal expressions. However, if the task involves writing a formal or semi-formal letter, email, message or note, students should not use contractions or informal language. Remind students that even if their writing is grammatically correct, if it is not in the correct style, they lose marks.
- With more confident classes, discuss the idea of register with them in more detail. Elicit or point out that an informal text will usually contain phrasal verbs; abbreviations; verb phrases; short, simple sentences and common words.

Homework > Workbook page 36

4 TAKE CARE!

Test yourself p55

Grammar test

1 Answers
1 taken 2 Have 3 since 4 ever eaten 5 never
6 for 7 long

2 Answers
1 Lily has just washed the dishes.
2 Lily has already bought the bread.
3 Lily hasn't taken the rubbish out yet.
4 Lily hasn't rung Mum at work yet.
5 Lily has just made the beds.
6 Lily has already made something for dinner.

3 Answers
1 Anne went ~~has been~~ to Brazil last year.
2 Did you see ~~Have you seen~~ Anna last week?
3 Has ~~Did~~ your little sister ever ridden ~~ride~~ a horse?
4 correct
5 My brother's 18. He's been ~~went~~ to Dublin three times.
6 correct

Vocabulary test

1 Answers
1 stomach 2 mouth 3 forehead 4 throat
5 elbow 6 shoulder

2 Answers
1 sore 2 swollen 3 bruise 4 temperature 5 scratch
6 ache 7 flu

3 Answers
1 chair 2 kit 3 poisoning 4 killer 5 health 6 disease
7 burn 8 eye

Exam success Units 3–4 p56

Reading

2 Answers

1 **C**; 'learning English and … learning as much as possible about the local culture and history' – *lessons … mix English, history and culture*; *students have guided visits to museums, monuments and castles*; *they can also go to … the biggest arts festival in the world*

2 **E**; 'group sports' – *you can do different kinds of sports, like football, basketball and volleyball*; 'school accommodation where you share a room with students from different countries' – *three to four students of different nationalities share a room*

3 **H**; 'prepares her for an international English-language exam' – *exam-preparation courses*; 'two weeks' – *courses that can last from two to eight weeks*; 'private lessons' – *one-to-one lessons*; 'stay with a host family' – *accommodation with a host family*

4 **A**; 'also has courses for his parents and his teen sister' – *family courses for teenagers and their parents*; 'semi-intensive course' – *20 hours of morning lessons*; 'includes visits to interesting places' – *'extra-curricular activities … full-day excursion … to see the most interesting places in and near the city'*

5 **F**; 'spend eight weeks studying' – *four, eight or twelve weeks*; 'visit more than one city' – *start your course in England and finish it in Spain*; 'learn another language' – *you don't have to … study the same language in only one place*; *English, French, German, Italian and Spanish*

- If you wish, go to page 145 to continue working through the Exam success section for these two units.
- See the Exam trainer, Workbook page 95, for more information and practice on this Preliminary for Schools task.

Collaborative project 2 p57

International words

1 SPEAKING

- Students work in groups of three to four. If possible, make sure these groups are different to the ones students worked in on the previous Collaborative project. If you have students of different nationalities within your class, consider grouping them according to their first language. This will make the final Project time presentations more varied.
- After students work in groups, ask them to share their ideas with the class and collate on the board some of the most common English words and expressions in students' daily lives.

2 SPEAKING

- Students continue to work in their groups from exercise 1.
- If you selected one project type (A–D) for the whole class to work on in Collaborative project 1, choose a different type here. If groups chose their own project type, encourage them to discuss their experience with their new group briefly, and try a new type, as far as possible.
- After reading the *Research areas*, ask students to consider which ones they may be able to find word lists online for (all except the first one). Write *false friends* on the board and ask students which bullet point these refer to (the third). Point out that this will be a useful search term in their research.
- Remind students that when they do their research online, they should keep a list of the sites they consult in case they need to check anything later.

3 Ask individuals to read aloud the tips and discuss them with the class.

- In the *Intercultural awareness* section, make sure students understand that the questions are asking them to go beyond simple lists of words, and include information in the project about attitudes to English words being used in their language.
- In the *Collaboration* section, elicit from students what the purpose of these phrases is (responding positively) and elicit other possible phrases. Students can also use the phrases for distributing work from Collaborative project 1.
- After reading the *Academic skills* section, give students time to practise working with dictionaries in class, using some of the words/expressions on the board from exercise 1. Make sure they understand that words are listed by part of speech (noun, verb, adjective, etc.) and start with the most common usage.

4 SPEAKING

- Remember to establish a clear plan for the project (interim dates/deadline; stages to be done at home/ in class). Remind students that as much discussion as possible should be in English, both in and out of class.

5 If students mark the projects of their classmates, encourage them to share and justify their marks.

Virtual Classroom Exchange

- Connect with teachers and students in other countries and encourage students to present their projects to each other.

5 SCREEN TIME

Vocabulary in context p58
Using a range of lexis to talk about TV and online video

> **Warmer**
>
> Books closed. Write or project this text on the board:
> *When I was a teenager, all my friends had one of these in their bedroom. Doctors said it could cause health problems. Some of my friends wanted to appear on it. Our parents thought it was a bad influence on us!*
> Ask students to read and guess what the object is (TV). Ask which, if any, students have a TV in their bedroom. Ask how much TV students watch and how they access content. Discuss briefly how the world of TV and video is different for teenagers today compared to your experience.

1 SPEAKING 34

- Accept students using their own language in this exercise as they give examples. The objective is for students to process the vocabulary for TV programmes and series.
- During class feedback, give the English titles of international series where appropriate, e.g. *The Voice, Big Brother, Survivor, Game of Thrones*.
- Follow up by asking: *How and where do you usually watch programmes and series? Do you watch things at the same time as your friends? How do you find out about new things to watch?*

Language notes
The news looks like a plural, but it is not used with a plural verb and cannot be used with *a*. To refer to a single part of the whole, we use *a news story* or *a piece of news*.

2a 35

- Point out that students need to change the form of some items. For less confident classes, clarify that this means they need to use plurals.
- When checking answers, check the spelling of the plurals.

> **Answers**
> 1 streaming service 2 mobile devices 3 screen
> 4 binge-watching 5 channel 6 seasons 7 episodes
> 8 viewers 9 contestant 10 spoilers

2b 36

- When checking answers, ask students to correct the false sentences.

> **Answers**
> 1 False – <u>Hulu</u>® *was the first TV streaming service*. [It was launched in 2008.] 2 True 3 True 4 True 5 True 6 False – *The US sitcom The Big Bang Theory stopped after <u>12</u> seasons*. [It ran from 2007 to 2019. A total of 281 episodes.] 7 False – *There <u>haven't</u> been over 1,000 episodes of The Simpsons*. [It has run since 1990. Over 30 series and hundreds of episodes, but still some way off the 1,000 mark.]

> 8 False – *In <u>1969</u>, about 600 million TV viewers around the world watched a live programme showing the first astronauts to walk on the moon*. [The moon landing was one of the first events to be televised around the world and remains one of the most impressive broadcasting achievements of the 20th century.] 9 True 10 True

3 37

- After checking answers, ask students for other adjectives they know which can be used to describe TV programmes. Write suggestions on the board, check meaning, spelling and pronunciation, and elicit if they are positive, negative or both.

> **Possible answers**
> **Positive:** brilliant, entertaining, funny, informative, inspiring, moving, original
> **Negative:** annoying, awful, dull, violent
> **Both:** scary

Mixed ability
Tell more confident students to complete the exercise individually as the instructions state. Assign less confident students four words each – i.e. one row of the box – and tell them to use their dictionaries to check the meaning.
During class feedback, nominate students to say whether words are positive or negative or both. Include less confident students in the feedback stage by asking them to explain words you know they checked.

4 SPEAKING

- After students do the task, ask pairs to share opinions they have in common with the class, e.g. *We both think cartoons are dull, they are for younger kids. We like fantasy series, but not if they are really scary!*

Use it … don't lose it!

5 SPEAKING

- Before students do the task, tell them about one of your favourite TV programmes as a model, making sure you include vocabulary from all three sets in the lesson.
- After students do the task, ask some students who have spoken about different programmes and series to tell the class. The other students listen and see which words from exercises 1, 2a and 3 they use.

Culture notes
The first episode of *Doctor Who*® was broadcast by the BBC in 1963. The original series ran, with seven different actors playing The Doctor, until 1989. The series was revived in 2006 and has been immensely popular since. There have now been 13 'Doctors', and – for the first time – the current Doctor is a woman. She travels through time in a machine called a TARDIS® (*made to look like a British police telephone box*). It has also inspired various spin-off series, including *Torchwood*.

54

SCREEN TIME 5

Reading p59
Reading for gist and specific information

Warmer

Books closed. Ask students to write down as many adjectives to describe TV programmes as they can in one minute.
Put them in pairs to compare their lists, then elicit the words and write them on the board, checking spelling and pronunciation.

1 SPEAKING

- After students do the task in pairs, discuss the questions as a class. Elicit ideas for what the shows pictured may be about and why students think that, e.g. *I think the first picture could be from a survival show – I don't want to know what the man is eating.* Elicit that 'reality' TV, despite its name, doesn't always feature very real people or situations.

Culture notes

The left-hand picture shows *I'm a Celebrity ... Get Me Out of Here!*. It has run on British TV since 2002 and has been licensed to many other countries. Contestants have to survive in the Australian jungle and complete challenges to earn food. The right-hand picture shows *Whisker Wars*. It featured teams from different countries preparing for the World Championship, by growing the best beards and moustaches.

2
- Before students do the task, make clear that they do not need to understand every word. They only need to read for gist.
- After students do the task, elicit which words/expressions helped them understand the writer's general feeling, e.g. *some producers create drama and tension, false idea, One of the saddest things, unrealistic*.
- Elicit possible titles for the text and make sure students understand there is no 'right' answer.

Answer
The writer generally has a negative opinion of reality TV.

3 🔊 38
- Before students do the task, make clear they now have time to read the text more carefully and understand it more fully. Point out that the question numbers match the paragraph numbers.
- Pre-teach any words students may have problems with, not including the underlined words, e.g. *attract* (make someone interested in something so that they see or do it), *on purpose* (deliberately) and *rediscover* (remember you like something when you do it again after a long time).

Answers

1 a correct – The initial quote in the text implies that people don't watch reality TV, but the survey data from OnePoll contradicts this, so option a is the correct answer. **b incorrect** – The paragraph doesn't talk about the quality of the programmes. **c incorrect** – The paragraph mentions *popular examples ... singing ... or cooking*, but these are not the reason why people watch reality TV.

2 a incorrect – The sentence *Others use ... members of the public – they're much cheaper than actors* shows that option a is not correct as members of the public are 'cheaper'. **b correct** – The paragraph says some shows *use ordinary members of the public*. **c incorrect** – Only *some shows ... use professional actors*.

3 a correct – The sentence *The producers need contestants who attract viewers ... by starting arguments* shows that **option a** is correct. **b incorrect** – The producers don't argue with the contestants. **c incorrect** – The paragraph mentions *talent shows, one of the most popular types,* but this is not saying that talent attracts viewers.

4 a incorrect – There are examples of something that never really happened (*they say they are in one place when ... they are filming in a different location* and *they 'surprise' the contestants with things they knew about already*) but not all the examples are of this. **b correct** – This applies to all the examples. **c incorrect** – While *they say they are in one place when ... they are filming in a different location,* this is the only example of this in the paragraph.

5 a incorrect – This might be inferred from the general negative opinion of the writer, but it is not stated directly. **b incorrect** – The paragraph suggests stopping watching reality TV, but it's not suggesting a ban on reality TV itself. **c correct** – It paraphrases *we can't tell the difference between what's real and what isn't*.

Fast finishers ▶▶

Ask students to look at the incorrect options for each question. Tell them to refer back to the text and think about why these could seem to be correct answers. When checking answers, ask students to explain why certain options are incorrect, rather than explaining it yourself.

4 Answers

beard – hair on a man's chin and cheeks
actually – in fact, emphasising what is really true
ordinary – normal, not famous
edit – make changes to a piece of film or video
In spite of – referring to a fact that makes something else surprising
survey – set of questions you ask a large number of people
producers – people who organise the work and money for a TV programme
judges – people who decide who the winner is
manipulation – behaviour that controls something in a dishonest way

5 🧠 Critical thinkers

- Before students do the task, remind them to justify their opinion and give suitable examples.
- If you feel your students need more support, write these prompts on the board:
  I'm certain/not sure (that) ... because ...
  I (really) believe/feel/think (that) ... because ...
  In my opinion, ...
  Speaking personally, ...
  I would say ...

 Homework Workbook page 41

55

5 SCREEN TIME

Grammar in context 1 p60
Using comparatives and superlatives; less ... than, (not) as ... as

> **Warmer**
> Ask students to work in small groups and race to think of an adjective for every letter of the alphabet (except x and z). Set a time limit of four minutes. The group with the most correct adjectives wins the game. Ask students if they know the comparative/superlative forms of any of the adjectives.

> **Possible answers**
> **a**wful, **b**rilliant, **c**lever, **d**ull, **e**ntertaining, **f**unny, **g**reen, **h**appy, **i**nformative, **j**ealous, **k**ind, **l**oud, **m**oving, **n**ice, **o**riginal, **p**opular, **q**uiet, **r**eal, **s**cary, **t**all, **u**nusual, **v**iolent, **w**et, **y**oung

1a Answers
1 cheaper 2 the saddest 3 the scariest 4 more unusual
5 the best

1b Answers
b 2 c 3 d 1 e 5

1c Answers
1 funnier, the funniest 2 more informative, the most informative
3 duller, the dullest 4 worse, the worst 5 thinner, the thinnest
bad is irregular.

1d Answers
1 than 2 in

➕ **Extra activity**
Ask students to choose three comparatives and three superlatives from exercises 1a and 1c and write six sentences.

Language notes
In spoken English, people don't always apply the rules for comparatives strictly, and *more* + adjective is often used with some two-syllable adjectives, e.g. *more clever* instead of *cleverer*, *more friendly* instead of *friendlier*.

2a Before students do the task, make clear that they should complete the sentences so they are true for them. To avoid using *less ... than* at this point, this may mean changing the order of the two things, e.g. for question 1, *I think **talent shows** are more interesting than **food programmes**.*

2b SPEAKING
- Before students do the task in pairs, drill pronunciation of the weak form *than* (/ðən/). Point out that the main stresses are on the two things being compared and the adjective, e.g. *I think TALENT SHOWS are MORE INTERESTING than FOOD PROGRAMMES.*

> **Possible answers**
> 2 I think playing sport is better than watching sports programmes on TV. 3 I think watching series on a mobile device is worse than watching series on a TV. 4 I think game shows are more entertaining than chat shows. 5 I think comedies with real actors are funnier than cartoons. 6 I think streaming services are more popular than traditional TV channels.

3a Point out that sometimes more than one of the adjectives in box A can be used with the phrases in box B. If possible, students should try to use the adjectives in box A once only. However, the most important thing is that all six sentences make sense.

> **Possible answers**
> The best actor in my country is ...   The happiest day I can remember is ...   The most exciting film I've ever seen is ...   The most important moment in my life was ...   The most popular streaming service is ...

3b SPEAKING
- Before students do the task, drill pronunciation of the weak form *the* (/ðə/).

4 Point out that the sentences are based on sentences from the reading on page 59.

> **Answers**
> a *much* – big difference; *slightly* – small difference
> b *much* = *a lot, far*; *slightly* = *a bit*

5 Ask some students to tell the class the sentences they wrote. Point out that the modifiers are also stressed in these sentences, e.g. *I think TALENT SHOWS are FAR MORE INTERESTING than FOOD PROGRAMMES.*

> **Possible answers**
> 2 I think playing sport is far better than watching sports programmes on TV. 3 I think watching series on a mobile device is a lot worse than watching series on a TV. 4 I think game shows are a bit more entertaining than chat shows. 5 I think comedies with real actors are slightly funnier than cartoons. 6 I think streaming services are much more popular than traditional TV channels.

6a SPEAKING
- Elicit an example for the first item from the class, but don't confirm if it is correct or not. Encourage discussion about the two actors before students work in pairs to change the other words in bold.

6b 🔊 39
- Follow up by asking: *Did any of the facts surprise you?* Encourage students to answer in full sentences.

> **Answers**
> 1 True 2 True 3 False – *Superman* [created in 1938] *is a lot older* than Spider-Man [created in 1962]. 4 True 5 True

SCREEN TIME 5

7
Answers
a less … than, not as … as   b less … than, not as … as
c as … as

- After checking answers, refer back to the sentences students wrote in exercise 2a and show how these can be rewritten with these new structures without a change in meaning, e.g.
I think **talent shows** are <u>more interesting than</u> **food programmes**. =
I think **food programmes** are <u>less interesting than</u> **talent shows**. =
<u>I don't</u> think **food programmes** are <u>as interesting as</u> **talent shows**.

Language notes
For adjectives which form the comparative with *more*, both *less … than* and *not as … as* can be used. However, for one-syllable adjectives which form the comparative with *-er*, we only use *not as … as*. For example, *Maria is not as tall as Kate.*

8
- Before students do the task, ask them what they know about the series *Stranger Things*. Revise vocabulary by asking: *What type of programme is it?* (fantasy/science-fiction series); *Where can you watch it?* (It's a Netflix Original series available on the streaming service.); *If you've watched it, how would you describe it?* (brilliant, entertaining, original, scary, violent).
- Highlight the fact that in exercise 7 students saw different ways to say the same thing and point out that sometimes more than one answer is therefore possible.

Answers
2 Season 1 isn't as long as season 2.   3 Season 1 is as exciting as season 2.   4 Season 1 is less violent than season 2./Season 1 isn't as violent as season 2.   5 Season 1 was less expensive to make than Season 2./Season 1 wasn't as expensive to make as season 2.   6 Season 1 is less scary than season 2./Season 1 isn't as scary as season 2.

🌐 Culture notes
Stranger Things has run since 2016 and is one of Netflix's most popular series. Set in a fictional small town in the US, it deals with supernatural events centred around a mysterious girl called Eleven and the group of teenage boys she makes friends with. Set in the 1980s, it has a retro feel which evokes films and TV series that were popular in that period.

Use it … don't lose it!

9 SPEAKING
- Before students do the task, drill pronunciation of the weak form *as* (/əz/).
- After students do the task in pairs, extend to a class discussion by asking some students to share their opinions with the class. Make sure students listen to each other and agree or disagree using suitable phrases.

Developing vocabulary p61
Using adjectives ending in *-ing* and *-ed*

Warmer
In pairs, students take turns to compare objects on their desks with those of their partner, using a different comparative adjective each time and, where possible, a modifier from the previous lesson, e.g. *My folder is slightly messier than yours. My rucksack is a bit smaller than yours.* etc.

1
Answers
moving, moved, *-ed*

- After students do the task, give them more examples and ask them to compare the two sentences in each pair.
My friend is bored. (= My friend feels bored.)
My friend is boring. (= My friend is a boring person.)
I am confused. (= I don't understand something.)
I am confusing. (= I will cause you to be confused.)

2a
Before students do the task, make clear that some of the adjectives are correct and do <u>not</u> need to be changed.

Answers
a bored   b *correct*   c depressing   d disappointing   e tired
f gripping   g *correct*   h *correct*   i embarrassing

➕ Extra activity
Write the adjectives on the board in three groups and drill them:
annoyed, bored, surprised, tired
depressed, embarrassed, gripped, relaxed
disappointed
Elicit that in the first group, the *-ed* ending is pronounced /d/ and in the second group it's pronounced /t/. Only in the third group is an extra syllable (/ɪd/) added.
Point out that the pronunciation rules are the same for *-ed* adjectives as for regular past simple forms.

2b
Students answer the question in pairs or as a class.

3
Give an example for the first item which is true for you.
- Remind students to think carefully about whether the words in brackets should end in *-ing* or *-ed*.

Answers
1 inspired   2 fascinating   3 moving   4 confusing
5 frightening   6 annoying

Use it … don't lose it!

4 SPEAKING
- Before students do the task, check the spelling of the six adjectives, particularly items 2–4 which drop the final *-e* before adding *-ing*, and item 6 where the final *-y* may cause confusion.

Homework Workbook page 43

57

5 SCREEN TIME

GREAT LEARNERS GREAT THINKERS p62

Thinking about how TV and online videos can influence us

Warmer

Books closed. Tell students you are going to answer two questions. Explain that they should listen to you and work out what the questions are. Answer the two questions in exercise 1 so they are true for you. Depending on the level of your students, adjust your answers to reflect more/less closely the wording in the questions, e.g. to make it easier, keep your answers short and start *Well, I spend more time watching TV, definitely. I ...*, and *When I watch online videos, I usually watch ...*

When you have finished, put students into pairs to discuss what they think the questions were. They then compare with the questions in exercise 1.

1 SPEAKING
- Before students do the task, check they remember the word *channel*, from Vocabulary in context on page 58.

2 VIDEO
- If your class is less confident, look at the gaps together first and elicit whether each is a word or a number, and any answers they think might be logical for the gaps, e.g. *1 their homes/houses*, *2 the world/the US*, etc.

Answers
1 their bedrooms   2 the UK   3 45   4 dialogue   5 playground
6 musicians   7 want

3
Students work individually in this step as preparation for the Great thinkers exercise.
- Tell students that, as well as deciding if they agree or disagree with each opinion, it is essential that they make notes of their arguments in each case.

GREAT THINKERS

4 SPEAKING
- The *Share-Wait-Think-Discuss* thinking routine allows students to systematically *share* in groups their views on questions/topics they have thought about individually. It emphasises how valuable it is to *wait* and *think* about what others say before they start to *discuss* it. It's also a routine that asks students to consider different perspectives and encourages them to give reasons for their views. (Note that this routine may be referred to elsewhere as *Think-Pair-Share*, starting with the *Think* step, currently in exercise 3.)
- Students work in groups of three or four.
- Before students do the task, tell them that you will ask them at the end to explain the views of someone else in their group. Remind students that this means they need to listen actively and make notes. They should not rely on memory to explain someone else's arguments.

- When doing the task, students should all first share two of their ideas and explain why they agree or disagree with the people in exercise 3. They should allow time between each person to think about what he/she has said before moving on to the next, and there should be no discussion until all the students in the group have shared their ideas.

5a
If it's possible, allow students to select a short clip to share in exercise 5b. Make sure students understand the clip is secondary and that the focus here is on preparing to talk about the three areas.

5b SPEAKING
- Students work in groups of three or four.
- Although this is not further practice of the Great thinkers routine, remind students how valuable it is to always let someone finish *sharing*, then *wait* and *think* before they start to *discuss* what the person has said.

GREAT LEARNERS SEL

- Elicit from students that there are often positive and negative sides to situations. Learning to see both of these will help students to understand situations better and make more informed decisions.

LEARNER PROFILE

- Ask students to read the statement and the question in the Learner profile on page 142, and then grade themselves from 1 to 5. Explain that here 1 means 'I don't often question my own attitudes and behaviour', and 5 means 'I frequently question my own attitudes and behaviour'.
- If appropriate for your class, get students to share their grades with a partner or small group and, if they wish, to give their reasons. Encourage students to share suggestions for questioning their own attitudes and behaviour more. Alternatively, ask students individually to think of ways to question their own attitudes and behaviour more.

SCREEN TIME 5

Listening p64

Listening for gist and specific information

> **Warmer**
>
> Books closed. Write *binge-watching* on the board. Ask students to tell you types (not titles) of TV programmes and series (e.g. crime series, dramas, fantasy series, reality shows, science-fiction series) which people typically binge-watch.

2 🔊 40

- Before students do the task, make clear that they do not need to understand every word. They will be able to listen again for more detail in the next exercise.
- If your class is less confident, pause after each speaker, give students time to think and then answer the question together before moving on.

> **Answers**
> 1 No 2 Yes 3 Yes 4 No

3 🔊 40

- **Exam tip** To answer the question in the Exam tip box, the speakers will probably express the same ideas using different words and expressions, not the exact words that are in the questions. Thinking of synonyms for the words in the statements helps students identify the answers.
- Students shouldn't worry if they don't understand everything the first time they listen. In most exams, students listen twice. They should use the second listening to find the answers they missed the first time and to check the answers they already have.
- Pre-teach any words students may have problems with, e.g. *rest* (spend time relaxing after doing something tiring), *reckon* (believe something is true), *live* (/laɪv/) (something you can watch or listen to at the same time as it happens), *ending* (the way a story or film ends) and *switch off* (stop something such as a light or a machine working).

> **Answers**
> A Lee says: *Some mornings I didn't have enough energy to study much! It was awful.* B Holly says: *I'm a teacher. Sometimes my students are so tired in the morning and often it's because they watch TV until late at night.* C Jenna says: *I think there's more binge-watching because of streaming services.* D Noah says: *sometimes I binge-watch because I don't want to have problems with spoilers.* E Lee says: *I give myself a time limit before I start watching. ... Or I decide how many episodes I can watch that evening.* F Holly says: *Parents need to be careful with the number of hours kids watch TV.* G Noah says: *What happens to me is that a friend tells me about a great series that I've never heard about, ...* H Jenna says: *I'm old enough to remember when we just had three or four channels ...*

🔵 Mixed ability

Tell less confident students, or the whole class, to answer only questions A–D and to use each name only once. Repeat the process with questions E–H.

4 ✳ **Critical thinkers**

- When students share their ideas, make sure they listen to each other and agree or disagree using suitable phrases.

🏠 **Homework** > Workbook page 43

Grammar in context 2 p64

Using *so*, *such*, *too* and *(not) enough*

> **Warmer**
>
> Draw three weights on the board – one of 500g and two large weights, both 1 kg. Label them A, B and C. Then write: *B and C are … A.*; *B is … C.* and *A is … B and C.*
> Say the word *heavy* and point at the first sentence outline. Use this to elicit: *B and C are heavier than A.* Then elicit: *B is as heavy as C* and both: *A is not as heavy as B and C.* and *A is less heavy than B and C.*
> Draw a fourth weight of 100 kg on the board. Then write: *D is …* and use this to elicit: *D is the heaviest.*

1
- You may have set the Flipped classroom video for homework, but if not watch the video in class before working through the activities.
- Point out that the sentences are from the listening in the previous section.

> **Answers**
> a such b so c such

🌍 **Culture exchange**

2 Before students do the task, ask them to scan the text and find all the names of programmes and actors. Ask them which programmes they have seen and what they know about the actors.

> **Answers**
> a so b such c so d such e such f so g so

🌐 Culture notes

Blue Planet II is a sequel to the original *Blue Planet* series. It is presented by David Attenborough.
Sherlock is a 21st century version of the Sherlock Holmes stories.
Victoria is a drama about Queen Victoria, and her relationship with Prince Albert and key figures from the period.
Dancing with the Stars is the American title for the show originally known as *Strictly Come Dancing* in the UK. It has been licensed to over 40 countries and is known by numerous names, including *Mira quien baila* in Mexico and *Bailando con las Estrellas* in Spain.
Millie Bobby Brown (2004–) shot to international fame with her role as Eleven in *Stranger Things*.
Freddie Highmore (1992–) is well known for starring as *The Good Doctor* in the series of the same name.
Coronation Street has run since 1960. Set in a fictional street in Manchester, UK, it follows the lives of various people living in the area.
Countryfile has run since 1988. At its highest point it had nearly ten million viewers.

5 SCREEN TIME

3a Point out that the sentences are from the listening on page 64.

3b Answers
1 c 2 a 3 b

3c Answers
1 before 2 after 3 before

4 Before students do the task, make clear that this exercise revises all the grammar covered in the unit so far.
- If your class is less confident, have them complete exercise 5 first, which focuses only on *too* and *not ... enough*.

Answers
a most b enough c as d too e not f enough g less h unusual i in j easy

🌐 Culture notes

Got Talent was first broadcast in the US, in 2006, where it has run ever since. In 2014, it was awarded the Guinness World Record when it reached 59 versions in 58 countries (Belgium has versions in both French and Belgian-Dutch). In 2019, a new format was created, *Got Talent: The Champions*, which brings together past winners from around the world to compete for the ultimate title of world champion.

➕ Extra activity

Divide the class into two groups, one to work on the text in exercise 2 and one to work on the text in exercise 4. Tell students to form pairs with another student from the same group and write comprehension questions about their text to ask other students, e.g. text 2 *How many different types of programme are mentioned in the text?*; text 4 *What reasons are there in the text for the success of* Got Talent *around the world?*
Regroup students in pairs or groups of four. Students take turns to ask and answer the comprehension questions.

5 If your class is less confident, follow up each question by asking: *1 How old does Brad need to be to watch the series?* (18); *2 Would the person prefer the game to be easier?* (yes); *3 Does the person feel hot or cold?* (hot); *4 Does the person think a story should be easy or difficult to understand?* (easy); *5 What other, less polite, adjective could we use to describe the contestant?* (stupid).

Answers
2 is too difficult 3 is/'s too warm 4 is/'s too confusing
5 wasn't clever enough

6 Pre-teach any words you think students may have problems with, e.g. *stunt performer* (*a person who does dangerous actions in a film or TV programme*); the adjectives *calm* (*not affected by strong emotions such as excitement, anger, shock or fear*), *brave* (*able to deal with danger, without seeming to be frightened*) and *fit* (*healthy, strong and able to exercise without getting very tired*); and the expression *have what it takes* (*have the specific skills and qualities to do a specific job or task*).

Use it ... don't lose it!

7 SPEAKING
- After students do the task, identify the students who think they are brave enough to be a stunt performer. Ask the other students to challenge them with *Would you ... ?* questions and find out where their limits are, e.g. *Would you jump off a bridge into a deep river in freezing cold weather?*

SCREEN TIME 5

Developing speaking p66
Negotiating

Warmer

Books closed. Write *free time* on the board.
Ask students to write down as many free-time activities as they can in one minute. Put them in pairs to compare their lists, then elicit the words to the board. Make sure that all of the following, which appear in the listening in 2, are included: *cooking, doing sport, playing a musical instrument, playing video games, reading, running* and *watching TV*.

1a SPEAKING

Possible answer

I think she feels tired and maybe a bit stressed. She's too busy and hasn't got enough time to do everything.

1b Before students do the task, quickly check the words for the free-time activities in the photos.

1c SPEAKING

- After students do the task, elicit suggestions to the board, check meaning, spelling and pronunciation, and elicit if the adjectives are positive or negative related to the different activities, or if they can be both.

2 🔊 41

- Before students do the task, explain that the recording is a section from a speaking exam and is a common exam format.
- After students do the task, remind them how important it is to listen carefully to what the teacher/examiner tells them to do in a speaking exam (question 1) and to question and clarify if necessary. Tell them it is also important to try and complete the task set (question 2), but to make sure they always discuss all the options carefully before reaching a conclusion.

Answers
1 The teacher asks the students to talk about the different activities and to choose which one would be the most relaxing.
2 Watching TV.

3a 🔊 41

- When checking answers, check the spelling of the six adjectives.

Answers
1 great, tiring 2 tiring, boring 3 brilliant, difficult

Fast finishers »

Ask students who complete the task in exercise 3a after listening only one time to listen carefully when you repeat the recording. The second time they should write down in what order they hear the other three activities in the photo discussed and what the students say about them.

Answers
1 watching TV (discussed after 'reading': much more relaxing; you don't have to think much) 2 playing video games (discussed after 'running': better; really gripping; bad for your eyes) 3 cooking (discussed after 'playing video games' above: interesting; not very easy)

3b SPEAKING

- When checking answers, ask students to share their ideas for other adjectives to describe the activities and check pronunciation.

4 🔊 41

Answers
All of the expressions are used.

Language notes

What do you think about ... ? is usually followed by an *-ing* form, e.g. *What do you think about reading?* It can also be followed by a noun, e.g. *What do you think about my idea?*
Let's ... is followed by an infinitive without *to*, e.g. *Let's decide which one is the best.* It could also be used earlier in this exam task, e.g. at the beginning *OK. Let's start.*, or to change topic *OK. Let's talk about running.*
Why don't we ... ? is also followed by an infinitive without *to* and is a synonym of *Let's ...*, e.g. *Why don't we choose TV then?* (= *Let's choose TV then.*)

5 SPEAKING

- ✓ **Exam tip** In this type of exam task, there isn't usually a right or wrong answer. The examiner wants to hear the candidates speaking together (which is why, to answer the Exam tip question, it's very important for students to listen to their partner) and see how well they interact.
- Tell students that if they can't think of anything to say, then they can still show how fluent they are by asking their partner a question (e.g. *What do you think?*), using fillers (e.g. *Well ..., Hmm ..., Let me think ...*) and giving a fuller explanation for an opinion or idea.
- Tell students it is essential in this exam task to use the phrases for responding to opinions and suggestions to show that they are listening actively to their partner. If they don't understand, using questions like *Sorry, can you say that again?* or *Sorry, could you speak more slowly?* prove that students know how to interact and are fluent even in challenging circumstances.

6 Before students do the task, remind them how important it is to use any preparation time they are given in exams to think about what they could say (or what they might hear in a listening exam).

- If your class is less confident, collate ideas from this preparation stage on the board.

Practice makes perfect

7 SPEAKING

- Before students do the task, check they have understood the task by asking: *What is the first thing you have to do?* (talk about the photos); *Which of the photos should you talk about?* (all of them); *What do you need to do at the end?* (make a decision together).

Homework › Workbook page 45

61

5 SCREEN TIME

Developing writing p67
Writing an article 2

> **Warmer**
> Books closed. Write
> 4 D 3 C 5 T 2 1 N
> 4 N T 4 R T 5 2 N M 4 N T on the board. In pairs, students try to 'break the code'. Tell them to put their hands up when they have worked it out, not call out the solution.
> Follow up by asking: *Can you think of anything that is both education and entertainment?*

Answers
1 O 2 I 3 U 4 E 5 A (EDUCATION ... ENTERTAINMENT)

Culture exchange

2 Before students read the article, make sure they understand the advert and the things they need to read for. Ask: *How many things do you need to find out?* (four – two names of shows, games or apps; reasons why the writer likes them; and things the writer thinks you can learn from them)

- Pre-teach any words students may have problems with, e.g. *puzzle* (a game with questions or problems that you have to answer by thinking carefully), *solve* (find the answers to a question or problem in a game), *portal* (a science-fiction 'door' to another place, time or dimension), *gravity* (the force that makes objects fall to the ground) and *friction* (the force that makes it difficult for one surface to move over another).

Answers
The Witness and *Portal 2*.
The Witness is visually amazing. The characters in *Portal 2* are funny.
The Witness teaches you to solve puzzles on your own – you learn to listen and look at everything carefully. *Portal 2* makes you think about gravity and friction, like in physics.

Culture notes

The Witness was released in 2016. In the game, players have to solve numerous puzzles on a mysterious island where they wake up alone with amnesia. The more players explore and the more puzzles they solve, the more they can use what they learn to solve puzzles they had to leave unsolved earlier in the game. The ultimate objective is for the player to find his/her way home.

Portal 2 was released in 2011. It is a sequel to the original cult *Portal* game, released in 2007. There are two separate stories within the game, one for single-users the other as part of a two-player co-operative game. Both are set in the fictional Aperture Science Labs and feature a range of characters, including a murderous computer called GLaDOS who guides players through the game.

Both games regularly appear in lists of the greatest video games of recent years.

Extra activity

Check comprehension of the *Playing is learning* text by asking the following questions:
According to the writer, which game ...
... *looks great?* (The Witness)
... *makes players work individually?* (The Witness)
... *makes players interact with other people?* (Portal 2)
... *do you learn most from?* (The Witness)
... *has puzzles related to science problems?* (Portal 2)
... *makes you really look at the details of things?* (The Witness)

3 **Answers**
far as, In my, don't believe, Why don't

Language notes

Personally, *As far as I'm concerned* and *In my opinion* are all usually followed by a comma in written English. They are followed by a complete clause with its own subject and verb. *Personally* is always followed by a clause with 'I', but *As far as I'm concerned* and *In my opinion* can both be followed by a different subject, e.g. *As far as I'm concerned, **the best and most educational game** is ...*; *In **my** opinion, **it's** ...*
Why don't you ... ? is followed by an infinitive without *to*. It is similar to *Why don't we ... ?* (seen in the Speaking bank on page 66), but it is a suggestion for the listener only, and does not include the speaker.

4a Before students make notes to answer the questions, elicit some examples of educational shows and educational apps and make sure students understand that they do not have to write about games.

4b SPEAKING
- When students discuss their answers, encourage them to make notes of anything their partner/group says that they think would be good to use in their own article.

Practice makes perfect

5 Before students do the task, draw attention to the paragraph structure of the *Playing is learning* article. Tell students to follow the same format, i.e. paragraph 1: show/game/app 1; paragraph 2: show/game/app 2; Paragraph 3: final comment and conclusion.

Homework › Workbook page 46

SCREEN TIME 5

Test yourself p69

Grammar test

1 Answers
1 My school is a bit ~~more~~ bigger than this school.
2 You look slightly thinner than the last time I saw you.
3 Football is a lot more popular than badminton.
4 The Volga is the longest river in Europe.
5 Ethan is ~~a~~ much worse at German than Jake.
6 Do you think this exercise is the most difficult in the book?

2 Answers
1 Spain isn't as big as the US.
2 A kilo of sugar is as heavy as a kilo of iron.
3 To be a doctor, philosophy is less important than/isn't as important as anatomy.
4 Jamie isn't as old as Brad.
5 Playing tennis is less dangerous than/isn't as dangerous as parachuting.

3 Answers
1 such a   2 so   3 such   4 so

4 Answers
1 is/'s too high   2 aren't strong enough   3 is/'s too young
4 isn't warm enough   5 is/'s too slow

Vocabulary test

1 Answers
1 contestant   2 cartoon   3 viewer   4 spoiler   5 the news

Note
Answers in 1 have double points – one for remembering the word and one for correct spelling.

2 Answers
1 awful (–)   2 dull (–)   3 original (+)   4 moving (+)

3 Answers
1 tired   2 annoying   3 surprising   4 embarrassing
5 frightened   6 relaxed

6 CHANGING CLIMATES

Vocabulary in context p70

Using a range of lexis to talk about geographical features and the environment

Warmer

Books closed. Draw or project on the board illustrations of:
- a footprint, e.g. a simple outline
- the greenhouse effect, e.g. the section of the Earth showing the country where you are teaching; the sun in the sky; a simple dotted line to show the limit of the atmosphere and a series of arrows curving from the Earth to the limit and then bouncing back towards the Earth
- the symbol for recycling, e.g. three arrows forming the three corners of a triangle.

Ask students what they think the pictures represent and how they are connected. Elicit that they are connected to environmental issues and assess students' knowledge of vocabulary on the topic. Then focus on the title of the unit, and ask students what ideas and themes they think they might study in this unit.

Possible answers
We use the word *footprint* to describe an individual's impact on the environment through the use of carbon or water (*carbon footprint*, *water footprint*). When we burn fossil fuels, the greenhouse gases in the atmosphere increase, leading to the *greenhouse effect* and global warming. The symbol refers to *recycling* – the process where materials are reused, not thrown into landfill.

1 SPEAKING 42

- Point out the different pronunciation, and stress for these two words: *desert* (n., *a dry region with little water*) /ˈdezə(r)t/ and *dessert* (n., *the sweet course at the end of a meal*) /dɪˈzɜː(r)t/.
- When checking answers, ask students to try and name a famous example either from their country or from around the world for each of the geographical features in the box, e.g. *Copacabana Beach* (Brazil), *Altamira Cave* (Spain), etc.

3a 43

- Pre-teach any words students may have problems with, e.g. *temperature* (*how hot or cold something is*), *greenhouse gases* (*a gas, e.g. CO_2 that stops heat escaping from the atmosphere*), *goal* (*something that you hope to do*) and *useless* (*has no purpose*).

3b 44

- After checking answers, draw attention to the word *sensible* and elicit the meaning, i.e. 'reasonable and practical'. If this word is a problem in students' own language, contrast it with *sensitive* (*about a person, likely to become angry or upset easily*).

Answers
a reduce b save c waste d recycle e reuse f consume
g throw away

4 SPEAKING 45

- If you wish, allow students to use dictionaries.
- Before students do the speaking task, make sure they understand there is no 'right' answer.

Possible answers
The second photo shows melting ice – it might be part of one of the ice caps. This is a result of global warming and is causing sea levels to rise.
The third photo shows pollution. Some of it could be toxic waste.

Fast finishers ››

Ask students to write definitions of words related to the environment, either from the Student's Book or any other words they know. They then read their definitions for the class to guess the word, e.g. *waste*, *save*, *drought*, *flood*, *deforestation*, *acid rain*, etc.

5 Pre-teach *wind power* and *solar power* by drawing a simple picture of a windmill and a sun shining on a solar panel on the board.

Answers
1 change 2 warming 3 renewable 4 save 5 recycle
6 reduce, emissions, waste

Use it ... don't lose it!

6 SPEAKING

- After students do the task, have a show of hands to see how many people are optimistic about the planet's future and how many are pessimistic.

Homework Workbook page 48

CHANGING CLIMATES 6

Reading p71
Predicting content, reading for gist and detail

Warmer

Write the following words in two columns on the board:
turn off   less
switch off   school
fly   lights
recycle   more
walk to   taps

Ask students to work in pairs and match the words to make phrases. Then ask them to say what the phrases relate to (being green/protecting the environment). Ask students if they try to do any of these things.

Answers
turn off taps   switch off lights   fly less   recycle more
walk to school

1

 **Culture notes**

The central photo shows the Palace of Westminster in London as it would be if the River Thames were to flood dramatically. This possibility was explored in a novel by Richard Doyle in 2002, which was then adapted into a film in 2007.
The right-hand photo shows the Maeslantkering, a sea gate in the Netherlands. It took six years to build and opened in 1997. It protects the area of Rotterdam. It is one of the biggest moveable mechanical structures in the world, which can be seen in the photo by looking at the size of the ship, top right.

2 SPEAKING
- Pre-teach *fake news* (*a story that is not true but is designed to make people think that it is*).
- After students do the task, elicit their ideas for each question but don't confirm if they are correct or not.

3 Pre-teach any words students may have problems with, not including the underlined words, e.g. *factor* (*one of the things that explains why something happens*), *take up* (*fill a particular space or time*) and *combat* (*try to stop something bad or solve a difficult problem*).

Answers
1 A   2 E   3 B   4 D   5 C

 **Mixed ability**

To simplify the activity, tell less confident students, or the whole class, to answer only the question *Were any of your answers in exercise 2 similar to the answers in the text?* and not to match the questions to the answers.

4
- With less confident classes, give students the correct alternatives, and ask them simply to reread the text and find the paragraphs which contain the information.
- Before students do the task, remind them that if they are not sure that they have found the correct answer, they should read the other sections again in more detail before making a final decision.

Answers
1 more, B; *... NOAA statistics show that the amount of sea level rise caused by melting has increased dramatically ...*
2 a lot more, A; *Their statistics also show that in many places along the US coast, flooding is much more frequent than it was 50 years ago.*
3 can't, D; *... it is clear that we will need to spend money on other ways to protect these coastal areas because rising sea levels will still continue to cause problems.*
4 coastal areas, C; *... 275 million people live in areas which are going to be at risk from rising sea levels.*
5 a variety of different, E; *... engineers and architects are always coming up with different solutions, big and small.*

5 Answers
According to – in someone's opinion
average – the quantity that is typical for something
amount – quantity
expands – gets bigger and bigger
at least – not less/fewer than
face – experience and have to deal with
move away – go to another place
floating – sitting on water

6 Critical thinkers
- Before students do the task, remind them that the objective is to justify their opinion and give suitable examples.

Possible answer
I'm certain that where I live – Madrid – sea level rise won't affect me directly. It's hundreds of kilometres to the sea and we are hundreds of metres above sea level! However, I really feel that we need to do more about the environment and to stop sea levels rising. In Spain, the coast and the Canary Islands are going to be very affected if we don't take action. The two-metre rise the NOAA talks about is really worrying. And we're now getting some very big storms, and they are doing terrible damage. I would say the government isn't doing enough to combat this problem.

Flipped classroom
You may want to ask students to watch the Flipped classroom video for Unit 6 as homework, in preparation for the grammar lesson.

Homework › Workbook page 49

65

6 CHANGING CLIMATES

Grammar in context 1 p72
Using *will*, *be going to* and present continuous for future; using *will*, *may* and *might*

> **Warmer**
>
> Ask students to choose some of the words from Vocabulary in context, exercises 3a and 4 (page 70) and some of the underlined words from the Reading text (page 71) and write a gapped sentence for each, e.g. *We need to stop burning _____ immediately or the environment won't recover.* (fossil fuels), *How much homework do I get? I think the _____ is about an hour each day.* (average), etc. They then read out their sentences for their partner to guess the word that fits the gap.

1a If you didn't set the Flipped classroom video for homework, watch the video in class before working through the activities.

- Point out that the sentences are based on sentences from the reading text on page 71.

1b Remind students of the popular spoken form of *going to*: *gonna*. They hear this form in films, on TV and in songs but they should not use it in written English.

> **Answers**
> 2 b 3 a 4 e 5 c 6 d

Language notes
Explain to students that the key difference between *will* and *be going to* is that if you make a decision at the moment you speak, you use *will*, e.g. *Do you want to go to the cinema tonight? Sure. I'll see you there at 8 pm.* The negative form of *will* is *won't* (*will not*). It is used to make predictions about things we don't expect to happen in the future, e.g. *I won't see Sarah at the party.*

In normal everyday speech, *will* is rarely used; the contraction *'ll* is much more common. Encourage students to use the contracted form rather than the full form unless they are speaking in more formal situations. If they use the full form, remind them not to stress it unless they have a very strong intention to do something. *'ll* is pronounced with a dark /l/ sound, i.e. it sounds like *ull* in *full* rather than the *l* in *light*.

2 Before students do the task, ask them: *What happens to the verb* be *in the structure* be going to? and elicit that they will need to use *am*, *are* or *is* according to the subject.

- After checking answers, remind students that it is the content words that are usually stressed. Ask students to look at the sentences and underline the stressed words, e.g. *Experts believe that temperatures will continue rising.* They then practise saying the sentences using the correct sentence stress.

> **Answers**
> 2 's going to be, 4 3 'll help, 1 4 's going to die, 4 5 's going to study, 5 6 'll be, 2 7 will have, 3 8 'm revising, 6

3a If you feel your students need more support, suggest they think about what is in the diary app on their phone and what is in their 'to-do' list. If students are still unsure about the two forms, draw a page from a diary on the board and label it 'present continuous' and a sticky note and label it 'be going to'.

3b SPEAKING

- After students do the task, ask them to share any plans and intentions they had which were similar with the class and see if any other pairs also had similar sentences.

+ Extra activity
Write these problems on the board:
1 I can't decide what to do after school today.
2 I don't know what to buy my friend for his birthday.
3 I don't know what to wear to the party tonight.
4 I'm tired of being a teacher but I don't know what job to do.
Ask students to call out ideas for how to solve each problem using *I know! I'll ...*, e.g. *1 I know! I'll read a book.*; *I know! I'll play football with my friends.*; etc.

4a Point out that the sentences are based on sentences from the reading on page 71.

- When checking answers, ask: *Which four expressions have a similar percentage of certainty?* (perhaps ... will, it's possible that ... will, may, might); *Which word makes* will *or* won't *really strong?* (definitely); *Which word makes* will *or* won't *less strong?* (probably).

> **Possible answers**
> 2 100% certain 3 50% certain 4 50% certain 5 50% certain
> 6 50% certain 7 70–80% certain 8 100% certain

4b
> **Answer**
> *Definitely* and *probably* come just after *will* but just before *won't*.

5 In sentence transformation activities, students are given a sentence and must complete a second sentence so that it means the same as the original sentence. In some exercises, students must also use a word they are given. In this case, they cannot change the form of this word. Generally, students can only use between two and five words, including the word given.

- Before writing their sentence, tell students to read the original sentence carefully. They should think about the meaning of the sentence, the type of structure(s) used, the tense(s) used, etc. If students are given a word, they should think about its meaning. They should also think about the grammatical function of the word and whether it always or usually goes with another word or tense.

- ☑ **Exam tip** To answer the question in the Exam tip box, when they finish, students should check that they have not changed the meaning of the original sentence, have not changed the form of the word they are given and have not used more than the maximum number of words permitted.

> **Answers**
> 2 will definitely reuse 3 summers might not be
> 4 will probably be 5 will probably want to 6 's possible that it will

Homework Workbook page 50

CHANGING CLIMATES   6

6 Possible answers
2 There may be sharks near the UK coast.
3 We might not drive cars in the future.
4 We definitely won't have terrible droughts.
5 It's possible they will clean all the plastic from our seas.
6 We will definitely stop using fossil fuels.

Developing vocabulary p73
Using different uses of *get*

Warmer

Books closed. Write or project the following sentences on the board:
They hoped to _____ tickets for the concert before they sold out.
Jo, can you _____ me that dictionary from the cupboard?
I have a Saturday job, but I only _____ £6 an hour.
We usually _____ up at seven o'clock on school days.
Ask students to think which word can complete all four sentences. Tell them to put their hands up when they have worked it out, not call out the solution. Elicit the answer (*get*), and explain that there are many different uses of *get* and that students are going to look at some of these in more detail.

1 Pre-teach *conference* (*a large meeting, often lasting a few days, where people interested in a subject come together to talk about it*).

Answers
1 a 2 c 3 b 4 g 5 f 6 d 7 e

Language notes
The verb *get* has many different meanings in English. It is also part of many phrasal verbs. When we use *get* with a direct object (a noun or pronoun), it often means *receive*, *obtain*, *bring*, *catch*, *give* or something similar, e.g. *I got your email yesterday.*, *Last week she got a book about pollution.*, *Can you get me that pen that's on the desk?* When we use *get* before an adjective, it often means *become*, e.g. *Summers are getting very hot.* These uses of *get* are generally more informal than the alternatives.
Get often means *travel*, and when we use it before a word like *up*, *out*, *to* or *away*, it usually refers to a movement of some kind, e.g. *Are you going to get away this summer?*

2a With less confident classes, write the structure:
is/are getting   adjective + *-er* (*than*)
                    less adjective (*than*)
on the board. Ask students: *Which adjectives in B have a change in spelling?* Elicit that in *hot* and *wet* we double the final *t*, i.e. *hotter* and *wetter*; and that in *dirty* and *sunny* the ending is *-ier*, i.e. *dirtier* and *sunnier*. Ask: *Which adjective in B uses* less*?* Elicit *extreme*.

2b SPEAKING
- When students share their ideas, encourage turn-taking, and make sure they listen to each other and agree or disagree using suitable phrases.

Use it ... don't lose it!

4 SPEAKING
- Before students do the task, write the various meanings of *get* from exercise 1 on the board, i.e. *arrive*, *bring*, *become*, etc. Students copy these down and, while they listen, they tick off the uses they hear in each dialogue.

+ Extra activity
Students write a story using *get* as many times as possible. With less confident classes, you could brainstorm collocations with *get* and write them on the board for students to use in their stories, e.g. *get dressed*, *get ill*, *get bored*, *get on*, *get over*, *get under*, *get a shock*, etc.

Homework Workbook page 51

67

6 CHANGING CLIMATES

GREAT LEARNERS GREAT THINKERS p74

Thinking about the impact of plastic on the environment

Warmer
Draw three columns on the board, *fruit* on the left, *vegetables* on the right and *grey area* in the middle. Tell students to copy the columns into their notebooks and classify the words you give them. Dictate 10–12 items, e.g. *melon, carrot, peach, tomato, strawberry, broccoli, spinach, pineapple, grape, pepper, cabbage* and *cucumber*. If useful for your class, adapt the wordlist to cover any typical fruit and vegetables grown where students live which they may not know in English.

Answers
Fruit: melon, peach, strawberry, pineapple, grape; **Vegetables:** carrot, broccoli, spinach, cabbage; **Grey area:** tomato, pepper, cucumber (These are usually classified botanically as fruits but by chefs as vegetables.)

1 SPEAKING
- Extend the discussion by asking: *Do you know anyone who grows their own fruit and vegetables? What do they grow? Where? Have you ever tried any of the things they grow?*

2 VIDEO
- After checking answers, ask students if they can remember the term used in the video for the area where fruit and vegetables are grown to be sold. Elicit/Teach *market garden*.

Answer
The south of Spain is very hot and dry. However, cheap fruit and vegetables are grown for Europe in plastic greenhouses.

3 VIDEO
- If your class is less confident, project the text on the board and highlight the eight mistakes before students watch the video again to correct them.

Answers
The video shows the 1 ~~south~~ *eastern* coast of Spain. It's dry and 2 ~~one of~~ Europe's only deserts. The temperatures can reach 3 *50°C* ~~45°C~~. You 4 ~~can't~~ *see plants, or vegetation* ~~and the Mediterranean Sea~~ from up in the sky. Plastic has become part of the earth in this area. It comes from 5 *the greenhouses* ~~rubbish that local people throw away~~. The plastic becomes smaller and smaller and finally goes into the sea. About 7% of 6 *the world's* ~~Europe's~~ plastic is in the Mediterranean. This plastic ~~only~~ affects fish and sea life 7 *and gets into our food and drinking water*. The plastic greenhouses in this area 8 ~~only~~ bring us *both* positive *and negative* consequences.

GREAT THINKERS

4 The *Think-Question-Explore* thinking routine encourages students to *think* about what they already know about an area; think of related *questions* they would like the answers to; and consider how they can *explore* the area further, answer those questions and learn more. (Note that this routine may be referred to elsewhere as *Think-Puzzle-Explore*.)

- Students work individually at first and can then share their ideas in small groups or as a class.
- Students may include common misconceptions, but these are still a valuable contribution to the *think* stage as they can later be reconsidered.
- This routine can be used in later lessons to introduce new topics. Before starting work on a new unit, reading text, listening section, etc., consider asking students to think about what they already know about an area and what questions they would like the answers to. At the end of the lesson/unit, they can then see which of their questions have been answered and discuss how they could find the answers to the questions which haven't.

5 SEL
- Discuss as a class to what extent the text confirms what students already knew, what new information it includes and if students included any common misconceptions in their notes in exercise 4. Most importantly, discuss which questions remain unanswered and how students might learn more about the area.

6 SPEAKING
- Students work in pairs before feeding back to the class. Elicit that it is extremely hard to make your life plastic-free but that small changes are better than nothing.

GREAT LEARNERS

- Remind students that it may be best to take 'baby steps', i.e. be realistic about the changes they can make. Suggest they choose just one idea which they will try over the next week. They can then feed back to the class and, if they've been successful, try making additional small changes.

LEARNER PROFILE

- Ask students to read the statement and the question in the Learner profile on page 143, and then grade themselves from 1 to 5. Explain that here 1 means 'I don't often think globally or act locally' and 5 means 'I always think globally and act locally'.
- If appropriate for your class, get students to share their grades with a partner or small group and, if they wish, to give their reasons. Encourage students to share suggestions for thinking globally and acting locally more. Alternatively, ask students individually to think of ways to think globally and act locally more.

# CHANGING CLIMATES 6

Listening p76

Listening for gist and detail

Warmer

Books closed. Write on the board: *chillax, hangry, froyo, plogging, screenager* and *snaccident*. Elicit what the words have in common (they are blends), and remind students that they learnt about blends in the Reading in Unit 3. Point out that one of the blends is new and ask students which it is. Explain that they will learn more about this blend in the listening. Put students into pairs to try and remember what two words are combined in each of the other blends.

Answers
plogging is new
chillax = chill out + relax   *hangry* = hungry + angry   *froyo* = frozen yoghurt   *screenager* = screen + teenager   *snaccident* = snack + accident

1a SPEAKING

Possible answer
I can see two people in sports clothes picking up litter. There's a man in the background riding a bike.

1b Before students do the task, remind them that they can write both *yes/no* questions and *wh-* questions with *Who, What, Why, When, Where, How*, etc.

2 🔊 47
- If possible, use a map to check that students are clear about where *Sweden* is, and elicit the nationality *Swedish*.

3 🔊 47

Answers
1 True – *It's a blend of the words 'plocka upp', which is Swedish for 'pick up', and 'jogging'.*
2 False – *… it was the idea of a Swedish man called Erik Ahlström. He started a community of ploggers in Stockholm.*
3 False – Carol says *I began because I wanted to get fit.*
4 False – *Each year it costs (local authorities) a billion pounds to clear up litter in the UK!*
5 True – *With 'plogging' … you bend down, stretch, get up again and then carry the rubbish. And we all know that you use up more calories if you move more.*
6 True – *… just picking up a bag or two of rubbish doesn't really make a big difference to the environment. … people will drop MORE litter in the street if they know that people like you will pick it up.*
7 False – Carol says *perhaps it is a small step but it can make a real difference. And it will make a massive difference if lots of people do it.*
8 True – Carol says *when you finish running, you feel good because you feel healthier. But ploggers feel even better because they know they're also doing something good for their neighbourhood and for the planet.*

4 🔊 47

Possible answers
1 'Plogging' combines running and picking up the rubbish you find on your way. The name is a blend of words. It was the idea of Erik Ahlström and started in Stockholm, Sweden.
2 'Trash running' was a similar thing that used to take place in the US.
3 You just need your usual running equipment, some gloves and a bag to put the rubbish in.
4 Eighty-one percent of British people are angry about litter in the streets. Each year it costs a billion pounds to clear it up.
5 Some people think plogging doesn't make that much of a difference. Other people may not care about throwing litter if they know that ploggers will pick it up.

> **Homework** > Workbook page 51

Grammar in context 2 p76

Using the zero conditional; using the first conditional

Warmer

Write the following sentence beginnings on the board:
If I'm hungry, …
If I'm tired, …
Ask students to suggest ways to complete them so they are true for them. Assess whether what students say is something that happens to them or something they do, e.g. *If I'm hungry, I get hangry.* (something that happens to them); *If I'm tired, I go to bed early.* (something they do). Then circle the *If* at the start of each sentence, and elicit what type of sentence this word introduces (a conditional).

1a Point out that the sentences are from the listening in the previous section.

Answer
things that are generally true

1b   **Answers**
1 present simple, present simple   2 no   3 after the first half of the sentence when the sentence starts with *if*

Language notes

The zero conditional is often used to talk about scientific facts and general truths. *When* can often be used instead of *if* without changing the meaning.

2   **Answers**
1 f   2 d   3 a   4 b   5 c   6 e

6 CHANGING CLIMATES

3a With less confident classes, have students complete the sentences in pairs. Then work in different pairs for exercise 3b.

> **Possible answers**
> 2 you get sick 3 your vocabulary improves 4 something bad happens 5 you practise a lot 6 you pay attention in class

4a Before students do the task, ask: *What will you do if it rains all weekend?* Elicit suggestions with *If it rains all weekend, …*, e.g. *If it rains all weekend, I'll go to the cinema with my friends.*, and then elicit that this is a first conditional.

- Point out that the sentences are from the listening in the previous section.

> **Answer**
> possible

4b
> **Answers**
> 1 the present simple 2 will or won't

Language notes
When we use the first conditional, we're talking about a particular situation in the future and the result of this situation. There is a real possibility that this conditional will happen.

5 Pre-teach *drastically* (having a very big effect).

- Follow up by asking: *Have you ever been on a cruise? Where did you go? Did you enjoy it? Why/Why not? Would you like to go on an Arctic cruise? Why/Why not? Are there lots of cruise ships in your country? Do you think they are damaging the environment? Why/Why not? In which areas is it getting to be a problem?*

> **Answers**
> 1 melt, will be 2 is, will want 3 will sail, want 4 sail, will be 5 will melt, is 6 melts, will change 7 will become, changes

6 Before students do the task, write the following contractions on the board: *'ll, 'm, 're, 's* and *'ve*. Elicit the verb in each case (*will, am, are, is/has, have*), and ask students which contractions they expect to see in the first conditional (*'ll*; possibly *'m, 're, 's* for *is*).

- Remind students that we usually use contractions after subject pronouns, e.g. *I, you, she*, etc. We also sometimes use them after nouns and names but only in informal situations.

> **Answers**
> a happens b 'll need c want d 'll become e won't be f continue g is h will copy i produces j 'll help k will get l grow

+ Extra activity
Introduce the idea of Murphy's law: the opposite of what you want or expect is what usually happens.
Ask students to complete the following sentences using the first conditional and thinking about the concept of Murphy's law:
1 If I don't take an umbrella, …
2 If I don't wear a warm coat, …
3 If I study hard for a test, …

> **Possible answers**
> 1 it will rain.
> 2 it will be really cold.
> 3 the teacher will forget about it and we'll watch a video instead!

Use it … don't lose it!

7 SPEAKING

- Before students do the task, make sure they understand that the second part of sentence 1 becomes the first part of sentence 2, then the second part of sentence 2 becomes the first part of sentence 3, etc.
- Check students have understood the task fully by asking: *When are you going to stop?* (ideally never, the idea is they should keep linking sentences until you stop them); *When should you start again?* (if they get completely stuck and can't think of a way to continue).

Homework — Workbook page 52

CHANGING CLIMATES 6

Developing speaking p78
Making arrangements

Warmer

Books closed. Draw or project a simple page from your 'diary' on the board with three (invented) appointments, e.g.

Saturday 13th Feb

9:00	Shopping with Jon	Supersave, shopping centre
11:15	Meet Cathy	Café Fiorentina, High Street
13:30	Family lunch	Mum and Dad's house

Elicit a sentence from the class for each appointment, e.g. *At nine o'clock you're doing the shopping with Jon at Supersave in the shopping centre.; At quarter past eleven, you're meeting Cathy for coffee at Caffè Fiorentina in the High Street.; At half past one, you're having a family lunch at your mum and dad's house.*
Point to the diary and ask students: *What are these?* to elicit 'arrangements' and ask them which tense they were using (the present continuous).

1 SPEAKING

- Follow up by asking: *Which of the activities in the photos can you do where you live? How far do you have to travel to do them?*

2 48

Answers
1 to the beach
2 They're going to meet at 11 o'clock at the station.
3 They're going to take some sandwiches.
4 Speak on the phone and do something else.

3 48

- After checking answers, highlight *be up to* in Jamie's first question (*Are you up to anything ...?*), and elicit the meaning of this (*doing*). Point out that the end of the question can be changed for any logical time expression and elicit examples, e.g. *this afternoon, tomorrow, on Monday evening, after the swimming competition*, etc.

Answers
a good b beach c 11 o'clock d station e sandwiches
f have lunch on the beach g rains h ring i ring j 11

4 After checking answers, suggest a few activities to different students in the class and ask them to accept or reject them using a phrase from the Speaking bank.

Answers
Do you fancy verb + -ing?, What time shall we meet?, Why don't we meet at …?, Sure., Fine., OK., Good idea., Not really.

5a PRONUNCIATION

- Play the recording again up to and including the line: *What time shall we meet?*. If possible, repeat the individual phrases: *Do you fancy coming?* and *Sure*, and highlight the variations in pitch the speakers use to show enthusiasm.

Answer
To show enthusiasm speakers vary the pitch substantially.

Language notes

Intonation can be described as the movements or variations in pitch which affect the level (high/low) and tone (falling/rising) of our voices. Rising intonation means the pitch of the voice increases; falling intonation means that the pitch decreases. Intonation can be difficult to teach, so here students are simply introduced to the idea of pitch movement to show enthusiasm.

5b SPEAKING

- If your class speaks a language with more limited intonation patterns, tell students that if they don't feel slightly silly doing this activity, then they need to exaggerate it more.

Mixed ability

To make the activity more challenging, tell the more confident students that they need to practise the dialogue without looking at exercise 3 or the Speaking bank. Give them a few moments to memorise the useful expressions, then tell them to role-play the dialogue using only their answers to the questions in exercise 2. If students have problems, allow them to quickly refer to exercise 3 and the Speaking bank as they work, but encourage them to do as much as possible without referring to the Student's Book.

6 SPEAKING

- With less confident classes, collate ideas from this preparation stage on the board.

Practice makes perfect

7b SPEAKING

- Remind students to show enthusiasm as they saw in exercise 5a.
- After each pair acts out their dialogue for the class, elicit the key details of each arrangement from the rest of the class, e.g. time, place, other people involved, etc.

Homework Workbook page 53

71

6 CHANGING CLIMATES

Developing writing p79

Writing an opinion essay

> **Warmer**
>
> Books closed. Write the following expressions on the board:
> - *I think … because …*
> - *Some parents think …*
> - *Many people say …*
> - *All in all, I believe …*
>
> Ask students: *Where do you think you might see expressions like these? In what sort of text?*
>
> Elicit that they are all expressions for giving opinions and check the meaning of *essay* (a short piece of writing on a particular subject).

2 When discussing answers, if students think the statistics would be different for their country, ask them to give more detail, e.g. *In my country, I don't think any children spend 60 minutes playing outside each day. We spend a lot of time outside, but not playing – maybe talking with friends or …; I think there are probably a lot of teenagers here who have never been to a beach.*

🌐 Culture notes

Persil® is a brand of laundry products. Originally a German brand, it was the first laundry detergent sold and has existed for over 100 years. It is well-known around the world.

4 After students read the opinion essay, ask them to put their hands up if the writer's opinion is similar to their own. Then elicit from those students which ideas the writer mentions that they thought of in exercise 3.

5
> **Answers**
> Sequence: Secondly, Finally
> Addition: What's more
> Contrast: Nevertheless

Fast finishers »

Ask students if they know any other linkers, and tell them to add them to their lists, e.g. *then*, *besides*, *in addition*, *on the one hand/other hand*, *moreover*, etc.

Language notes

Linkers (sometimes called connectors) are words that join sentences with others. Some frequent linkers are *and*, *but*, *or* and *so*. Linkers have different functions (in this unit students see three groups, to express sequence, addition and contrast). Remind students that a logical argument needs few linkers and they should not overuse them.

Nevertheless and *however* have similar meanings, but *nevertheless* is slightly more formal. They are both normally placed at the beginning of a sentence when contrasting two ideas. They can also come in the middle or at the end.

Furthermore and *what's more* also have similar meanings, but *furthermore* is quite formal and *what's more* is more idiomatic.

6 With less confident classes, put students into pairs to discuss whether they agree or disagree with the statement and make notes together. Tell them that even if they don't share the same opinion they can still help each other generate ideas.

Practice makes perfect

7a Before students do the task, draw attention to the paragraph structure of the opinion essay in exercise 4, i.e. paragraph 1: introduction clearly giving the writer's opinion; paragraph 2: reason 1; paragraph 3: reason 2; paragraph 4: reason 3; paragraph 5: conclusion clearly restating the writer's opinion. Tell students that they definitely need to include the first and last paragraphs in their essay, but they may have only two paragraphs in the middle, depending on how they structure their arguments.

- If you wish, you could do this activity as an exam simulation.

7b Remind students that when they write in exam conditions, they can't usually use a dictionary or grammar book.

- ✓ **Exam tip** To answer the question in the Exam tip box, if students do not know a word, they should think of a similar word or a more basic or general word. They should never leave a gap or write the word in their own language. If necessary, students should change what they were going to say. If students are not sure how to use a grammar structure, they should think of a different way to say the same thing.

- Remind students, too, that they should always answer the question. They might not get any points if they don't answer the question properly.

- Students should also pay attention to the maximum and minimum number of words in the instructions. They should plan and organise their essay before they write and check it carefully for mistakes when they finish.

Homework › Workbook page 54

CHANGING CLIMATES 6

Test yourself p81

Grammar test

1 **Answers**
1 The students are going to go on an excursion.
2 What are your plans? What are you doing/are you going to do do you do tomorrow?
3 They say it's going to rain raining next week.
4 I can't meet you tomorrow because I'm doing/I'm going to do I'll do an exam.
5 I don't know what to do now … I know! I'll see I'm seeing Joe!

2 **Answers**
1 definitely   2 might   3 The problem will probably   4 may not
5 will see

3 **Possible answers**
1 If you mix blue and yellow, you get green.
2 If you are late for school, you get into trouble.
3 If you never brush your teeth, they start to decay/they fall out.
4 If you run every day, you get fit.

4 **Answers**
1 shines   2 finishes   3 will/'ll get   4 comes   5 's   6 won't bring

Vocabulary test

1 **Answers**
1 waterfall   2 cliff   3 glacier   4 island   5 stream   6 rainforest

2 **Answers**
1 renewable energy   2 rise   3 melt   4 waste
5 drought   6 carbon emissions   7 throw away
8 global warming

3 **Answers**
1 buy/obtain   2 arrive   3 bring   4 understand   5 becoming
6 received

Exam success Units 5–6 p82

Listening

2 🔊 ES2

> **Answers**
> 1 A **correct** – The girl says *There was something about the cave. I couldn't stop looking at it.*
> B incorrect – The boy says he *liked the one of the really high cliffs by the coast*, but the girl isn't particularly interested in it.
> C incorrect – The boy says *the photo of the small island was cool*, but the girl isn't particularly interested in it.
> 2 A incorrect – The girl says *I'm bored of binge-watching TV* and the boy says *I'd like to take a break for a while*, so this is happening at the time of speaking.
> B incorrect – The girl says *Let me just finish my sandwich*, so they have already made lunch.
> C **correct** – The boy says *How about we go skateboarding?* and the girl agrees *(Why not?)*.
> 3 A incorrect – The boy asks *Did you go with your family to that new restaurant in town?*, but the girl replies *No*.
> B **correct** – The girl says *I went hiking with my parents* and *I'll show you a photo I took of a waterfall. This is where we hiked …*
> C incorrect – The girl says *We were going to see an art exhibition in the city, but the weather was too nice to be inside a museum all day.*

3 🔊 ES3

> **Answers**
> 1 A incorrect – The boy says he doesn't *usually watch shows like that. They're usually too slow and serious*, but this one is *entertaining*.
> B incorrect – The boy says *the stories in the series aren't the same as the historical facts*.
> C **correct** – The boy says *the actors who play the main characters – Queen Victoria and her husband – play their roles so well.*
> 2 A **correct** – The girl says *you can actually learn something from them and I also discover stuff that can help me in my everyday life.*
> B incorrect – not stated on the recording
> C incorrect – not stated on the recording
> 3 A incorrect – The boy says *I'll do almost anything to avoid watching TV.*
> B **correct** – The boy says *I'd rather see my friends than waste my time watching stuff that doesn't mean anything to me.*
> C incorrect – The boy says *I'll even practise the piano for hours, that always makes my mum happy*, but it is not his preferred activity.

Speaking

4 If your class is less confident, before they do the task, elicit the different activities they can see in the pictures (clockwise round the main picture of the school: picking up litter, recycling, planting new plants and trees, hanging bird feeders, painting a recycling mural, growing fruit and vegetables).
- Pre-teach *grounds* (*the area around a building or group of buildings, in this case a school*).
- If you wish, go to page 146 to continue working through the Exam success section for these two units.
- See the Exam trainer, Workbook pages 100 and 103, for more information and practice on these Preliminary for Schools tasks.

Collaborative project 3 p83

TV and online video in your country

1 **SPEAKING**
- Students work in groups of 3–4. If possible, make sure these groups are different to the ones students worked in on the previous Collaborative projects.
- Nominate one student in each group to refer to the Culture exchange text, while the others work with their books closed. Groups start their discussion by trying to remember what was in the text before contrasting it with their country.

2 **SPEAKING**
- Students continue to work in their groups from exercise 1.
- Encourage students to try a different project type (A–D) for this Collaborative project.
- Point out that for the last research area, groups could prepare a small survey themselves, e.g. to ask ten teenagers and ten parents, in order to include some original research findings in their project.

3 Ask individuals to read aloud the tips and discuss them with the class.
- After reading the *Digital skills* section, remind students that when they do their research online, they should keep a list of the sites they use. When they plan to use a specific piece of information, this means they should note both sources.
- In the *Collaboration* section, remind students that they can also use the phrases from the previous Collaborative projects.

4 **SPEAKING**
- Remember to establish a clear plan for the project (interim dates/deadline; stages to be done at home/in class). Remind students that as much discussion as possible should be in English, both in and out of class.

5 Explain that Presentation here means the way a project has been created and done, e.g. the quality and general attractiveness of the layout and design of a poster or leaflet, or the clarity and coherence of a spoken presentation or video message.

Virtual Classroom Exchange

- Connect with teachers and students in other countries and encourage students to present their projects to each other.

GET TO THE TOP! 7

Vocabulary in context p84
Using a range of lexis to talk about jobs, work and personal qualities

Warmer
Elicit different ways of asking about someone's job, e.g. *What do you do? What is your job? What do you do for a living?* As a class, discuss the meaning of the unit title *Get to the top!* and elicit that it has both a literal meaning, e.g. when you are climbing a tower, mountain or similar and you reach the highest point, and also a more abstract meaning in the context of work, where it means 'be the best or most important in your company or profession'.
Ask students what they think the unit is going to be about and elicit ideas from around the class.

1 Before students do the task, make clear that they do not need to think about the people the sentences are talking about at this point. They should focus only on the meaning of the words in bold.

> **Possible answers**
> *outdoors* – not in a building
> *the public* – people in general
> *paperwork* – the part of a job that involves written documents
> *look after* – make sure someone/something is OK and has everything he/she/it needs
> *manual work* – physical work using your hands
> *Teamwork* – work that you do together with other people
> *figures* – numbers you need to count or calculate
> *earn* – receive money for work that you do
> *salary* – a fixed amount of money that you receive each month/year from your job
> *overtime* – extra hours that someone works at their job
> *retail* – the business of selling things in a shop
> *finance* – the business of investing money

2 SPEAKING 49

- Before students do the task, look at the example together, and point out that sometimes various answers are possible for the sentences in exercise 1 and that the jobs in exercise 2 can be used more than once.

> **Possible answers**
> 2 photographer, vet 3 journalist, lawyer 4 au pair, nurse
> 5 mechanic, plumber 6 chef, firefighter 7 economist, receptionist 8 architect, lawyer 9 company director, police officer 10 economist, shop assistant

Mixed ability
To make the activity more challenging, tell more confident students to complete the exercise using all the jobs at least once.
To simplify the activity, tell less confident students to repeat the jobs as necessary.
During class feedback, ask any students who think they have been able to use all the jobs at least once to put their hands up. Nominate one of these to read out their answers for the rest of the class to check if they agree and if the student has been successful. Make sure you include other students in the feedback stage by asking them which other jobs they think match each sentence.

3 SPEAKING

- After checking answers, extend work on the jobs in exercise 2 by asking half the class to order them from least to most stressful and the other half from worst to best paid. Extend to a class discussion or put students into new pairs, with one from each group, to share their ideas.

4a 50

- With less confident classes, before students do the task, look at the personal qualities together and match them to the jobs in exercise 2 to help consolidate meaning.
- Pre-teach any words students may have problems with, e.g. *carefully* (*thinking about what you do so that you avoid problems*), *vital* (*very important or necessary*), *depend on someone* (*trust someone to do something/rely on somebody*) and *success* (*a person who achieves a lot*).

4b 51

> **Answers**
> a well-organised b flexible c creative d sociable/friendly
> e friendly/sociable f reliable/responsible g responsible/reliable h calm/patient i patient/calm j ambitious

5 SPEAKING

> **Possible answers**
> You're *clever/bright* if you can quickly find solutions to tricky problems.
> You're *confident* if you believe you can do something and don't feel nervous or frightened.
> You're *determined* if you know what you want and how to achieve it.
> You're *fit* if you're healthy and strong.
> You're *hard-working* if you put a lot of effort into your work to do it properly.
> You're *sensitive* if you think about other people as well as yourself.
> You're *strong* mentally if you are able to deal with problems without them affecting you.
> You're *strong* physically if you are powerful and healthy.

Use it ... don't lose it!

6 SPEAKING

- After students do the task, extend to a class discussion by asking some students to tell the class which of the things in exercise 1 they would like in their future job. The class can then suggest jobs they think the student would be interested in and would definitely not be interested in doing.

Homework Workbook page 58

75

7 GET TO THE TOP!

Reading p85
Predicting content, reading for gist and detail

Warmer

Books closed. Ask students to brainstorm jobs they think are 'safe' and 'dangerous'. Write the suggestions on the board and ask the class to vote for the 'safest' and the 'most dangerous' jobs. Then look at the two photos and ask students how safe or dangerous they think the two jobs are.

Language notes

Job and *work* have similar meanings. *Job* is countable. In most cases *work* is uncountable so rarely comes after *a* or a number, and it is rarely used in the plural.

1 SPEAKING

- Remind students that they saw personal qualities in exercise 4a on page 84, and check the meaning of *skills* (*the ability to do something well, usually as a result of experience and training*).
- After students do the task, discuss the question as a class.

2a Before students read the texts, explain that in the next exercise they will need to tell their partner the key information from their text. Tell them that they can make short notes to help them but that they will not be able to look at the original text when they share the information.

2b SPEAKING

- Books closed. Explain that students should first tell each other the key information from their text using their notes. They should then discuss the questions.
- After students do the task, ask some pairs to tell the class about the things they think the two people have in common.

Possible answers

They have both overcome difficult situations. They are both very talented at what they do. They have both won awards.

3 🔊 52

- Remind students that in an exam they should always read the text(s) quickly to get a general idea first.
- ✓ **Exam tip** To answer the question in the Exam tip box, students should then read the sentences that they need to prove true or false. They should find the parts of the text where the information comes and read them again in more detail.
- Remind students that if there is no information to say a sentence is true, they should mark it false.

Answers

1 False – *in comparison with Alan Geaam, most other Michelin star winners have it easy* does <u>not</u> mean that Michelin changed the rules for him.
2 False – *He found work as a* <u>construction worker</u> *during the day and worked part-time* <u>delivering pizzas</u> *and* <u>washing dishes</u> *in a restaurant at night.* No mention is made of problems finding work.
3 True – *One night, the chef in the restaurant where Alan worked cut his hand and went to hospital. So, Alan cooked for the customers and everyone loved his dishes.*
4 True – *You just have to believe in yourself …*

5 False – *Ami feels a photographer should 'live the story'* means she has done dangerous things to get a better photograph <u>not</u> because she likes danger.
6 False – *… Ami* <u>doesn't</u> *see herself as a nature photographer …*
7 True – *Ami has helped to create an organisation that allows women around the world … to tell their stories.*
8 False – *Ami believes that you don't have to travel abroad to find interesting stories* means that it is <u>not</u> hard.

4 Answers

overcoming adversity – getting past a difficult situation
penniless – having no money
delivering – giving/taking things to people
privileged – having many opportunities/being lucky
awards – prizes for doing something well
contracted – became sick from a disease or infection
abroad – in another country

5 🧠 **Critical thinkers**

- Before students do the task, remind them that the objective is to justify their opinion and give suitable examples.

Possible answers

Speaking personally, I think Ami's story is the most inspiring. Alan's achieved something amazing, but I feel that a restaurant with a Michelin star is not something that everybody can enjoy. On the other hand, Ami's photographs are something we can all see, either on the Internet or in magazines. What's more, she seems to be very interested in people and has done a lot for women. In my opinion, photographs are a universal language, and I really believe a picture can tell a story in a way words can't.

➕ **Extra activity**

Divide the class into small groups and ask them to discuss these questions: *What kind of work do you want to do in the future? What would your dream job be? What do you need to do in order to get this job? Which jobs wouldn't you like to do? Why? What was your dream job when you were a child?*

▶️ **Flipped classroom**

You may want to ask students to watch the Flipped classroom video for Unit 7 as homework, in preparation for the grammar lesson.

Homework — Workbook page 59

GET TO THE TOP! 7

Grammar in context 1 p86
Using modal verbs of obligation, prohibition and advice

> **Warmer**
> Read the following sentences to the class and ask students to guess the job. Tell them to put their hands up when they think they know, not call out the answer.
> *To do this job, you don't have to go to university.*
> *You shouldn't have a problem with manual work or working with the public.*
> *You should be sociable and friendly because teamwork is very important.*
> *You must be able to stay calm in dangerous situations.*
> *You have to be very fit and strong.*
> *You mustn't be scared of going into burning buildings!*
> After checking the answer (firefighter), ask students if they noticed anything about the sentences you used (they all talked about obligation, prohibition or advice) and if they know the name for the types of verbs often used to talk about these (modal verbs).

1a If you didn't set the Flipped classroom video for homework, watch the video in class before working through the activities.
- Point out that the sentences are based on sentences from the reading text on page 85.

1b **Answers**
2 d   3 c   4 a, f

Language notes
should/shouldn't for giving advice
Should and *shouldn't* are used when we want to give a strong opinion, telling someone the best thing to do. We can request advice by asking *Do you think I should ...?* or *Should I ...?*

have/has to for obligation
Have/has to and *must* mean the same when we are talking about rules and obligations. We can also say *I have got to ...* and this also has the same meaning.

don't/doesn't have to for no obligation
Make clear that this is not the same as *mustn't*, which is used for prohibition. *Don't/doesn't have to*, on the other hand, means it is not necessary to do something, but you can do it if you wish.

must/mustn't for obligation or prohibition
Must is not very common in question forms; we usually say *Do I have to ...?* instead.

1c **Answer**
the infinitive form of the verb without *to*

2a PRONUNCIATION
- Before students do the task, check they have understood by eliciting the silent letter 'l' in *should*. Explain that all the words have one silent letter.

2b 53
- With more confident classes, you might want to point out that the letters are silent, but sometimes their presence influences the pronunciation of the words, e.g. *calm* would be *cam* /kæm/ without the 'l'; *know* would be *now* /naʊ/ without the 'k', etc.

Answers
1 shou~~l~~d   2 firefi~~gh~~ter   3 s~~c~~ientist   4 mus~~t~~n't   5 dis~~c~~ipline
6 desi~~g~~ner   7 plum~~b~~er   8 ca~~l~~m   9 si~~gh~~t   10 lis~~t~~en   11 ~~h~~ours
12 ta~~l~~k   13 ~~k~~now   14 s~~c~~ene   15 colum~~n~~   16 ~~w~~rist
17 thum~~b~~   18 ~~w~~rap

+ Extra activity
Tell students that silent letters are 'hiding' everywhere in English. Write these words on the board: *calf, knee, climb, island, foreign, Wednesday, drought*. Students find the silent letter in each word.

Answers
ca~~l~~f   ~~k~~nee   clim~~b~~   is~~l~~and   forei~~g~~n   We~~d~~nesday   drou~~gh~~t

2c SPEAKING
- After students do the task, ask some of them to share their sentences with the class, and see if the other students can identify all the silent letters.

3 Before students do the task, check they have understood fully by asking: *How many gaps are there in the text?* (7); *How many pieces of advice are there?* (8); *What do you do with the extra piece of advice?* (nothing); *What other words do you need to add?* (should/shouldn't).

Answers
1 E; should do a lot of sport and exercise
2 B; should learn to fly
3 A; should speak one or more foreign languages
4 F; shouldn't have bad eyesight
5 C; should study science, technology, maths or engineering
6 D; shouldn't panic in difficult situations
7 G; shouldn't be tall

4 **Answers**
a both   b don't have to   c has to   d sit   e have to
f both   g mustn't   h mustn't   i have to

Homework Workbook page 60

7 GET TO THE TOP!

5 Remind students that in sentence transformation activities, they are given a sentence and must complete a second sentence so that it means the same as the original sentence. In the previous unit (page 73), they also had to use a word they were given. In this exercise, they do not need to include a specific word (though they do need to use a modal verb from the section), and there is no word limit.

- When checking answers, make sure students remember the silent 'l' in *should* and the silent 't' in *must(n't)*.

> **Answers**
> 2 must/have to wash their hands
> 3 should learn a foreign language
> 4 we mustn't run in the corridor
> 5 shouldn't use informal language in a job interview
> 6 don't have to wear a tie here
> 7 must/have to stay calm

6 Before students do the task, make sure they understand that they should make notes for all four areas: obligation, no obligation, prohibition and advice/recommendation.

Use it ... don't lose it!

7 SPEAKING

- Before students do the task, point out that they are now going to ask each other questions to try and guess what job their partner made notes for in exercise 6. Remind students that they can ask about anything using the modal verbs in order to guess the job. Also, tell students they can ask as many questions as they need.

Developing vocabulary p87
Using compound adjectives

> **Warmer**
> Write these words from Units 1–6 on the board: *nosebleed, painkiller, rainforest, waterfall, sunburn, homework, wheelchair, toothache.* Ask students what they all have in common and elicit that they are compound nouns.
> Remind students that they studied compound nouns in Unit 4, and tell them that they are now going to learn about compound adjectives.

2a 54

- After checking answers, point out that all the words are connected with a hyphen, and explain that this makes compound adjectives much less problematic than compound nouns, which can be written as one or two words.

> **Answers**
> badly-paid badly-behaved blue-/brown-/green-eyed easy-going
> full-/part-time good-looking long-/short-haired right-/left-handed
> well-paid well-behaved well-known

2b PRONUNCIATION 54

> **Answer**
> The stress is usually on the second word.

Language notes
Rules regarding hyphenation of compound adjectives are complex, and, as there is no official language academy for English, there are often differences between dictionaries, and native speakers themselves often don't agree. The general rule is that compound adjectives are usually hyphenated when they come before the noun they refer to, e.g. *He's a very good-looking young man.* but not hyphenated when they are used on their own, e.g. *I saw this young man at the shopping centre. He was very good looking.* For simplicity, all the compound adjectives presented in this section come before a noun so they are hyphenated.

3 When checking answers, point out that *18-year-old* is a flexible expression, and the age, '18', can be changed as necessary to describe the person. Elicit the meaning of *well-off* (rich or having enough money to live well), and ask students to find the opposite in the text (*modest*, line 2).

- Follow up by pointing out that Reggie Nelson is a real person and asking: *What do you think of Reggie's strategy for getting a job? Do you think it would work where you live? Why/Why not?*

> **Answers**
> a hard b full c 18-year d well e well f badly g forward

Use it ... don't lose it!

4 SPEAKING

Fast finishers »
Ask students to think of other famous people from a variety of areas, e.g. music, film, sport, science, politics, etc., and to practise describing them with the compound adjectives.

78

GET TO THE TOP! 7

GREAT LEARNERS GREAT THINKERS p88

Thinking about the different things we want from a job

Warmer

Ask students to work in small groups and race to see if they can think of a job for every letter of the alphabet (except x and y). Set a time limit of four minutes. Students share their jobs with the class at the end and the group with the most correct jobs wins the game.

Possible answers
architect, **b**utcher, **c**hef, **d**etective, **e**conomist, **f**irefighter, **g**oalkeeper, **h**airdresser, **i**nventor, **j**ournalist, **k**ing, **l**awyer, **m**echanic, **n**urse, **o**fficer (e.g. police, prison), **p**lumber, **q**ueen, **r**eceptionist, **s**hop assistant, **t**axi driver, **u**nemployed, **v**et, **w**riter, **z**oologist

1 SPEAKING
- After students work in pairs, briefly discuss as a class what options students would prefer and why. Find out how much consensus there is in the class, if any.

2 VIDEO
- Before students do the task, make sure they understand that the answers are the same for both the young man and the young woman.
- After checking answers, ask students: *Could you live like the people in the video? Why/Why not?*

Answers
1 Working outdoors
2 Having flexible working hours
3 Working individually
4 Working with no technology
5 A satisfying job, the salary is not important

3 VIDEO
- Check students understand the meaning of *primitive* (something very simple, not usually involving modern technology) and *gadget* (a small piece of equipment, often technological, that does something useful).
- Before students do the task, make sure they understand that the information does not all come together in the video. They will need to make notes about Jess and Zeki and then decide at the end whether the statements are true about one or both of them.

Answers
1 J 2 J 3 B 4 Z 5 Z 6 B 7 B

GREAT THINKERS

4a The *Step inside* thinking routine encourages your students to think about situations, events and issues from a viewpoint different from their own.
- Divide the class into pairs and tell them to choose who is Jess and who is Zeki. They then work individually thinking about how to answer the questions from Jess or Zeki's perspective.

4b SPEAKING
- Students work in pairs and take turns to give their answers as 'Jess' and 'Zeki'. If your class is more confident, allow students to go beyond the questions in exercise 4a, and improvise further, talking about 'their' lifestyle.
- Follow up by asking students if the exercise has changed their view of Jess/Zeki, and if so, how.

5 Before students do the task, make sure they understand they can repeat the marks. The task is not to order the comments (a–f) from 0–5.

6 SPEAKING
- If possible, in this step pair each student with another student who you expect to have marked the statements in exercise 5 in a different way. This will give them more room for discussion in this exercise and in recommending jobs in the next.

7 Remind students how important it is to look at things from a different perspective. To complete this task successfully, even if they find their partner's choices strange, they need to give sensible suggestions taking into account their partner's preferences.
- If your class is less confident, refer students to the jobs in Vocabulary in context on page 84. Students can select from these jobs to make suggestions for their partner.

GREAT LEARNERS SEL

- Encourage students to use the suggestions their partner made in exercise 7 to see how closely they listened in exercise 6. Ask them to tell each other how good they thought their suggestions were, and give reasons.

LEARNER PROFILE

- Ask students to read the statement and the question in the Learner profile on page 143, and then grade themselves from 1 to 5. Explain that here 1 means 'I don't always listen actively to others', and 5 means 'I always listen actively to others'.
- If appropriate for your class, get students to share their grades with a partner or small group and, if they wish, to give their reasons. Encourage students to share suggestions for listening more actively to others. Alternatively, ask students individually to think of ways to listen more actively to others.

7 GET TO THE TOP!

Listening p90

Predicting content, listening for gist and detail

Warmer

Elicit from students which skills and qualities are important for many jobs, e.g. *communication skills, honesty, teamwork, motivation, flexibility, computer skills, analytical skills, organisational skills*, etc.
Ask students: *What makes a job enjoyable? Is it more important to have an enjoyable job or a well-paid job? Should you do a job you don't really like just for the money?*

1 SPEAKING

- Use the photo to pre-teach *raven* (a large bird with shiny black feathers).

2 55

- After checking answers, ask students: *Would you like to do the jobs? Why/Why not?*

3 55

- Remind students that they should read the different answers before they listen. These can give students ideas about the topic of the text and the vocabulary they are going to hear in it. Point out that sometimes the difference between two answers is just one word.
- **Exam tip** To answer the question in the Exam tip box, students usually hear the recording twice so tell them not to panic if they do not understand information the first time. If they don't hear the answer to one question, they should start listening immediately for the answer to the next question.
- Students should use the second listening to find the answers they didn't hear the first time and to check the answers they already have.
- When students finish, they should check that they have an answer for each question. They should never leave answers blank in an exam.

Answers

1 a incorrect – Harry says *I like having an ice cream or two in the summer …*
  b incorrect – Harry talks about putting on weight with ice cream, and Layla talks about the sugar in ice cream, but these are not the main reasons for Harry not being enthusiastic.
  c **correct** – Harry says *if I did that job I'd get tired of it … you wouldn't want to eat it all through the winter.*
2 a incorrect – *Louise travels a lot* but this is not the reason why Layla likes Louise's job.
  b **correct** – Layla says *She's always looking for new flavours and ideas and that's the part that sounds the most interesting to me.*
  c incorrect – no mention of Layla enjoying eating all types of ice cream
3 a **correct** – Harry says [referring to the legend] *that's why it's so special. You're responsible for the future of the country!*
  b incorrect – The ravenmaster is *the man who looks after* the ravens *at the Tower of London.*
  c incorrect – no mention of writing books and stories being typical of a ravenmaster
4 a **correct** – *You must have at least 22 years of military experience.*
  b incorrect – The ravenmaster must have more than 20 years *of military experience.*

  c incorrect – *What I'd love about the job is that you live inside the Tower of London!*
5 a incorrect – Different foods are mentioned, but Harry is not saying that visitors should give them to the ravens.
  b incorrect – Harry says the ravenmaster *has lots of marks on his arms where the ravens have attacked him*, but says the ravens *steal* things from visitors; no mention of ravens attacking visitors.
  c **correct** – Christopher says … *it isn't a good idea to get too close to them.*

 **Homework** Workbook page 61

Grammar in context 2 p90

Using the second conditional and *unless*

Warmer

Write the following sentence beginnings on the board:
If I had a million pounds, …
If I could fly a plane, …
Ask students to think of ways to finish them and write their ideas down as full sentences. Ask some students who you know have completed the second conditional sentences correctly to share their ideas with the class, and elicit that this is the second conditional. Remind students that they saw the zero and first conditional in the previous unit.

1a Point out that the sentences are based on sentences from the listening in the previous section.

Answers
a improbable and imaginary b the present or future
c give advice

1b Remind students that when the *if* clause comes first, we use a comma after it. When the *if* clause comes second, there is no need for a comma, e.g. *I'd choose a different dream job if I were you.*

Answers
1 the past simple 2 would(n't) + infinitive 3 can
4 'if … not' or 'except if'

2a Answers
1 If I were you, I would go to bed early.
2 If I were you, I wouldn't eat lots of sweets.
3 If I were you, I would do more exercise.
4 If I were you, I would study more vocabulary/vocabulary more.
5 If I were you, I wouldn't go there.
6 If I were you, I would watch films in English.

80

GET TO THE TOP! 7

2b SPEAKING

- After students do the task, discuss as a class what each person's problem could be.

3 Before students do the task, draw their attention to the photo, and ask them what they think the person's job could be. Then ask them to scan the text and find out (section 3, dog-surfing instructor).

- Remind students that *if/unless* can come at the start or in the middle of a conditional sentence but that wherever in the sentence it occurs, the grammar associated with it remains the same. Ask: *What do we use in the part of the sentence with if or unless?* (the past simple); *What do we use in the other part of the sentence?* (would(n't) + infinitive). Point out that in this exercise, *if/unless* does not always come at the start of the sentence.
- After checking answers, ask students how they would feel doing the four jobs in the text, e.g. *I think I would feel sick as a 'snake milker'. That sounds disgusting!*

> **Answers**
> **a** liked **b** 'd become **c** wouldn't do **d** paid **e** wouldn't be
> **f** had to **g** lived **h** had **i** 'd need **j** 'd learn **k** wanted
> **l** would help

4 After checking answers, ask students to close their books. Then elicit the sentences orally to see if students can remember them, e.g. *If I wasn't at school, I'd work.*, and highlight the contracted form of *would* ('d) in sentences 1 and 5.

> **Answers**
> 1 wasn't 2 unless 3 would repair 4 unless
> 5 sang 6 if

Language notes

We often use the contracted form of *would* ('d) when we speak, and this can make it difficult to hear. The best way to hear if someone is using a first or second (or third) conditional is by focusing on the tense of the verb after *if*. In the case of a second conditional, this will be the past simple.

5

To simplify the activity, tell less confident students, or the whole class, to work on only half of the situations. Elicit the words *odd numbers* for 1, 3, 5 and 7 and *even numbers* for 2, 4, 6 and 8. Tell half the students to work on the odd-numbered items and the other half on the even-numbered items.

For exercise 6, pair up the students so there is one person who worked on the odd numbers and one who worked on the even numbers in each pair. Students can then read the four new situations and listen to the sentences their partner wrote for each.

Use it ... don't lose it!

6 SPEAKING

- When students discuss their ideas, encourage turn-taking, and make sure they listen to each other and agree or disagree using suitable phrases.

Homework Workbook page 62

7 GET TO THE TOP!

Developing speaking p92
Giving detailed personal information

> **Warmer**
> Write the following question beginnings on the left of the board:
> 1 What's your
> 2 How often do you
> 3 Do you like
> and the following question endings on the right of the board:
> a see your grandparents?
> b playing video games?
> c favourite school subject?
> Ask students to match the question halves. Then ask students: *What sort of information are all three questions asking for?* (personal information), and remind them that they saw how to ask for personal information in the Unit 1 Speaking section. Explain that in this section they will learn how to give more detailed personal information about themselves.

Answers
1 c   2 a   3 b

1 SPEAKING

- Check students understand that *ICT* stands for *Information and Communication Technology*.
- Follow up by asking: *Are you in a sports team? What do you play? Who with? Have you ever had to help someone older than you with technology? What did they want to do? How did you help them?*

Fast finishers »
Ask students to look back at pages 84 and 87 and see what words from the vocabulary sets match the photos.

Possible answers
Picture A: fit, sociable/friendly, strong
Picture B: calm, caring, clever/bright, patient, sociable/friendly, easy-going

2 56

- When checking answers, elicit the three questions to answer question 1, write them on the board and make sure all students have copied them in their notebooks. They are an essential part of exercise 5, exercise 6 and exercises 7a/b at the end of the section.
- Ask students what they think the context of the listening is. Elicit that these are the sorts of questions you might be asked as part of an interview, e.g. for a part-time job or to be a volunteer. Amelia gives detailed information about the things she has done and gives detailed examples, and these are both things we would expect in an interview situation.

Answers
1 What do you like doing in your free time? What skills have you learned from that? And what qualities do you think you have that help you?
2 She is playing in the school basketball team and training the school's youngest girls' team.
3 Yes – She's learned to motivate others.
4 No, she gives two: she's friendly and caring and she's good at organising people.

3 56

- After checking answers, tell students to close their books. Ask them if they can remember any of the expressions Amelia used before she gave the examples. Students can compare the expressions they remember with the Speaking bank before listening again if necessary.

Answers
Motivating others: just seven girls in the team at beginning, now 12
Friendly and caring: good relationship means that team try harder for her
Good at organising: team didn't know when to train, so she made a timetable

4 56

Answer
A good example is …

5
Before students do the task, remind them of the three questions they copied in their notebooks in exercise 2 to answer question 1. These are the three questions they should answer. Point out that the focus is not on the interviewer, it is on the person answering the questions.
- With less confident classes, allow students to prepare the answers to the questions in pairs before practising individually.

6
Make sure students understand that they need to choose a free-time activity which has helped them develop personal skills and qualities. Explain that if they can't match their free-time activity to three items from the list in exercise 1, they should think about a different free-time activity.
- With more confident classes, allow students to use personal skills and qualities not covered in exercise 1, as long as you think they are suitable and logical.

Practice makes perfect

7b Before students repeat the task, give them a few minutes to look at their notes from exercise 6 again and think about what they did well in exercise 7a and what could be better. Allow them to make any small changes they think necessary before continuing.

Homework Workbook page 63

GET TO THE TOP! 7

Developing writing p93
Writing a job application

> **Warmer**
>
> Books closed. Put students into pairs, and ask them to try and remember all the jobs they have seen in the unit, both 'traditional' (e.g. chef, construction worker, nurse, shop assistant) and 'unusual' (e.g. astronaut, ice-cream taster, ravenmaster, big-cat dentist).
>
> After students do the task, ask them if they could choose one job from the unit to apply for, which it would be and why.

1 SPEAKING

- If it is not common for teenagers to work in their country, follow up by asking: *What age do people usually get their first job in your country? Is it usually a part-time or a full-time job? Is it usually a good job? Do people at university often work and study at the same time? Why/Why not?*

2 Pre-teach any words students may have problems with, e.g. *disappearing* (stopping happening) and *lifeguard* (someone whose job is to save swimmers who are in danger, either at a swimming pool or the beach).

> **Answers**
> 1 Yes, but it is not as common as it used to be.
> 2 working in retail or in restaurants, creative jobs like singing or acting and working as a lifeguard

3 SPEAKING

- Pre-teach *mission* (an objective that is very important to an organisation).
- After students do the task, take a show of hands to find out which of the two jobs is more popular.

+ Extra activity

Write these words on the board: *badly-paid, boring, depressing, relaxing, tiring, well-paid*. Put students into pairs to decide which adjectives they would use to describe each job and to add other words to the lists. Remind them that in Developing vocabulary in Unit 5 (page 61) they saw adjectives ending in *-ing* and *-ed*. Point out that adjectives ending in *-ing* usually describe things and the effect they have on your feelings.

4 Students answer the question in pairs or as a class.

- Point out that the main section of the job application (*I do many different sports ... learning French at school.*) contains very similar detailed personal information to what students practised giving in the Speaking section on page 92. Highlight that the letter gives detailed information about the things Olivia has done, gives detailed examples and explains what skills and qualities she has developed.

> **Answer**
> Yes, this person is suitable for the job because they love many different sports and have experience of working with children. Furthermore, they speak more than one language.

5 With more confident classes, ask students what they should do if they don't know the name of the person they are writing to. Elicit that in this case we use *Dear Sir/Madam* and *Yours faithfully*.

> **Answers**
> Ms, look forward, sincerely, contractions, Could you

Language notes

Some people continue to make distinctions between married and unmarried women. Students may be surprised to see that men are always addressed as *Mr*, while women may be addressed as *Mrs* (married) or *Miss* (unmarried). While students will almost certainly see both of these, suggest they use the 'neutral' form *Ms* (/məz/), which gives no indication of a woman's marital status, if the woman does not make the distinction herself.

6 SPEAKING

- With less confident classes, collate ideas from this preparation stage on the board.

Practice makes perfect

7a Before students do the task, draw attention to the paragraph structure of the job application. Tell students to follow the same format, i.e. *Dear ...,*; paragraph 1: reason for writing; paragraph 2: detailed personal information; paragraph 3: short close; *Yours ...,*.

- Draw students' attention to the email address in the Faster Food! advert. Point out that in 'a.daly@ ...' Daly is a surname. With less confident classes, elicit possible first names, e.g. Antonio or Agata, and tell students that they need to decide if they are writing to a man or a woman.

Homework Workbook page 64

7 GET TO THE TOP!

Test yourself p95

Grammar test

1 Answers
1 mustn't   2 must/has to   3 don't have to   4 have to/must
5 mustn't   6 doesn't have to   7 mustn't

2 Answers
a look   b Should I   c would send   d shouldn't   e would

3 Answers
1 I saw a bear, I'd take a photo of it.
2 my brother were/was angry, he'd shout.
3 my parents won the lottery, they'd give me a present.
4 I understood French, I wouldn't watch a French film.
5 we didn't have phones, we'd talk face to face more.
6 he were/was very good at football, he wouldn't play professionally.
7 I lived in Italy, I'd speak Italian.
8 we had wings, we'd be able to fly.

Vocabulary test

1 Answers
1 salary   2 Construction workers   3 journalists   4 manual
5 outside   6 au pair   7 overtime   8 receptionist

2 Possible answers
1 … he wants to be successful and well-paid.
2 … can adapt to any situation.
3 … always texts his mum when he is going to be late.
4 … keeps trying until he finds a solution.
5 … can be trusted to do what you say you are going to do.
6 … are able to solve problems easily.

3 Answers
1 paid   2 going   3 known   4 year-old   5 looking   6 time

FRIENDLY ADVICE   8

Vocabulary in context p96
Using a range of lexis to talk about feelings and friendships

Warmer
Write or project the following quotes about friendship on the board:
'A friend is someone who knows all about you and still loves you.' Elbert Hubbard
'The best mirror is an old friend.' George Herbert
'The only way to have a friend is to be one.' Ralph Waldo Emerson
In pairs, ask students to decide what they think the quotes are saying about friendship, and choose their favourite one. Elicit ideas from different students. Tell students they are going to study the topic of friendship in this unit.

1 🔊 57
- When checking answers, explain that all the words form adjective/noun pairs, e.g. *angry* (adj)/*anger* (n), *boredom* (adj)/*bored* (n). Point out that there is one 'unusual' pair, where the words are very different: *afraid* (adj)/*fear* (n), and that *upset* (adj) does not have a matching noun.

Answers
Adjective – Positive feeling: delighted, excited, happy, proud, relieved
Adjective – Negative feeling: afraid, angry, bored, confused, disappointed, embarrassed, lonely, sad, upset
Noun – Positive feeling: delight, excitement, happiness, pride, relief
Noun – Negative feeling: anger, boredom, confusion, disappointment, embarrassment, fear, loneliness, sadness

🔵 Mixed ability
To address different levels within your class, work through the words in the box together. Do not discuss meaning but elicit if each word is an adjective or a noun. Tell more confident students to classify all the words, divide less confident students into two groups, and tell one group to classify the adjectives and one to classify the nouns.
During class feedback, nominate students to say whether words are positive or negative. Make sure you include less confident students in the feedback stage by asking them to explain words you know they checked.

2
Before students do the task, make sure they understand there is no 'right' answer.

Possible answers
1 delight, pride
2 boredom, disappointment, loneliness, sadness
3 disappointment, loneliness, sadness
4 pride, delight, excitement, happiness

4a 🔊 58
- Before students do the task, point out that they need to change the form of some items. With less confident classes, clarify that this means they need to use plurals and different verb forms.

4b 🔊 59
- Point out the different pronunciation and stress for *close* (v, the opposite of 'to open') /kləʊz/ and *close* (adj) /kləʊs/.
- After checking answers, draw attention to the six verbs with *with*. Ask students to find these verbs in the text (c, e, f, g, i, j), and elicit from students when we use *with* (when the verb is followed by a person, e.g. *c hang out with them; g got on well with him*). Show students how these verbs can also be used without *with*, e.g. *My friends and I hang out at my house after school.*, and how the other verbs can be used with *with*, e.g. *I see eye to eye with Leo on lots of things.*

Answers
a circle of friends b classmates c hang out d close
e see eye to eye f have in common g got on well h ups and downs i have arguments j fallen out k make up l through thick and thin

5
Answers
1 of 2 with, up 3 out 4 in 5 on, with 6 through

Use it ... don't lose it!
6 SPEAKING 👥
- After students do the task, flip the activity by allowing the students to interview you using the questions. Elicit the necessary change in question 5 (*classmates* to *colleagues*).

Homework Workbook page 66

85

8 FRIENDLY ADVICE

Reading p97
Predicting content, reading for gist and detail

> **Warmer**
>
> Ask students to think about the most important friendships in their lives. Ask students to talk about these friendships in pairs, saying why they are important. Ask them to include how they know their friend, why this person is special and to describe a memory they have of them, e.g. *My relationship with my best friend is important to me because I can tell him everything and he always gives me good advice. We met at primary school when we were six years old. I remember playing football with him on the first day we met.*
> If students wish to do so, they can share some of their thoughts and ideas with the class.

1 SPEAKING
- After students do the task, collate ideas from this preparation stage on the board.
- The central picture shows Pepper, a real humanoid robot designed by SoftBank Robotics. He is the first robot to be able to start a conversation when he sees a person. He can speak 15 languages and interact with people through speech and the touchscreen on his chest.

2 Culture notes

Isaac Asimov (1920–92) was born in Petrovichi, Russia, but moved with his family to the US when he was three. He taught biochemistry at Boston University but is most famous as a writer of science fiction novels and science books for the general public.
WALL-E and R2-D2 are famous fictional robots. The first, WALL-E, from the Disney/Pixar® film of the same name; the second, R2-D2 from the *Star Wars*™ series.
PARO is a real robot in the form of a fluffy baby seal, like a child's cuddly toy. It was designed so that patients who could benefit from animal therapy could receive this in places like hospitals and care homes where real animals are not allowed.

3
- Pre-teach any words students may have problems with, not including the underlined words, e.g. *forced labour* (hard physical work that someone makes you do), *seal* (large sea animal that eats fish and usually lives in cold parts of the world) and *living beings* (a person, animal, bird, etc. that is alive, rather than something like a stone which was never alive).
- After checking answers, ask students if they think they could ever be best friends with a robot. Encourage students to share their opinions with the class and explain why or why not.

Answers
1 Robots are no longer just machines for work but are now being designed as toys for children.
2 She was worried at first until the robot saved her child's life.
3 They are examples of friendly robots that exist in fiction that may confuse children.
4 Robots are now capable of real interaction with children and can show sadness and disappointment, as well as getting upset.
5 It responds to a person's voice and touch, and it makes people with dementia feel less lonely without ever having an argument with them.
6 A group of people had to interact with a robot which then begged them not to switch it off.
7 It showed how some of the people in the experiment formed an emotional connection with the robot which was so strong in some people that they refused to switch the robot off.

Fast finishers
Students write two more comprehension questions about the text to ask the rest of the class.

4 Answers
divided opinions – different points of view among a group of people
inanimate – not alive (and never having been alive)
shake – move something quickly from side to side or up and down
modify – change
surroundings – what is around you
companion – friend
begged – asked repeatedly
hesitated – paused before doing something

5 Critical thinkers
- Before students do the task, remind them that the objective is to justify their opinion and give suitable examples.

Possible answer
I'm not sure about this issue at all because I can see positives and negatives. In the future I think we will be interacting with robots and machines more and more, so maybe children need to learn that from when they are very young. Speaking personally though, I reckon that a lot of teenagers today spend too much time looking at screens and not enough time with real people in the real world. I think that's a pity. So, I think parents giving young children robot companions could make the problem worse, as children might stop interacting with each other completely.

Homework — Workbook page 67

FRIENDLY ADVICE 8

Grammar in context 1 p98
Using the past perfect

> **Warmer**
>
> Books closed. Write the following sentence on the board:
> *I ¹was paying at the supermarket when I ²put my hand in my pocket and ²realised …*
> Elicit the names of the two tenses used (1 past continuous; 2 past simple), and then ask students to suggest ways to complete the sentence. Write one example with the past simple on the board, e.g. *I ²didn't have my wallet.* If no students offer an ending with the past perfect, ask them to complete the sentence using *forget*, e.g. *I ³had forgotten my wallet.* Explain that this sentence is more sophisticated as it contains three different tenses, and elicit or teach that the third is the past perfect.

1a **Answer**
The green actions happened first.

1b **Answer**
before

1c **Answer**
have, past participle

Language notes
The past perfect is used when we are already talking about the past and we want to go even further back in time. It makes it clear that something happened before another point in the past. Students may find the following timeline useful for exercise 1a sentence 2:

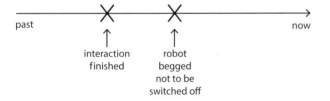

Point out to students that sometimes native speakers avoid the past perfect by using the words *before* and *after* to make the order of actions clear, e.g. *After I did my homework, I went to bed.*
There are, however, many instances when the past perfect is necessary. Point out, or mark on a timeline, the differences between the sentences:
When I arrived, John left. (= John left at the same time as I arrived, i.e. the two actions happened simultaneously.)
When I arrived, John had left. (= John left before I arrived.)

➕ Extra activity
Ask students to write down what they have already done today with a time next to the action, e.g. *7.00 had a shower, 7.30 ate breakfast, 8.00 went to school*, etc. They then use their notes to write sentences about what they had already

done by the time they did an action, e.g. *When I got to school, I'd already eaten breakfast.* Students can also ask and answer questions about their day in pairs, e.g. *Had you already had lunch when you went to the science lesson?*

2 Before students do the task, make clear that they need to use both the past simple and the past perfect once in each sentence.

> **Answers**
> 1 had put, left   2 corrected, had done   3 had finished, asked
> 4 fell, had told   5 wasn't, had lost   6 had left, went   7 was, had switched   8 had passed, felt

3
> **Answers**
> a was   b had died   c knew   d 'd trained   e was   f had invited
> g appeared   h had manipulated   i had had   j met

4a
> **Possible answers**
> 2 I had passed my driving test
> 3 they had won the competition
> 4 my friend had cancelled our cinema trip
> 5 somebody had broken their car window
> 6 the show had been postponed
> 7 I had found out my favourite band was playing in town
> 8 it had started to rain

4b
Language notes
The contracted form of *had* is usually used in spoken language because using the full form can seem too emphatic. Both *had* and *would* are contracted to *'d*, but *had* in the past perfect is followed by a past participle, while *would* is followed by an infinitive.

5 Highlight the use of *by the age of (five)* in the example, and check students understand that it means 'when I reached the age of five'.

> **Possible answers**
> 3 I'd learned/learnt to read by the age of five.
> 4 I'd swum in the sea by the age of eight.
> 5 I'd started to ride a bike by the age of six.
> 6 I haven't been/gone on a holiday without my parents yet.
> 7 I'd met my current best friend by the age of 12.
> 8 I'd done a part-time job by the age of 14.

Use it … don't lose it!
6 🗣 SPEAKING

• After students do the task, discuss some of the most interesting and varied items as a class, e.g. find out when students started to learn English (interesting, but probably a similar age), when they first travelled to a different country (more likely to be a spread of ages), etc.

🏠 Homework Workbook page 68

8 FRIENDLY ADVICE

Developing vocabulary p99
Using the noun suffixes -ness, -ship and -dom

Warmer

Books closed. Write *connect*, *differ* and *embarrass* on the left of the board and the suffixes *-ment*, *-ion* and *-ence* on the right of the board. Ask students to match the words to the correct suffixes. After checking answers, remind students that they saw these three suffixes in Developing vocabulary in Unit 1 (page 9), and explain that in this section they are going to look at three more common noun suffixes.

Answers
connection   difference   embarrassment

1b When checking answers, highlight the spelling change (y to i) in *lonely – loneliness* and the spelling and pronunciation changes in *wise* /waɪz/ – *wisdom* /ˈwɪzdəm/.

Answers
-ness: brightness, darkness, kindness, loneliness, madness, weakness
-ship: citizenship, friendship, leadership, membership, partnership, relationship
-dom: boredom, freedom, kingdom, stardom, wisdom

✚ Extra activity

Ask students to underline the stressed syllables in the nouns in exercise 1b and practise saying them using the correct word stress.

Answers
-ness: <u>a</u>wareness, <u>bright</u>ness, <u>dark</u>ness, <u>kind</u>ness, <u>lone</u>liness, <u>mad</u>ness, <u>weak</u>ness
-ship: <u>ci</u>tizenship, <u>friend</u>ship, <u>lea</u>dership, <u>mem</u>bership, <u>part</u>nership, re<u>la</u>tionship
-dom: <u>bore</u>dom, <u>free</u>dom, <u>king</u>dom, <u>star</u>dom, <u>wis</u>dom

Language notes

The suffix *-ness* is perhaps the most common in the English language and can be attached to many adjectives to make abstract nouns, e.g. *happiness*, *friendliness*.
The suffix *-ship* denotes a state or condition and is similar in meaning to *-dom*. Base words for *-ship* are usually connected to social groups, e.g. *friendship*, *relationship*, *apprenticeship*.

2 Pre-teach any words students may have problems with, e.g. *residents* (people who live in a particular place). Check the pronunciation of *nyctophobia* (/ˌnɪktəˈfəʊbɪə/).
- The Tower of London was built by William the Conqueror. Many British people don't know this.

Answers
1 Citizenship   2 wisdom   3 kingdom   4 Membership
5 boredom   6 stardom   7 darkness

Culture exchange

3 Make sure that students understand that exercise 2 focused on the meaning of the words and this exercise focuses on the form. Tell students they should look carefully at the words before and after each alternative to help them decide what type of word they need.
- Check students know what a *postcard* is (*a small card that you write on one side of and send someone by post; it usually has a picture on the other side and is sent from a place you are visiting*). If possible, bring in a postcard you have received or show a postcard on screen to elicit the meaning.
- When checking answers, check students understand that in (b) both words are nouns, a *friend* is a person, *friendship* is abstract – you can only send a postcard to a person, so the answer is *friend*; in (g) a *relation* is a person, a *relationship* is the connection you have with a person – the text is talking about connections between people, so the answer is *relationship*.

Answers
a happiness   b friend   c brightness   d illness   e loneliness
f sad   g relationship

4 With more confident classes, tell students to cover the rest of the page and try to add the noun suffixes from memory. When students finish, they can look back at the table in exercise 1b to check their answers.

Answers
1 ship   2 ness   3 dom   4 ship   5 ness   6 ness
7 ship, dom   8 ness

Homework > Workbook page 69

88

FRIENDLY ADVICE 8

GREAT LEARNERS GREAT THINKERS p100

Thinking about ways of making new friends and not letting people feel left out

Warmer
Write or project these questions on the board:
How many close friends do you have in your circle?
Do you have any friends who have been with you through thick and thin? Where did you meet?
Loneliness is a common feeling in the modern world. How do you deal with feeling lonely?
Students discuss the questions in pairs or small groups.

1 SPEAKING
- Follow up by asking: *Who do you think is more responsible for helping children who feel lonely?*, and discuss with the class the four options (1–4). Aim to elicit that no single person is more responsible than the others and that everyone has a part to play if they see a child looking lonely.

2 VIDEO
- After checking answers, ask students if they know of any systems that schools in their country use to help lonely children.

Answer
Buddy benches – children can sit on the bench and wait for someone to ask them to play with them. Yes, it appears to be working.

3 VIDEO
- Check students remember the word *playground* by showing a still from the video. Pre-teach *symbol* (something that represents a particular idea), *inclusion* (the action of including someone in a group), *stigma* (a feeling that something is wrong or embarrassing in some way) and *well-being* (the positive state someone should be in, including being happy, healthy and safe).

Answers
1 friendship 2 play 3 Ireland 4 247 5 feelings 6 40 7 90

4 SPEAKING
- Collate students' ideas on the board before they move on to the Great thinkers exercise.

GREAT THINKERS

5 The *Compass points (E-W-N-S)* thinking routine shows students how to think about an idea from different angles before forming an opinion on it.
- Encourage students to record their responses visually using the directions of the compass, i.e. *E* to the right, *W* to the left, *N* to the top and *S* to the bottom, rather than as a simple list.
- If your class is less confident, work together on one idea first: choose one of the situations from exercise 4; draw a compass on the board; then invite and collate students' suggestions for 1–4 around the compass.
- Note that the points (1–4) are intentionally ordered: E (*exciting*) → W (*worries*) → N (*need*) → S (*steps*). This is because students will probably find it easier to start with the *exciting* and positive aspects, before moving through the other categories and finishing with concrete *steps*. Therefore, do not change the order in this routine to work in a different order, e.g. clockwise around the compass.

6 Make sure students understand that in this case there are no 'correct' answers. They may have included different, and equally valid, steps in their answers to exercise 5.

7 SPEAKING
- Ask students who thought of other steps in exercise 5 to share these with the class and collate them on the board. Students can then include any ideas they like in their definitive list of tips.
- If appropriate for your class, put students into pairs or small groups to produce a leaflet with tips on dealing with loneliness. They can display these around the classroom and students can vote on the one they think contains the most 'professional' advice.

GREAT LEARNERS SEL

- Extend the discussion by asking students to look back on their time at primary school and think about what things the teacher did to try and help them show empathy and kindness.

LEARNER PROFILE

- Ask students to read the statement and the question in the Learner profile on page 143, and then grade themselves from 1 to 5. Explain that here 1 means 'I don't often show empathy and kindness to others' and 5 means 'I always show empathy and kindness to others'.
- If appropriate for your class, get students to share their grades with a partner or small group and, if they wish, to give their reasons. Encourage students to share suggestions for showing empathy and kindness to others. Alternatively, ask students individually to think of ways to show empathy and kindness to others.

8 FRIENDLY ADVICE

Listening p102

Listening for gist and detail

Warmer

Ask students to read the statements in exercise 1. Then give a short response yourself to one of the statements, without repeating the original wording of the statement too obviously, e.g.
I don't agree with this at all. I've got a few really good friends who I don't see very often. They live a long way away and if I didn't use Facebook and Twitter it would be really hard to stay friends. In fact, sometimes when I'm home alone they stop me feeling lonely!
Students guess which statement you are talking about. (Statement 3)

1 SPEAKING

- After students do the task, explain that some people might describe the statements as *myths* (*things that people always say but that aren't perhaps true*).

2 🔊 61

Answers
1 All three speakers both agree and disagree.

3 🔊 61

- Remind students that in multiple-choice exercises they should read the different answers before they listen. Give them time to do this before listening again.

Answers
1 a incorrect – Sally says *up to a point, yes, I agree* but then talks about a friend of hers who has different interests.
 b **correct** – Sally says *That doesn't mean you have to have exactly the same tastes* and gives the example of a friend who likes a different activity to her.
 c incorrect – *That doesn't mean you have to have exactly the same tastes …*
2 a incorrect – No mention of this, but Sally talks about having *lots to talk about* because you do different things.
 b incorrect – Sally says *Some Saturdays we both go shopping and others we both go running*, but they are not introducing each other to something new here.
 c **correct** – Sally gives the example of how she compromises with her friend *Some Saturdays we both go shopping and others we both go running!*
3 a incorrect – Mark says *I'm not interested in counting my friends.*
 b incorrect – Mark says *I'm not interested in counting my friends.*
 c **correct** – Mark says *What IS a friend, anyway? How close do you have to be?*
4 a incorrect – No mention of 'as many people as possible'.
 b **correct** – Mark says *the only important thing is feeling comfortable and happy with the person or people that you spend your free time with.*
 c incorrect – Marks talks about *feeling comfortable and happy with the person or people that you spend your free time with*, not the people around you.
5 a **correct** – Maya mentions *misunderstandings on social media* and saying *inappropriate things* and says *if you say anything on social media, you should also be prepared to say it to a person's face …*
 b incorrect – No mention of whether people do or don't read what their friends write.
 c incorrect – No mention of people saying too much.
6 a incorrect – Maya says *it's a bad idea to spend too much time* on social media, but she is not saying that it is a 'waste of time'.
 b **correct** – Maya talks about the friends she can't see very often and says *Without social media, it would be difficult to keep those relationships alive.*
 c incorrect – *Some people get lonely …*

4 💡 Critical thinkers

- Before students do the task, remind them that the objective is to justify their opinion and give suitable examples.

🏠 **Homework** Workbook page 69

Grammar in context 2 p102

Using gerunds and infinitives

Warmer

Ask students to give you five gerunds and five infinitives and write them on the board. Next, ask students to write at least two sentences with gerunds and two with infinitives. When they have finished, elicit examples and ask the class to correct any errors.

1a You may have set the Flipped classroom video for homework, but if not watch the video in class before working through the activities.

- Point out that the sentences are based on sentences from the listening in the previous section.

1b Before students do the task, point out that they will need to leave one cell in the table blank.

Answers
We use the gerund: e, f, g
We use the infinitive: b, c, d

Language notes

Gerunds and infinitives are both common verb forms. Gerunds end in *-ing*, e.g. *walking*, and act as nouns. Infinitives are the basic verb form with the particle *to*, e.g. *to walk*. The terms *-ing* form and present participle are also commonly used for words ending in *-ing*. The grammatical distinction between these is complex, so for simplicity in this section, all the words used are gerunds.

2a **Answers**
2 g 3 b 4 d 5 f 6 g 7 e 8 c 9 a 10 f

FRIENDLY ADVICE 8

3a Before students do the task, point out that the correct use of gerunds and infinitives is one of the grammar areas that is often tested in exams, so students should spend time and effort getting this right.

- In order to decide whether they need a gerund or an infinitive, remind students to pay close attention to what happens before or after a word, e.g. after an adjective we use the infinitive. Explain that this is a reason why students should write example sentences alongside new vocabulary rather than trying to learn words out of context.

Answers
1 to make   2 to say   3 giving   4 to relax   5 shopping
6 Doing   7 listening   8 talking

3b SPEAKING

- With less confident classes, write or project the following example dialogue on the board, so students have an idea of the type of conversation expected:
   A: I think sentence 1 is probably true for you. Am I right?
   B: Yes, you are! And I think this one is true for you too. You said earlier that you like meeting new people.
   A: Exactly, I do!

4 After students do the task, ask them to imagine how they would feel in Aron's situation, living on an isolated island. Discuss as a class if there are any regions of students' countries where there might be young people as isolated as Aron.

Answers
a living   b swimming   c cycling   d spending   e to go
f Studying   g letting   h to help   i Getting   j appearing
k staying

5 Before students do the task, focus their attention on the photo. Ask if any students recognise the two tennis players (left: Serena Williams; right: Caroline Wozniacki), and elicit anything they know about them.

- Point out that there are two types of mistakes in the text: sometimes the text uses a gerund where an infinitive is needed, and sometimes the text uses an infinitive where a gerund is needed. However, not all the gerunds and infinitives are incorrect.

Answers
Professional sport is obviously very competitive. **1 To get** ~~Getting~~ to the top, you have to work incredibly hard. But it's important **2 to remember** ~~remembering~~ that it's still just sport. Everybody wants **3 to win** ~~winning~~, of course. But, winning isn't everything. So, in the world of tennis, it's been great to see that top players like Serena Williams and Caroline Wozniacki could be rivals on the court, but friends when the match finished. **4 Having** ~~To have~~ respect for your rival is the important thing. It's normal **5 to have** ~~having~~ occasional differences and arguments but at the end of the match you need **6 to forget** ~~forgetting~~ these. Many young people enjoy **7 watching** ~~to watch~~ sport and they look up to sports stars. By watching some of the top tennis players, they can learn that rivals don't have to be enemies.

Culture notes

Serena Williams (1981–) was born in Michigan, US. She has won numerous Grand Slam titles, both singles and doubles. At the 2012 London Olympic Games®, she won gold medals both in women's singles and in doubles, which she played with her equally famous older sister, Venus.

Caroline Wozniacki (1990–) was born to Polish parents in Odense, Denmark. She started playing at the age of 7 and turned professional when she was 15. Like Williams she has won numerous titles, including the Australian Grand Slam in 2018. She retired from professional tennis in early 2020 in order to pursue other interests.

6 Mixed ability

To simplify the activity, tell less confident students, or the whole class, to work on only half of the questions. Tell half the students to work on items 1–5 and the other half on items 6–10. Pair students in exercise 7 with a student who worked on the other questions. Remind students of the question *What about you?* which asks for the other person's ideas or opinions.

Use it ... don't lose it!

7 SPEAKING

- After students do the task, follow up as a class by nominating a student to ask each question and a different student to answer it.

Homework > Workbook page 70

8 FRIENDLY ADVICE

Developing speaking p104
Reporting a past event

Warmer

Give students a 'gerunds spelling test'. Read out the following words, repeating each one two or three times. Students write them down in their notebooks.
1 shopping, 2 swimming, 3 sitting, 4 planning, 5 having, 6 making, 7 cycling, 8 giving, 9 shouting, 10 relaxing, 11 happening, 12 staying

With more confident classes, put students into pairs or small groups to compare their answers. Tell them that, if their answers are correct, items 1–4 will have something in common, so will items 5–8 and so will items 9–12. Write or project all the words on the board for students to self-correct. Elicit or point out what the groups of items have in common.

Answers
1–4 all double the final consonant
5–8 all drop the final -e
9–12 add -ing to the infinitive (note: happen does not double the final consonant because it has the stress on the first syllable)

1 SPEAKING
- Pre-teach *theme park* (a large park where people pay to play games and have fun, e.g. Disneyland®) and *ride* (a general word for machines at theme parks which people go on for fun).
- Follow up by asking: *Have you ever been to a festival like this? Which? Have you ever been on a ride like this? Where?*

2 🔊 62
- With less confident classes, play the recording twice. First students listen and identify the questions they hear. Check which the speakers answer (1, 2, 4, 6, 7, 10) before students listen again to note details of the speakers' answers.

Answers
1 a pop music festival/the Fusion Festival
2 with mum, dad, Lily and Ryan
4 It was massive.
6 Yes, Jack and Claire.
7 It was the typical stuff. It was good, but it was a bit expensive.
10 about 10 pm.

3 **Answers**
1 b iii   2 c iv   3 d ii   4 a i

+ Extra activity

Draw the following timeline on the board:

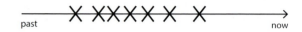

Ask students which verb form in bold in the Speaking bank it matches (*used to*). Elicit an example sentence that goes with the timeline, e.g. *When I was younger, I used to go skiing a lot, but I don't now.* (The crosses all indicate times I went skiing.)

Put students into pairs and tell them to think of one sentence combining past simple and past continuous, and one sentence combining past simple and past perfect. They then draw a timeline to illustrate each of these visually.

Answer
For reference, see the model timelines in this book on page 27 (past simple + past continuous) and page 87 (past simple + past perfect).

4 Remind students that they don't need to answer all the questions from exercise 2. The girl on the recording, for example, didn't answer questions 3, 5, 8 or 9. Students should make notes for the questions that are most appropriate for the event that they are talking about.

Practice makes perfect

5b SPEAKING
- In this type of activity, students have to talk about something (real or imaginary) that happened in the past. Students may need to speak alone or have a conversation with the examiner or another student.
- ✓ **Exam tip** To answer the question in the Exam tip box, students will be expected to use past tenses correctly. Tell them to refer back to exercise 3 if necessary.
- When reporting past events, students should also use expressions of time and sequence (*first, next, then, later,* etc.) to make the order of events clear; basic question words like *Who? What? When? Where? How? Why?* to help them think of more things to say; and fillers like *Well, Hmm* or *Let me think* to give them time to think of what they want to say next. They should also listen actively to what their partner or the examiner is saying.
- Remind students that if they don't understand what the examiner or their partner is saying, they should ask them in English to repeat or to speak more slowly. They should use expressions like: *Sorry, can you say that again, please?* or *Sorry, could you speak more slowly, please?*

FRIENDLY ADVICE 8

Developing writing p105
Writing an email of advice

> **Warmer**
>
> Write the phrasal verb *to fall out* on the board, and elicit the meaning (*to stop being friendly with someone because you have had a disagreement with them*). In pairs, ask students what they think the most common reasons to fall out with friends are. Elicit some ideas from students and ask which they think is the most and least serious reason.

1 Put students into pairs or project the photo and work as a class. Ask students to describe the photo and what they think is happening, e.g. *I'm not sure but I think the two girls have had an argument. The girl on the left looks upset and the girl on the right looks sorry. I think the girl on the right might be apologising because …*

- Before students read the emails, explain that in the next exercise they will need to tell their partner the key information from their email. Tell them that they will not be able to look at the original email as they share the information, only their notes.

> **Answers**
> **Student A:** Rachel doesn't have anything in common with her friend Ellie any more. She doesn't want to spend time with her because Ellie isn't interested in music. She feels bad about lying to her.
> **Student B:** Ellie doesn't see her friend any more because her friend is in a band and spends time with her new friends. Ellie misses her and feels lonely.

2 SPEAKING

- Books closed. Explain that students should first tell each other the key information from their email using their notes. They should then discuss the question.

> **Answers**
> **Similarities:** Both girls are talking about difficulties in their friendship.
> **Differences:** Rachel doesn't really want to hang out with Ellie, but Ellie wants to hang out with Rachel.

+ Extra activity

Give students time to read the email they didn't read in exercise 1, then check comprehension of the emails by asking the following questions:
Where did Rachel and Ellie meet? (at primary school)
When exactly did the problem start? (when Rachel joined a band)
What does Rachel do when Ellie asks if she can hang out with her and the band? (Rachel invents reasons why Ellie can't.)
How does each girl feel about the situation? (Rachel feels bad about lying to Ellie. Ellie misses Rachel and feels lonely.)
Have the two girls fallen out? Why/Why not? (No. They haven't really had a disagreement, it's just that they don't know how to adapt to the new situation. They both want to keep the friendship or they wouldn't be writing the emails.)

3 SPEAKING

- With less confident classes, collate ideas from this preparation stage on the board for students to use in exercise 7a.

5 Remind students that they saw both *If I were you, …* and *should* in Unit 7.

> **Answers**
> If I were you, I'd …
> you should …

Language notes

Explain has three main structures:
- I <u>explained that</u> it was a problem. (explain that + clause)
- I <u>explained how</u> we could solve the problem. (explain + question word)
- I <u>explained the problem to my friend</u> and asked for help. (explain something to someone)

Suggest also has three main structures:
- She <u>suggested talking</u> to him. (suggest + gerund)
- She <u>suggested that</u> I talk to him. (suggest that + clause)
- She <u>suggested what</u> I should do next. (suggest + question word)

6 After checking answers, highlight the comma after all the words and expressions.

> **Answers**
> First of all, Next, After that, Lastly

Practice makes perfect

7a Before students do the task, check they understand that they are writing a reply to Ellie, so their email will have the same format as the one in exercise 4, not the ones in exercise 1.

7b **Exam tip** To answer the question in the Exam tip box, in writing exams students lose marks if they do not answer the question. It is not enough to write a composition with no grammatical mistakes and with a wide variety of vocabulary. Students must also answer the question and include all the information asked for in the question.

- Tell students that reading the question carefully can also help them to decide which tenses and vocabulary they need to use.

Homework Workbook page 72

8 FRIENDLY ADVICE

Test yourself p107

Grammar test

1 Answers
1 had finished, brushed 2 had done, said 3 dried, had washed 4 took, had had 5 arrived, had started 6 had written, sent 7 went, had bought 8 was, had learned/learnt 9 had got, dried

2 Answers
1 to buy 2 seeing 3 Eating 4 running 5 cycling 6 to listen 7 opening 8 to help 9 to go 10 to stay

Vocabulary test

1 Answers
1 delight 2 fear 3 pride 4 boredom 5 anger 6 relief 7 happiness

2 Answers
1 see, eye 2 out with 3 ups and 4 on, with 5 out with 6 have, with 7 through, thin

3 Answers
1 weakness 2 wisdom 3 madness 4 relationship 5 stardom 6 freedom 7 leadership

Exam success Units 7–8 p108

Reading

2

Answers

1 **A** incorrect – The sign doesn't mention specific areas of the park. **B** incorrect – The sign mentions *hiking paths*, but says nothing about what is open/closed. **C correct** – 'not to go near' – *Never approach*; 'certain animals' – *bears or mountain lions*

2 **A** incorrect – Zoe is asking Tom to confirm if he wants to see the film. **B correct** – 'see if Tom is still interested' – *I'll go if you want to. Let me know what you think?* **C** incorrect – Zoe says *the reviews aren't great*, so she has already seen them.

3 **A correct** – 'be responsible for their waste' – *It shouldn't be someone else's job to pick up your rubbish.* **B** incorrect – 'new recycling rules' are not mentioned **C** incorrect – The sign tells students to deal with their own rubbish.

4 **A** incorrect – The class is looking for *new artists* but *professional painters* will help these new artists. **B correct** – 'suitable for inexperienced artists' – *places still available for new artists* **C** incorrect – 'particular painting techniques' are not mentioned

5 **A** incorrect – The notice mentions *volunteers* and *term time only*, but it is aimed at students, not volunteers. **B** incorrect – The notice uses the word *network*, but in the sense of a group of people, rather than 'online'. **C correct** – 'support with their schoolwork' – *free homework advice ... help in any subject*

Listening

3

Answers

1 **A** incorrect – Sarah's cousin *designs websites for movies* but Sarah didn't see an advert for this job. **B correct** – *My cousin ... told me about a production company that needed more actors for a film that they're about to start filming.* **C** incorrect – Evan asks about Sarah's *acting lessons*, but no acting teacher is mentioned on the recording.

2 **A correct** – *I haven't been told if I'm in one or loads of scenes, so I'm a bit anxious about that.* **B** incorrect – Sarah is *going to be an extra*, so she *won't have to remember any lines.* **C** incorrect – not stated on the recording

3 **A** incorrect – *it isn't one of those cool action movies* **B correct** – *It's about a really famous composer ... in the 18th century.* **C** incorrect – Evan asks *Is it one of those scary films?*, but Sarah replies that *it isn't*.

4 **A correct** – *I take any opportunity that I can to see how they act.* **B** incorrect – *I get acting tips just from watching them.* **C** incorrect – *Everyone wants to take photos with them, but I don't.*

5 **A** incorrect – *I earned quite a lot from it.* **B** incorrect – *I can't complain that I had to arrive at work when most people were still sleeping!* **C correct** – *I guess doing the same scene over and over again is what I found most difficult.*

6 **A** incorrect – Sarah mentions *good and bad films,* but is talking about being an extra in them, not watching them. **B correct** – *... don't expect to get the lead role in your first film! It takes a lot of hard work to even get small jobs ...* **C** incorrect – not stated on the recording

- If you wish, go to page 147 to continue working through the Exam success section for these two units.
- See the Exam trainer, Workbook pages 94 and 101, for more information and practice on these Preliminary for Schools tasks.

Collaborative project 4 p109

Jobs for teenagers in your country

1 SPEAKING
- Students work in groups of 3–4.
- After students work in groups, ask them to share their ideas with the class and collate these on the board in note form.

2 SPEAKING
- Students continue to work in their groups from exercise 1.
- Remind them that the information you collated on the board in exercise 1 is unverified, so they need to check any of this they decide to use.

3
- Ask individuals to read aloud the tips and discuss them with the class.
- After reading the *Academic skills* section, make sure students understand that if they use a graph or diagram they find on a website, or if they create their own graph or diagram using someone else's data, they need to credit the source.

4 SPEAKING
- Remember to establish a clear plan for the project (interim dates/deadline; stages to be done at home/ in class). Remind students that as much discussion as possible should be in English, both in and out of class.

5 If students mark the projects of their classmates, encourage them to share and justify their marks.

- Connect with teachers and students in other countries and encourage students to present their projects to each other.

9 FACTS ABOUT FICTION

Vocabulary in context p110
Using a range of lexis to talk about things we read, genres and book reviews

Warmer
In pairs, students discuss the meaning of the unit title *Facts about fiction* and what they think the unit is going to be about. Elicit that *facts* (*pieces of true information*) is the 'opposite' of fiction (*about imaginary events and people*). Elicit that the title of the unit suggests that the unit will contain lots of true information about books. Explain that *fiction* is a common genre, and elicit the opposite: *non-fiction* (*books about real events and people*). Ask students to tell the class the names of their favourite books and whether these are fiction or non-fiction.

1 SPEAKING 63
- After students do the task, take a show of hands to find out how many students read physical books and how many read electronically. Also read through the words in the box, and take a show of hands for each to find out which things students read the most and the least.

2 SPEAKING 64
- Accept students using their own language in this exercise as they give examples. The objective is for students to process the genres.
- When checking students' explanations, where necessary and possible, give them the English titles of any books they mention in their own language.

Answers
autobiography – a book about someone's life that they write themselves
biography – a book about someone's life that another person writes
crime/detective/spy fiction – a book about imaginary events with criminals/detectives/spies
fairy tale – a traditional children's story in which magic things happen
fantasy – an imaginative story very different to real life
historical fiction – a book about imaginary events in a historical setting
horror – a book intended to frighten people
mystery – a story in which events are not explained until the end
romance – a story about a romantic relationship
science fiction – a book about imaginary future events, often in space
thriller – a book that tells an exciting story, e.g. about a crime
YA (young adult) – a book written for teenagers

Fast finishers »
Ask students to classify the 'Things we read' in exercise 1 and the 'Genres' in exercise 2 as *fiction* or *non-fiction*.

4a 65
- Pre-teach *copy* (*a single book [or newspaper, magazine, video game, etc.] that is one of many that are all exactly the same*).
- Before students do the task, point out that they need to use the correct form of words or choose the correct part of phrases for some items. With less confident classes, clarify that this means they need to use plurals or choose one word from a longer expression.

🌐 Culture notes
Mortal Engines is by Philip Reeve (1966–present). Reeve was born in Brighton, UK, and is a well-known writer and illustrator of children's books. *Mortal Engines* is the first in a series of four books published from 2001 to 2006. To date, however, only the first novel has been adapted as a film.

4b 66
- Follow up by asking: *Have you read* Mortal Engines? *Did you enjoy it? Why/Why not? Have you seen the film? Did you enjoy it? Why/Why not? If you've read the book and seen the film, do you think it is a good adaptation? Why/Why not?*

Answers
a bestseller **b** awards **c** adaptation **d** set **e** main characters **f** plot **g** twists **h** ending **i** style **j** themes **k** masterpiece

5 Before students do the task, check they have understood fully by asking: *Do you need to think about a specific book at this point?* (No. The questions should be questions that work for any book.); *What questions are best in a questionnaire?* (questions which you can answer *yes/no, always/sometimes/occasionally/never*, etc.; or answer with a short simple answer).
- With less confident classes, have students write the questionnaire in pairs. Then put them in different pairs for exercise 6.

96

FACTS ABOUT FICTION 9

Reading p111
Predicting content, reading for gist and detail

Warmer
Write *J.R.R. Tolkien*, *Agatha Christie*, *William Shakespeare* and *J.K. Rowling* on the board. In pairs, students try to come up with the book title(s) – in English – and genre or each author is most famous for. Take class feedback, and ask students if they think these are the most famous authors for each genre.

> **Answers**
> **J.R.R. Tolkien:** fantasy (*The Lord of the Rings, The Hobbit*); **Agatha Christie:** crime/detective fiction (*Poirot, Miss Marple, Murder on the Orient Express*); **William Shakespeare:** plays (*Hamlet, Romeo and Juliet, Macbeth*); **J.K. Rowling:** fantasy (*Harry Potter and the Philosopher's Stone, Harry Potter and the Chamber of Secrets,* etc.)

2 Follow up by asking: *Is there a scheme like this where you live? If there is, have you tried it? If not, do you think it would be successful? Why/Why not?*

> **Answers**
> 1 It's a global project about sharing books on public transport.
> 2 Emma Watson is a keen reader and has shared books on the Underground and the Subway.

3 🔊 67
- In this type of activity, students have to fill gaps in a text with sentences taken out of the text. There are sometimes more sentences than spaces.
- Remind students that they should read the text quickly to get a general idea of what it is about. To do this type of exercise, they do not usually have to understand every word, so tell them not to panic if they don't understand everything.
- Students should then read the sentences which go in the text and ask themselves: *What does each sentence talk about?* They should then find the sections of the text which correspond to the information in the sentences and read them again slowly, in more detail. They should put each sentence in the most probable space.
- ✅ **Exam tip** To answer the question in the Exam tip box, when students finish, they should check by reading the text with their answers in the correct place. They should ask themselves: *Do the sentences go together logically? Do words like* this *or* it *make sense?* At the same time, they should check that they have an answer for each question. They should never leave answers blank in an exam.

> **Answers**
> a 6 *This* (= the hour she spent on the Underground) *gave her plenty of time …*
> b 4 *… she'd had reading it* (= the great YA novel she finished on her way to work)
> c 5 *The idea* was simple. *Find* a book …, *read it*, … *leave* it for somebody else.
> d 1 *It isn't only individuals who share their books. Publishers … also …*
> e 3 *They* (= some companies) *take photos or make videos … finding the books* (= the books the companies leave).
> f 7 *There* (= New York) *she* (= Hollie) *helped with …*
> g 2 *They* (= the 20 different schemes) *have local names* (= specific to the 14 countries, Spain, Mexico, Argentina, Poland, etc.).

➕ **Extra activity**
Check comprehension of the text further by giving students the following True or False statements:
There was nothing negative about Hollie's new job in London (False – It was *an hour on the Underground*, compared to *10 minutes* cycling.)
Lots of positive things came from Hollie's time on the Underground. (True – *This gave her plenty of time to read.*; She *realised how amazing and important reading a good book is.*; She had *the idea for 'Books on the Underground'*.)
Everyone who uses 'Books on the Underground' does it because they love reading. (False – *Some companies use the project to get publicity …*)
Hollie and Emma Watson run the scheme in New York. (False – *Hollie helped with 'Books on the Subway'*; Emma Watson *has shared books on … the Subway.*)
Emma Watson reads about 50 books a year. (True – *She tries to read one book a week.*)

4
> **Answers**
> *Tube* – an informal name for the Underground/metro in London
> *encourage* – motivate
> *sticker* – label with glue/adhesive
> *scheme* – project
> *publisher* – company which produces books
> *platform* – place in station where people get on train
> *expose oneself to* – become aware of

5 🧠 **Critical thinkers**
- Before students do the task, remind them that the objective is to justify their opinion and give suitable examples.
- If you feel your students need more support, write these prompts on the board:
  I'm certain / not sure (that) … because …
  I (really) believe/feel/think (that) … because …
  In my opinion, …
  Speaking personally, …
  I would say …

🔁 **Flipped classroom**
You may want to ask students to watch the Flipped classroom video for Unit 9 as homework, in preparation for the grammar lesson.

Homework > Workbook page 77

97

9 FACTS ABOUT FICTION

Grammar in context 1 p112
Using reported speech in statements

Warmer

Write *He/She* said ...* on the board (*pronoun to match your gender). Say some simple sentences in direct speech, e.g. *I like English. They're going to the bank.* Put students into pairs to try and report them as a sentence starting with *He/She said*. Assess how well students change the tenses, pronouns and possessive adjectives, e.g. *He/She said he/she liked English. He/She said they were going to the bank.* Elicit that these are examples of reported speech, and explain that in this section they are going to learn more about this.

1a If you didn't set the Flipped classroom video for homework, watch the video in class before working through the activities.

- Point out that the sentences are based on sentences from the reading text on page 111.

Answers
1a, 2a and 3a are direct speech. 1b, 2b and 3b are reported speech.

1b **Answers**
1 Most of the time they move one tense back in/into the past.
2 They usually change to the third person.
3 *Say* does not need a personal object; *tell* needs a personal object.
4 No.

Language notes

The most common verbs used to report statements are *say* and *tell*. When *tell* is used in reported speech, it is always followed by a noun/pronoun indicating the person spoken to, whereas *say* is not, e.g. *Jane told us (that) we were going to France. Jane said (that) we were going to France.*

2 Before students do the task, point out that the *'d* in sentence d is a contraction of *would* not *had*.

Answers
2 b 3 c 4 c 5 d 6 a 7 f 8 e 9 g 10 g

 **Mixed ability**

To address different levels within your class, before students do exercise 3, put less confident students into pairs and tell them to write example direct speech sentences for grammar forms 1, 3, 5, 6 and 9 in exercise 3. Tell more confident students to work individually. Do the same for grammar forms 2, 4, 7, 8 and 10.

During class feedback, elicit an example sentence for each tense from students, write it on the board, circle or underline the verb form and make sure students are clear about its name. You can also point out that the grammar forms in the Direct speech column (1–10) in exercise 3 match items 1–10 in exercise 2.

3 When checking answers, highlight that both the past simple (3) and the present perfect (4) change to the past perfect and that *have to* (9) and *must* (10) both change to *had to*.

- With more confident classes, point out that in a small number of cases we do not 'backshift' the verb tense. This is usually when the time being referred to is not yet finished, e.g. '*I'm going to the cinema on Friday evening.*' (said on Wednesday) – *Joe told me yesterday that he's going to the cinema tomorrow.* (said on Thursday).

Answers
2 past continuous 3 past perfect or past simple 4 past perfect
5 would 6 could 7 might or may 8 should 9 had to 10 had to

4a When checking answers, highlight the words that follow each gap, and make sure students are clear that (a) *the children*, (d) *them* and (e) *the students* are nouns/pronouns indicating the people spoken to, while (b) *the building* and (c) *it* are part of what the person originally said.

Answers
a told b said c said d told e told

4b **Answer**
A library. Because it can help you to travel through your imagination.

4c Follow up by asking: *What is Isaac Asimov's feeling about libraries and books?* (He thinks they are really important.); *Do you agree with his opinion? Why/Why not?*

Answers
a 'It's a spaceship that will take you to the farthest reaches of the universe.'
b 'The building is a time machine that will take you to the far past and the far future.'
c 'It's a teacher that knows more than any human being.'
d 'It's a friend that will amuse you.'
e 'This library is a gateway to a better, happier and more useful life.'

5 **Answers**
2 here 3 today 4 yesterday 5 tomorrow 6 tonight
7 next (week/month/year) 8 last (week/month/year)
9 a (week/month/year) ago

Language notes

When we use reported speech, we have to take into account how circumstances have changed since the speaker originally spoke the words. For instance, we may now be reporting what was said from a different time or place and a different point of view. The person reporting the speech may also be different to the original speaker. This will affect the choice of pronouns and/or adverbials of time and place.

Homework — Workbook page 78

FACTS ABOUT FICTION   9

6 Before students do the task, make clear that this exercise covers both moving tenses one back in/into the past (the table in exercise 3) and changing other words (the table in exercise 5).

- When checking answers, make sure that students have changed *these* to *those* in item 2, and point out that this is the plural of *this* and *that* (item 1 in the table in exercise 5).

> **Answers**
> **1** (that) there were books of which the backs and covers were by far the best parts.
> **2** (that) those books had been a way of escaping from the unhappiness of his life.
> **3** (that) she had been in every line he had ever read.
> **4** (that) he would never cry for her again.
> **5** (that) it had been the best of times, it had been the worst of times.
> **6** (that) she hoped that real love and truth were stronger in the end than any evil or misfortune in the world.
> **7** (that) a very little key would open a very heavy door.

Use it ... don't lose it!

8 SPEAKING
- Before students share their sentences, tell them they are not allowed to write anything down and will need to try and remember who said what in the next exercise.

9 Before students do the task, remind them that they need to think about three areas: moving tenses one back in/into the past, using *say* and *tell* correctly and changing other words.

Developing vocabulary p113
Using phrasal verbs connected with reading and writing

> **Warmer**
> Books closed. Write or project the following sentences on the board:
> *I flicked through the book in the shop before I bought it.*
> *When I finished Mortal Engines, I immediately wanted to read on and finish the series.*
> *Rafael, could you read out your answer to question 2, please?*
> *No, don't scroll down the page, scroll up. It's at the top!*
> *Please sit down but don't turn over the exam paper until I say you can start.*
> Ask students: *What kind of words are the underlined words?* (phrasal verbs) Put students into pairs to look at the phrasal verbs, and try to work out their meanings from the context. Don't check answers as a class, have students match the phrasal verbs with the definitions in exercise 1.

1 68

> **Answers**
> **1** read out   **2** read on   **3** turn over   **4** flick through
> **5** scroll down/up

Language notes

Associating phrasal verbs with a topic, e.g. reading and writing, can help students remember them more easily. This section focuses on the meaning of the phrasal verbs without focusing on the complicated grammar.

When phrasal verbs take an object, they can either be separable (*cross out, fill in, look over, make up, read out, turn over, write down*) or non-separable (*flick through*). A separable phrasal verb can have the object between the verb and the particle (*cross **the mistake** out*) or after the particle (*cross out **the mistake***), if the object is a noun. However, it must have the object between the verb and the particle if it is a pronoun (*cross **it** out* not *cross out **it***). A non-separable phrasal verb will always have the object after the particle (*flick through **the book/it*** not *flick **the book/it** through*).

2
> **Answers**
> **a** turn over   **b** read on   **c** scroll down   **d** flicking through/to flick through   **e** reading out

3 69
- With more confident classes, divide students into five groups. Assign each group one of the phrasal verbs. They work in their groups and first find the meaning (1–5) and then write an example sentence using the verb. Ask one student from each group to share their sentence with the class, for students to match each phrasal verb to its definition. With less confident classes, you may wish to give examples for the phrasal verbs yourself.

> **Answers**
> **1** fill in   **2** write down   **3** make up   **4** look over   **5** cross out

4
> **Answers**
> **1** make up   **2** write down   **3** fill in   **4** look over   **5** Cross out

Use it ... don't lose it!

5 SPEAKING
- After students do the task, extend to a class discussion by asking some students to share their opinions with the class. Encourage turn-taking, and make sure students listen to each other and agree or disagree using suitable phrases.

+ Extra activity

Ask students to write a short text about learning English in the classroom and how to learn effectively, using as many of the phrasal verbs from exercise 1 and exercise 3 as they can.

Homework > Workbook page 79

9 FACTS ABOUT FICTION

GREAT LEARNERS GREAT THINKERS p114

Thinking about what book covers can tell us and then designing a book cover

Warmer

Books closed. Write or project the following phrase on the board:
'Never judge a book by its cover.'
Check the meaning of *judge* (*form an opinion or idea about something*) and *cover* (*the outside pages at the front/back of a book/magazine*). Discuss with the class what they think the phrase might mean (it's used for saying that you should not form an opinion about someone or something only from their appearance), how far they agree with it and in what situations they might judge a 'book' by its 'cover'.

1 SPEAKING

- If you used the Warmer, highlight that the phrase there was not really about books and their covers, but that the lesson is. Extend the discussion by asking students if they think they can judge a (real) book by its (real) cover, e.g. *I think you often can. The people who design book covers know how to make them interesting for the people who will like the book!*

2 VIDEO

- After checking answers, ask if any students have read the novel *Lord of the Flies* (1954) by William Golding (UK; 1911–1993), or seen either of the film adaptations (1963/1990).

Answers
1 a novel by William Golding
2 the daughter of William Golding
3 a professional artist and book cover designer

3 VIDEO

- Pre-teach *entry* (*something that you have to make or do when you take part in a competition*) and *tactile* (*connected to the sense of touch*).
- Follow up by asking students: *Do you agree with the customer in the shop? Do you prefer physical books to e-books? Why/Why not?*

Answers
1 in the 1950s
2 for teenagers; design a new cover for *Lord of the Flies*
3 She thinks the teens have really understood the novel's message.
4 He prefers physical books. He likes the feel and magic of physical books and can't make the emotional step to e-books.
5 They will turn books into beautiful art objects.

GREAT THINKERS

4a The *See-Think-Wonder* thinking routine encourages students to look carefully at visual input and make logical deductions from this. It then encourages them to ask further questions, be curious and continue investigating.
- Students work individually.
- Make sure students understand that step 3, even though it doesn't contain one of the key words for the routine, is very important for the process and therefore they should give it equal importance.

4b SPEAKING
- Students work in groups of 3–4.
- Students should take turns to respond using all three stems about one book, e.g. student A talks about *Gilded Cage*: *I see ... , I think ... , I wonder ...* Student B responds about the same book, etc. The *I see ...* sentence may be quite short, but the *I think ...* and the *I wonder ...* sentences will be longer as students share additional thoughts and questions. Students then repeat the process for a different book cover with a different student starting.
- Encourage students always to structure their ideas using the three stems *I see ... , I think ... , I wonder ...* , and to keep notes summarising their discussion and their questions to share with the class.

5 SPEAKING

- Make sure students understand that they should choose either option 1 or option 2 and should then follow the three bullet points for the option they have chosen.
- If possible, make sure each group has someone who can either draw well or knows something about design/drawing software.

GREAT LEARNERS SEL

- Elicit from/point out for students how thinking creatively stimulates a different part of the brain and can help us solve problems which don't have a clear answer.

LEARNER PROFILE

- Ask students to read the statement and the question in the Learner profile on page 143, then grade themselves from 1 to 5. Explain that here 1 means 'I don't often think creatively', and 5 means 'I frequently think creatively'.
- If appropriate for your class, get students to share their grades with a partner or small group and, if they wish, to give their reasons. Encourage students to share suggestions for thinking more creatively. Alternatively, ask students individually to think of ways to think more creatively.

FACTS ABOUT FICTION

Listening p116
Listening for gist and specific information

Warmer

Write these questions on the board: *How do you choose what to read? Do you judge a book by its cover?* Ask students to discuss the questions in pairs and then with the class.

Write the choices *1 reviews, 2 author's name, 3 prizes the book has won, 4 friend's recommendation, 5 information on the back of the book* on the board, and ask students which would influence their decision most in choosing a book and why. Find out which authors are most popular with the class.

1 SPEAKING

- After students do the task, elicit possible reasons for a writer using a pen name or pseudonym and collate these on the board.

Answer
1 A false/different name that an author or writer uses instead of their real name.

2 🔊 70

Answers
To remain anonymous.
So it isn't clear if they are a man or a woman.
To write a different type of book than they normally write.

3 🔊 70

- **Exam tip** To answer the question in the Exam tip box, students should always read the incomplete notes before they listen. This helps them to know what to listen for. Tell them to look carefully at the words that come just before or after each space because these can help them predict the type of word that is missing (noun, verb, adjective, adverb, etc.).
- Remind students that it is not usually necessary to understand every word that they hear. They should listen out for the sections which correspond to the information in the notes and pay special attention to these sections.
- Students usually only need to write one or two words in each space. They should be careful with spelling and their handwriting.
- Remind students not to worry if they don't understand everything the first time they listen. In most exams, students listen twice. They should use the second listening to find the answers they didn't hear the first time and to check the answers they already have.

Answers
a Italian b Friend c an author d on TV e grandmother's name f pen name/pseudonym g crime h 500 i the book j understand

➕ Extra activity

Write *famous cases, bestsellers, theories, two letters, previous ideas* and *fascinating area* on the board. Tell students to listen again and make notes about why these words appear in the podcast.

Answers
famous cases: the subject of the podcast, Elena Ferrante and J.K. Rowling; **bestsellers:** examples by Ferrante: *My Brilliant Friend* and *The Story of the Lost Child*; **theories:** different theories about who Ferrante is; **two letters:** the publishers wanted Rowling to use two letters for her name; **previous ideas:** Ferrante (and maybe Rowling) didn't want people to read their books with pre-conceived ideas; **fascinating area:** the topic of how relevant an author's private life is to a book.

4 🧠 Critical thinkers

- Before students do the task, remind them that the objective is to justify their opinion and give suitable examples.

🏠 **Homework** ▶ Workbook page 79

Grammar in context 2 p116
Using reported speech in questions

Warmer

Ask students to write three true and two false personal statements to tell their partner, e.g. *I went to Italy last year. I have four brothers. My dog's name is Patch. I speak four languages. I can ski.*

Then ask students to read their statements to their partner. Students say the sentences back to their partner using reported speech, and tell him/her which statements they think are false, e.g. *You said that you'd been to Italy last year, but I think that's false. You told me you'd been to Greece.*

1a Point out that the sentences are based on sentences from the listening in the previous section.

Answers
1 RQ 2 RQ 3 DQ 4 DQ 5 RQ 6 DQ 7 DQ 8 RQ

1b Answers
1 change 2 don't use 3 don't use 4 don't put 5 use

Language notes

Yes/No questions in reported speech always begin with the word *if* or *whether*, e.g. *I asked her if/whether she wanted to go to the cinema.*

Wh- questions in reported speech always begin with the question word and change from question word order to statement word order, e.g. *She asked me what time dinner would be ready.* Reported questions are not real interrogative questions, and, therefore, they do not need questions marks.

2 Before students do the task, make sure they understand that *if* and *whether* mean the same. The choice in this exercise is therefore either a question word or *if/whether*, students do <u>not</u> have to choose between *if* and *whether*.

Answers
1 who 2 what 3 how 4 if/whether 5 why 6 if/whether 7 if/whether

101

9 FACTS ABOUT FICTION

3 With less confident classes, ask a more confident student to read out the dialogue with you and check the meaning of any problem words, e.g. *masterpiece* (an excellent painting, book, etc.).

- Point out that when we use the reporting verb *replied*, we include the *that*. We can however omit the *that* after *said*.

> **Answers**
> Ruth asked why the Brontë sisters were so famous.
> The teacher said (that)/replied that it was amazing to find three sisters who had all been able to write masterpieces.
> Ruth asked what they had written.
> The teacher said (that)/replied that Emily had written *Wuthering Heights*, Charlotte had written *Jane Eyre* and Anne had written *Agnes Grey*.
> Ruth asked if/whether they had used pen names.
> The teacher said (that)/replied that at first they had called themselves Acton, Currer and Ellis Bell.
> Ruth asked if/whether they had been old when they had died.
> The teacher said (that)/replied that no, they hadn't. They had been 29, 30 and 39.
> Ruth asked if/whether it was possible to visit the place where they had lived.
> The teacher said (that)/replied that (yes,) it was. Their home was now a beautiful museum in Haworth in Yorkshire. They had lived there in the middle of the 19th century.

Mixed ability

To simplify the activity, tell less confident students to work only on Ruth's questions and not report the rest of the dialogue. After students do the task, put less confident students into pairs or groups with more confident students. The less confident students report what Ruth asked, and the more confident students report the teacher's replies.

Culture notes

Emily Brontë (1818–1848), Charlotte Brontë (1816–1855) and Anne Brontë (1820–1849) were all born in Yorkshire, UK, and are often referred to as the Brontë sisters. Their three most famous novels *Wuthering Heights*, *Jane Eyre* and *Agnes Grey* were all published in 1847. Charlotte also wrote *Shirley* and *Villette*, and Anne also wrote *The Tenant of Wildfell Hall*, but Emily died the year after her masterpiece was published. *Wuthering Heights* has inspired more adaptations than any other work by the sisters.

4 Before students do the task, show them how each reported speech item can be broken down into questions and answers, e.g. *1 The actor asked ... moment.* (= question); *He said ... soon.* (= answer). The breaks in items 1–3 are at the full stops between the sentences, in 4 the break is at the comma and in 5 it is at the *and*.

> **Answers**
> 2 Did you enjoy my book?
>   I think it's the most beautiful thing I've ever read.
> 3 Why won't you answer any of my questions?
>   I only want to talk about my songs and I'm not going to talk about anything else.
> 4 Can you write an essay for tomorrow?
>   We can't because we have to study for an exam and we won't have enough time.
> 5 How many English novels have you read?
>   I've read lots.

5a SPEAKING

- Ask students who they can see in the photo (Iron Man from the Marvel series). Elicit ideas for who the class could interview. Evaluate each suggestion, and check that all students know about the character – if they do, make a note of the character on the board. When you have a selection of names, take a show of hands to choose the most popular character to interview.

5b SPEAKING

- Before students do the task, remind them that they can ask both open questions and *yes/no* questions. Remind them that they have only five questions, so should choose what they want to ask carefully. Tell them that, in an interview, open questions are more likely to get longer, more interesting answers.

Use it ... don't lose it!

6a SPEAKING

- As a class, students take turns to interview the student they have chosen to be the character. Make sure that students ask questions one at a time and pause to note down the character's answers. Consider choosing a more confident student to be the character or changing student two or three times during the interview.

6b SPEAKING

- Students return to their pair from exercise 5b and use their notes from exercise 6a to report back the interview orally.
- Before students do the task, remind them that they need to think about various areas: moving tenses one back in/into the past, using *say* and *tell* correctly, changing other words, ordering the words in reported questions correctly and using *if/whether* where necessary.
- After students do the task, ask them to share with the class anything they learnt from the interview that they found surprising or amusing. Encourage students to self-correct any mistakes with reported speech and reported questions.

FACTS ABOUT FICTION 9

Developing speaking p118
Giving a presentation

Warmer

Books closed. Write some or all of the following book titles on the board:
The Adventures of Huckleberry Finn (Mark Twain), *The Alchemist* (Paulo Coelho), *Alice's Adventures in Wonderland* (Lewis Carroll), *The Da Vinci Code* (Dan Brown), *Don Quixote* (Miguel de Cervantes), *Harry Potter and the Philosopher's Stone* (J.K. Rowling), *The Little Prince* (Antoine de Saint-Exupéry), *One Hundred Years of Solitude* (Gabriel García Márquez), *A Tale of Two Cities* (Charles Dickens), *War and Peace* (Leo Tolstoy)
Ask the class if they have read any of the books, and extend the discussion where possible, e.g. *When did you read it?*, *Did it take you a long time?*, *Was it as good as you expected?*, etc. Then ask students what all the books have in common. Elicit that they all regularly appear on the lists of most loved books and as the books which have sold most copies.

2 🔊 71
- Before students do the task, tell them not to worry if they hear things that they are not sure how to spell. For this activity it is good enough to write down an approximate spelling.
- After checking answers, tell them that *Lemony Snicket* is, in fact, not the author's real name. Ask them: *How do we say the name a writer uses when they don't want to use their real name?* and revise *pen name* and *pseudonym*.

Answers
Title: *A Series of Unfortunate Events*
Author: Lemony Snicket
Type of book: young adult fiction
Liked because: The plot is complex and the story is clever. Lots of unusual twists and the story/ending is gripping. The style is brilliant. It's really funny, although it is tragic at times. Interested in the characters although some are annoying. You want to find out what will happen so you read on. Short chapters make it easy and fast to read. It's well written.

🌐 Culture notes

A Series of Unfortunate Events is a series of 13 children's novels published between 1999 and 2006. They are credited to 'Lemony Snicket', but this is in fact a pen name of Daniel Handler (1970–) a US writer and musician. A 2004 film adapted the first three books and a 2017–2019 Netflix series adapted all 13 books.

3 🔊 71
- With less confident classes, tell students to put up their hands every time they hear one of the useful expressions. Pause and repeat the recording as necessary until students have completed all the expressions.

Answers
of all, more, true, but not least, up

4 When checking answers, make sure students understand that the sentences are advice about giving a presentation, they are not expressions used in a presentation.

Answers
1 e 2 d 3 c 4 f 5 b 6 a

5 Tell students that they should use the book they chose in exercise 1, unless they now feel that they would find it easier to give their presentation about a different book.

Fast finishers »

Remind students that the key to a good presentation is looking at your audience and not looking at your notes. Tell students to continue working on their notes, finding ways to make them shorter, organising them as bullet points and memorising the key points they want to make.

Practice makes perfect

6a SPEAKING 👥
- With less confident classes, allow students to practise their presentation with a partner before giving it in front of the class or a larger group.
- If more than one student has chosen to talk about the same book, consider doing this step in groups and making sure that within each group there is as wide a variety of titles as possible.

6b SPEAKING 👥
- If you wish, and students have the technical resources, ask them to record their presentation for homework including the suggestions the audience made for improvements. Students can then share the recording with you for further feedback.

9 FACTS ABOUT FICTION

Developing writing p119
Writing a story

> **Warmer**
> Ask students to think of their favourite stories. In pairs ask them to make a list of what they think makes a good story. Elicit answers from different pairs, e.g. *a good ending, a strong character, a funny moment*, etc.

1 With less confident classes, project or write the first sentence on the board and complete the exercise together. Elicit ideas for the story, and collate these on the board so that students can compare these with the pictures in exercise 2.

3a After students do the task, discuss as a class the most logical order for the pictures in exercise 2.

> **Possible answers**
> 1 b 2 c 3 d 4 e 5 f 6 a

➕ Extra activity
Write or project the following actions on the board:
start cleaning the university, get a phone call, get up, study literature at university, be confused, play with her daughter, realise it is true, go home, finish cleaning the university, go to work, write and publish a novel
Put students into pairs to read the story in exercise 3a again, and put the actions into the order they happened. Remind students that in a story, the order actions happened in is not always the order they appear in the text.

> **Answers**
> study literature at university, write and publish a novel, get up, go to work, start cleaning the university, finish cleaning the university, go home, play with her daughter, get a phone call, be confused, realise it is true

3b Students answer the question in pairs or as a class. Ask them to say why they think the story is fact or fiction, e.g. *I think it's fiction. I don't think it's believable that a cleaner would write a bestseller.*

🌐 Culture notes
Caitriona Lally (/kəˈtriːnə ˈlæli/) (1979–) was born in Dublin, Ireland. She won the 2018 Rooney Prize, an annual award for Irish writers, with her first novel *Eggshells*. At the time she was working as a cleaner at Trinity College Dublin, where she also studied for her degree.

4
> **Possible answers**
> **Use a variety of past tenses:** Literature was Caitriona's passion.; … she had written and published a novel …; She was playing with her when the phone rang.; … somebody told her that she had won a special award …
> **Use words and expressions of time and sequence:** That morning; Then; A few years ago,; Later that day,; At first,; Finally,
> **Use adjectives and adverbs to make your writing more descriptive:** she immediately went home; Suddenly, somebody told her; the most amazing thing

Practice makes perfect

5a Before students do the task, make sure they understand that their story – unlike Caitriona's – doesn't have to be true. Remind them that they saw some advice for writing a story in Developing vocabulary exercise 4 on page 113.
- With less confident classes, have students think of ideas in pairs or small groups. They can then compare their versions of the story in the next lesson and see what similarities and differences there are.

 Homework Workbook page 82

FACTS ABOUT FICTION 9

Test yourself p121

Grammar test

1 Answers
1 My sister said (that) she was going to a concert the following week.
2 Daniel told the teacher (that) he was sorry but he would be late the next/following day.
3 Holly said (that) that was her dictionary.
4 Sylvia said (that) she had always wanted to write stories.
5 They told us (that) there was going to be a concert in that room then.
6 They said (that) the play would start at seven o'clock the next/following day.
7 The students told the writer (that) they hadn't read any of his/her books.
8 Tom said (that) he had written the article the day before.

2 Answers
1 She asked me if/whether I was from Mexico.
2 Jo asked Karim what time he was going to leave.
3 I asked Katie why she had been crying.
4 The teacher asked the students if/whether they had ever read that book.
5 Sandra's dad asked her if/whether she would help him the next day.
6 Abigail asked her dad if/whether the doctor had seen Mike the day before.
7 Our teacher asked us if/whether we knew the answer to that question.
8 I asked Steve how many pages that book had.

Vocabulary test

1 Answers
1 manual 2 biography 3 thriller 4 play 5 romance
6 fairy tale 7 historical 8 comic/graphic novel 9 Young adult
10 Poetry

2 Answers
1 plot 2 bestseller 3 is set in 4 main character 5 style
6 masterpiece 7 twist

3 Answers
1 g 2 c 3 f 4 e 5 b 6 d 7 a

10 COMPUTER UPDATE

Vocabulary in context p122
Using a range of lexis to talk about computers, accessories and the Internet

Warmer

Books closed. Play a quick game of *Shark!* with words connected to the theme of the unit. Divide the class into two teams. Choose a word, e.g. *computer*, and draw a short line on the board for each letter of the word. The first team says a letter. If it is in the word, write the letter in all the places it appears in the word and continue playing with the same team.

If the word does not contain the letter, draw a stick figure (wrong guess 1). The turn then passes to the other team. Repeat the process. If the team guesses correctly, write in the letter; if not, draw a wooden platform under the stick figure (wrong guess 2). Repeat, drawing a series of waves (wrong guesses 3–6); follow this with a shark fin (wrong guess 7); and, finally, by 'throwing' the man into the water (wrong guess 8) if students don't guess correctly. If/When a team guesses the word, it wins a point.

You can make the game easier or more difficult by varying the number of waves. However, the penultimate turn is always signalled by the shark fin appearing and you calling out a warning 'Shark!'.

When you have finished, ask students to look at all the words you played with, and guess what topic or topics they expect to cover in the unit.

Language notes

There are many two syllable words in English whose meaning and word class change depending on the stressed syllable, e.g. re<u>cord</u> (v)/<u>rec</u>ord (n); ob<u>ject</u> (v)/<u>ob</u>ject (n); pre<u>sent</u> (v)/<u>pres</u>ent (n).

If necessary, remind students that a word can only have one main stress and that we only stress vowels not consonants.

4 After checking answers, elicit whether *log in* (2) and *download* (4) are verbs or nouns (verbs). Then ask students where the stress is on each (*log <u>in</u>*, down<u>load</u>). Drill the pronunciation of questions 2 and 4, making sure that students stress the verbs correctly.

> **Answers**
> 1 desktop 2 log in 3 subscribe 4 download

Use it ... don't lose it!

5 SPEAKING

+ Extra activity

Ask students to think of more words connected to the unit theme, either in English or in their own language, and look them up in their dictionaries if necessary, e.g. *digital camera*, *hardware*, *screensaver*, *podcast*, *network*, etc. They should write a definition in English and/or an example sentence for each word. They can then 'teach' the rest of the class their words or read out their definitions or sentences (missing out the word) for the rest of the class to guess the words.

1 SPEAKING

- When checking answers, draw attention to the schwa sound (/ə/) at the end of *monitor*, *printer*, *scanner* and *speaker*.

2a Before students do the task, ask them what advice they would give to their parents or grandparents if they needed to set up a new computer. Discuss their ideas as a class, and then ask students to read the text for gist and see if it includes any of their ideas.

2b After checking answers, check the pronunciation of *install* (/ɪnˈstɔːl/), *browser* (/ˈbraʊzə(r)/), *antivirus software* (/ˌæntiˌvaɪrəs ˈsɒf(t)ˌweə(r)/), *delete* (/dɪˈliːt/), *subscribe* (/səbˈskraɪb/), *crash* (/kræʃ/) and *restart* (/ˌriːˈstɑː(r)t/). Explain that the other words are the focus of the next exercise.

3a When checking answers, explain that students need to learn which words are one word, which words are hyphenated and which words are two words on a case-by-case basis.

> **Answers**
> 1a V 1b N 2a N 2b V 3a N 3b V 4a N 4b V 5a V 5b N
> Sometimes the verb/noun is written as one word and sometimes it is two words. Sometimes we also use a hyphen.

3b PRONUNCIATION

> **Answers**
> 1a download 1b download 2a backups 2b back up 3a set-up
> 3b set up 4a updates 4b update 5a log in 5b login
> It is different; the stress falls on the second word when it is a verb.

106

COMPUTER UPDATE 10

Reading p123
Skimming and scanning for global and specific information

> **Warmer**
> Ask students to think of all the ways they have used the Internet in the last week, and collate their suggestions on the board. Ask them how they would do these things if the Internet didn't exist or if they would have to do something completely different instead. Discuss how reliant the modern world is on the Internet. Ask whether they have ever experienced an Internet 'blackout', either because they lost their connection at home or because of a wider issue.

1 SPEAKING
- After students do the task, discuss the questions as a class. Elicit ideas for the two situations, but don't confirm if they are correct or not.

2 Follow up by asking: *How do you think people in your country would react to switching off the Internet for these reasons? Why? How would you react?*

> **Answers**
> In Algeria and Mauritania, they switched off the Internet to prevent cheating in school exams.
> In Bali in Indonesia, they switched off the Internet to celebrate Nyepi, a festival of meditation and silence.

3 🔊 74
- Remind students that in this type of exam task, the incorrect options often include words and ideas which are taken from and related to the text, but are not actually the correct answer. Tell students to read all the answers carefully and note how the options are different.
- Pre-teach any words students may have problems with, not including the underlined words, e.g. *examination hall* (*a very large room in a school or university used when students take exams*) and *criticism* (*things people say to show they think something is bad or wrong*).

> **Answers**
> 1 a incorrect – five days, but *up to three hours a day*, so not five <u>complete</u> days
>   b **correct** – The blackout was *for up to three hours a day for five days*.
>   c incorrect – *up to* three hours a day, not <u>exactly</u> three hours a day
> 2 a incorrect – There was no Internet blackout in 2017.
>   b incorrect – not <u>all</u> the students, only those students that *arrived at their exams late*
>   c **correct** – *… the next year they decided to switch off the Internet for the first hour of each exam.*
> 3 a **correct** – People complained that there are easier alternatives to stop Internet cheating.
>   b incorrect – no mention of the country coming to a stop, only certain businesses
>   c incorrect – no mention of this
> 4 a incorrect – *… wi-fi was available to them* (= tourists) *in hotels.*
>   b **correct** – *… wi-fi was available to them* (= tourists) *in hotels.*
>   c incorrect – The paragraph stresses that everything is closed, including shops.
> 5 a incorrect – The paragraph gives various serious situations in which the Internet can be switched off in the UK.
>   b **correct** – *It* (the situation) *would need to be very serious though …*
>   c incorrect – The paragraph mentions the cost of Internet blackouts, but does not state that the cost means it can never happen.

4
> **Answers**
> *queries* – requests for information
> *blackout* – a period when power is stopped
> *travel agents* – businesses/people that organise people's travel arrangements
> *jammers* – devices that block signals to mobile phones
> *available* – able to be used
> *unplugged* – disconnected from a power supply

Fast finishers »
Ask students to find other new words in the text and use their dictionaries to write the real definition of the word and then create two false ones. Ask them to read their words and definitions out to the class for them to guess the real definition.

5 🧠 **Critical thinkers**
- Before students do the task, remind them that the objective is to justify their opinion and give suitable examples.
- When students share their ideas, encourage turn-taking, and make sure they listen to each other and agree or disagree using suitable phrases.

> **Possible answer**
> In my opinion, switching off the Internet in these situations is completely wrong and unfair. I agree that in some cases, like the ones mentioned at the end – public safety or health or national security – it could be necessary. But I'd say that it is not right to do it to stop students cheating in exams or because a government wants to force 'meditation and silence'! In the case of exams, I think there are other ways to deal with the problem anyway. For example, make sure the exam paper doesn't get online or don't let students into exams late. And in the case of national holidays, I don't think a government should ever force everyone to celebrate, even if it is important.

▶ **Flipped classroom**
You may want to ask students to watch the Flipped classroom video for Unit 10 as homework, in preparation for the grammar lesson.

Homework › Workbook page 85

10 COMPUTER UPDATE

Grammar in context 1 p124
Using the passive – present simple

> **Warmer**
> Books closed. Write the following groups of verbs on the board:
> 1 *bring, find, say*
> 2 *begin, drink, know*
> 3 *cost, cut, put*
> Put students into pairs and tell them to think about what the verbs in each group have in common. Tell them to put their hands up when they have worked it out, not call out the solution. If students need help, give them a clue and tell them to think about the past forms.
> Tell students you are going to give them some more verbs and they need to add them to groups 1–3: *buy, eat, grow, hit, make, send, spend, take, write*. Students can check their answers using the irregular verbs list on page 159.

> **Answers**
> 1 Verb changes in the past – past simple and past participle are the same (also *buy, make, send, spend*).
> 2 Verb changes in the past – past simple and past participle are different (also *eat, grow, take, write*).
> 3 Verb doesn't change in the past (also *hit*).

1a If you didn't set the Flipped classroom video for homework, watch the video in class before working through the activities.

- Point out that the sentences are based on sentences from the reading text on page 123.

> **Answers**
> 1 passive 2 active 3 active 4 passive 5 passive 6 active

1b
> **Answers**
> 1 True 2 True 3 True

1c
> **Answers**
> 1 the present simple of *be* + the past participle 2 *by*

> **Language notes**
> Four main steps are needed to form a passive sentence from an active sentence, e.g. *The boys always eat the pizza.* – *The pizza is always eaten by the boys.*
> 1 Move the receiver of the action from the direct object position of the sentence to the subject position. (*The pizza* …)
> 2 Insert the correct form of the verb *be* for the new subject. (*The pizza is always* …)
> 3 Change the main verb to its past participle form. (*The pizza is always eaten* …)
> 4 (Optional) Place the agent (= the 'doer') of the verb in the object position after the preposition *by*. (*The pizza is always eaten (by the boys)*.)

2a Before students do the task, make sure they understand that they only need to complete the gaps which are followed by a verb in brackets (i.e. the second gap in all the items, apart from item 2, where it is the first). They will complete the other gaps in exercise 2b.

> **Answers**
> 1 are downloaded 2 is hit 3 are eaten 4 are sent
> 5 are drunk 6 are killed 7 are watched 8 are bought
> 9 are taken

2c 🔊 75
- After checking answers, ask students if they guessed any of the numbers correctly. Follow up by asking: *Do any of the numbers surprise you? Which ones? Why?*

> **Answers**
> 1 375,000 apps are downloaded. 2 The earth is hit by lightning about 6,000 times. 3 About 21,000 slices of pizza are eaten in the US. 4 25,000 GIFs are sent via Messenger®. 5 14,896 cups of tea are drunk in London. 6 More than 190 sharks are killed by humans. 7 4.3 million videos are watched on YouTube™.
> 8 1 million plastic bottles are bought. 9 3,472 journeys are taken on the London Tube.

3 Before students do the task, make clear that the exercise mixes active and passive verbs. Not all the sentences need to be in the passive.

> **Answers**
> 1 Many computers <u>are</u> made in China.
> 2 Usually, smartphones are not allow<u>ed</u> in exams.
> 3 The word 'flash drive' <u>is</u> ~~are~~ used more than 'pen drive'.
> 4 Correct
> 5 Millions of dollars <u>are spent</u> ~~spend~~ on video games every year.
> 6 Correct
> 7 Thousands of packages are <u>sent</u> ~~send~~ in the post every day.
> 8 Text messages are often <u>written</u> ~~wrote~~ very fast.

4 Before students do the task, point out that they should only include *by* + agent when the passive sentence would not be clear without it.

> **Answers**
> 1 A lot of silicon chips are made in India.
> 2 Many people are employed in the computer industry.
> 3 Amazing new technology is invented every day.
> 4 Sony®, Nintendo® and Microsoft create most games consoles.
> 5 Computer games are played by millions of kids every day.
> 6 The use of the Internet is controlled by some governments.
> 7 A password isn't needed to enter this site.

➕ Extra activity

Students draw five or six pictures showing a process they are familiar with or have learnt about at school, e.g. making popcorn, making a cake, coal mining, steel production, etc. They write sentences in the present simple passive to describe what happens at each stage of the process.

COMPUTER UPDATE 10

Use it ... don't lose it!

5 SPEAKING

- Before students do the task, draw attention to the model dialogue, and point out that it is fine to speculate here if students don't have or can't find specific facts. The objective is to practise the passive, even if the information is not correct.
- If students have Internet access in class, encourage them to look up information about the US.

Developing vocabulary p125

Using collocations with *email* and *document*

> **Warmer**
>
> Books closed. Divide the class into two groups. In one group, students work in pairs to think of all the things you can do with an email, e.g. *send*; in the other group, students work in pairs to think of all the things you do with a document, e.g. *open*.
>
> Divide the board into three columns with these headings, from left to right: *email*, *both*, *document*.
>
> Elicit ideas from each group but before writing each on the board, confirm whether it can also be used with the other word. If it can, e.g. *write*, put it in the 'both' column.

1 🔊 76

- Before students do the task, point out that they need to change the form of some items. With less confident classes, clarify that this means they need to use different verb forms.

> **Answers**
> a send b bounced c address d account e junk
> f forward g inbox h checked i replied to j attachment

🔴 Mixed ability

To make the activity more challenging, tell the more confident students to cover the box and complete the text using suitable words.

Students repeat the process when completing the explanations in exercise 2.

2 🔊 77

> **Answers**
> 1 create 2 copy and paste 3 open 4 save 5 attach 6 cut

Use it ... don't lose it!

3 SPEAKING

- Follow up by asking questions using the collocations from exercise 1 and exercise 2, e.g. *Have you ever sent or forwarded an email to the wrong person? What happened? How did you feel? Have you ever found something important in your junk email? When did you find it? Was it too late? How fast are you at cutting, copying and pasting? Do you use the mouse for this or do you know how to do it with the keyboard?*

> **Answers**
> a reply to b forward c inbox d cut e copy and paste
> f open g save h attachment/attach

Homework ▸ Workbook page 87

109

10 COMPUTER UPDATE

GREAT LEARNERS GREAT THINKERS p126

Thinking about human–computer interaction and facial recognition by computers

Warmer

Write *feelings and emotions* in a circle in the centre of the board. Brainstorm with students words for feelings and emotions. If they suggest adjectives, elicit the noun form for each one and write these around the circle on the board. Elicit definitions (*This is what you feel when …*) and spelling, and model pronunciation as necessary. If possible, pre-teach/check the meaning of *arrogance*, *disgust* and *shock*.

If your class is less confident, give them definitions to revise the following words from the course: *anger*, *boredom*, *confidence*, *disappointment*, *embarrassment*, *enjoyment*, *excitement*, *loneliness*, *pain*, *pride*, *relief*, *surprise* and *weakness*.

1 SPEAKING

- Follow-up by discussing different virtual assistants which students are familiar with, e.g. Alexa®, Cortana®, Google Assistant®, Siri®. Ask students how well they think these understand human feelings and how well they express their own 'feelings'.

2 VIDEO

- When checking answers, point out that the technology is trying to read/display facial features and body language, so it's focusing on the physical aspect. It's not taking into account spoken language. Follow-up by asking students if they think facial features and body language are universal. If not, ask in what ways they think the 'language' varies from country to country.

Answers
1 Yes, by analysing our body movements
2 Yes, by showing feeling with a robot human head

3 VIDEO

- After checking answers, ask students: *Would you feel comfortable with a computer analysing your face and body like this? Why/Why not? How would you feel talking to Charles the robot?*

Answers
1 University 2 body 3 smile 4 412 5 happiness, colour
6 frustration 7 difficult

GREAT THINKERS

4 SPEAKING

- The *Chalk talk* thinking routine allows students to think about a topic in silence and respond in writing. The extended silence gives students time to think things through fully before engaging in a discussion.
- In step 1, students work individually and in silence.
- In step 2, depending on your class size, students either work as a class collating all their ideas on the board or in two or three large groups, each with a large sheet of paper. They should continue in silence, looking carefully at what the other students are writing and trying not to repeat ideas. Encourage students to respond to each other's comments in writing if they see something which they have an opinion on.
- In step 3, students reflect individually and in silence on what their classmates have written.
- In step 4, students can now speak. If you feel your students need more support, write these prompts on the board:

    I saw that someone wrote …
    I wanted to reply to something I read …
    I read one view that I really disagreed with …
    At first I thought … but then I read a comment and I …

5 Although this is not further practice of the Great thinkers routine, remind students how valuable it is to take some 'silent time' to formulate their ideas and opinions. Encourage them to make notes of their reactions to share in the next step.

6 SPEAKING

- Discuss as a class what the most common ideas and opinions are in the class. Try to focus students on the common conclusions they are reaching about FRT.

GREAT LEARNERS SEL

- Highlight how important it is, not just to give reasons for your opinions, but for these to be logical and well structured. To convince someone of your viewpoint, it is essential to explain your reasoning in a clear, systematic way.

LEARNER PROFILE

- Ask students to read the statement and the question in the Learner profile on page 143, then grade themselves from 1 to 5. Explain that here 1 means 'I don't often justify my opinions' and 5 means 'I frequently justify my opinions'.
- If appropriate for your class, get students to share their grades with a partner or small group and, if they wish, to give their reasons. Encourage students to share suggestions for justifying their opinions more. Alternatively, ask students individually to think of ways to justify their opinions more.

COMPUTER UPDATE 10

Listening p128

Listening for gist and specific information

Warmer

Books closed. In pairs, students make a list of activities they use a tablet or computer for, e.g. *writing essays, sending emails, watching movies, downloading music, chatting online, reading the news, playing games*, etc. Ask students to look at the photos and say which of the activities they think they could do with the inventions. Discuss briefly how they think previous generations lived without technology and the Internet.

2 🔊 78

- Pre-teach any words students may have problems with, e.g. *handwriting* (*the particular way that someone writes with a pen or pencil*).

Answers

The Apple Newton was a device on which you could write with a type of pen. It would make this into a document that you could print or email. It was invented in 1993.
The TeleGuide had a telephone, a basic computer screen and a keyboard. You could use it to make calls, find information and do shopping. It was sold for the first time in 1991.
The worst video game in the world and coloured ketchup are also mentioned.

3 🔊 78

- When checking answers, if possible, use a map to check that students are clear about where *Switzerland* and *Sweden* are.

Answers

1 The Museum of Failure is in Sweden ~~Switzerland~~.
2 It was opened by a 44- ~~42~~-year-old psychologist called Dr Samuel West.
3 The Apple Newton was not very ~~especially~~ good at recognising handwriting.
4 It was not one of the very first smartphones. It was one of the first handheld devices.
5 The TeleGuide didn't need the Internet to function.
6 It was too cheap ~~expensive~~.
7 It disappeared because the company lost money ~~people were not interested in the product~~.
8 The video game was a failure because it was the worst in the world/boring ~~very difficult to play~~.
9 People became tired of ~~didn't like the taste of~~ green ketchup.

➕ Extra activity

Check comprehension further by playing the recording again and asking the following questions:
How did Holly feel when she left the museum? (positive and inspired)
When was the Apple Newton available? (from 1993 to 1998)
Why was the Apple Newton important? (because it helped create the handheld devices we know today)
How long was the TeleGuide available for? (six months)
Which famous film character was the star of the video game? What did he have to do? (ET. He had to get out of holes he had fallen into.)
How many products are there in the museum? (over 60)

4 🧠 **Critical thinkers**

- Before students do the task, remind them that the objective is to justify their opinion and give suitable examples.

🏠 Homework ▸ Workbook page 87

Grammar in context 2 p128

Using the passive – other tenses; using *have something done*

Warmer

Write the following gapped sentences on the board:
1 The Internet _____ invented in 1989.
2 In 1990, the Internet _____ being used by scientists at CERN.
3 Millions of apps have _____ downloaded this year.
4 Facial recognition technology _____ being used right now.
Ask students to fill each gap with a suitable word. If students are confident with these basic forms, you could quickly move through exercises 1a–b, eliciting answers from students in open class.

Answers
1 was 2 was 3 been 4 is

1a Point out that the sentences are based on sentences from the listening in the previous section.

- After checking answers, make sure students remember the key points from Grammar in context 1 by asking: *What are the three reasons we use the passive?* (when we're more interested in the action than the person; when we don't know who does the action; when it's obvious who does the action); *What preposition do we use to say who or what did an action in the passive?* (*by*).

Answers
1 past simple passive 2 present continuous passive
3 present perfect passive 4 past continuous passive

1b **Answer**
the verb *to be*

Culture exchange

2

Answers
1 Some interesting scientific objects were collected in 1857.
2 Some new buildings were opened in 1909.
3 Over 7.3 million objects have been collected by the Science Museum.
4 About 300,000 objects are being moved to a new building in Wiltshire.
5 This machine was invented in the 1820s by Sir Charles Babbage.
6 The Science Museum is always being updated.
7 New objects are being added all the time.
8 In recent times, the Science Museum has been visited by over 3 million people each year.
9 'Astronights' are sometimes organised for children.

10 COMPUTER UPDATE

3 In this type of activity, students should first read the complete text without thinking about the gaps to get a general understanding of the text.

- **✓ Exam tip** To answer the question in the Exam tip box, students should then look again at the gaps and at the words which come just before and after the gap. They should ask themselves: *Do those words need a special preposition? Is an article or auxiliary verb missing?*; and then think about the type of word they need (noun, verb, pronoun, article, etc.) and the general meaning.
- Students should then fill in the gap with the word that they think is best. They should also read the sentence again with their answer in the gap to check it. They should check that the meaning is logical but also check that the word fits in grammatically. Tell students that sometimes there may be more than one possible answer but they only need to put one.
- When students finish, they should check that they have an answer for each question. They should never leave answers blank in an exam.
- Follow up by pointing out that Richard Appiah Akoto (/ˈrɪtʃəd ˈæpɪə ˈækʊtəʊ/) is a real person and asking: *How well do you think you could learn to use a computer if you didn't actually have one in front of you? Why would it be easy or difficult to learn in that situation?*

> **Answers**
> **a** where/whose **b** being **c** been **d** but **e** have **f** by **g** had **h** were **i** to **j** on

4 SPEAKING

- With more confident classes, ask students how questions 1 and 4 are different from questions 2, 3 and 5. Elicit that questions 1 and 4 are subject questions. Remind students that we can answer these questions without changing the word order of the original question, e.g. <u>Four</u> Avengers films have been made.; <u>Santander Bank</u> sponsors our national football team. Point out that these types of questions are common in trivia, and tell students to include some examples when they write their questions in exercise 5.

> **Answers**
> **1** Four **2** Rio de Janeiro, Brazil (2016) **3** Tom Holland **5** 16th and 17th centuries (approximately 1592–1614)
> *Correct at time of publication*

Use it ... don't lose it!

6 SPEAKING

- After students do the task, elicit some of the questions that students couldn't answer and see if the rest of the class know the answers.

7
> **Answers**
> **a** somebody or something does an action for us **b** past participle **c** are **d** by **e** can

8 With less confident classes, before students do the task, elicit who is the customer and who is the professional in each picture, e.g. *1 left: customer, right: professional; 2 left: professional, right: customer*. Remind students that the subject of a sentence with *have something done* always refers to the customer.

> **Answers**
> **2** She had/got her hair cut.
> **3** He had/got his eyes tested.
> **4** She had/got a dress made.

Fast finishers »

Ask students to think of their own examples, write a sentence for it with *have something done* and draw a picture to illustrate it. Ask any students with particularly good pictures to show these to the class and elicit the sentence that goes with it.

9a
- Before students do the task, point out that the mistakes can be either with word order or with the words used.

> **Answers**
> **1** Have you ever had <u>your computer fixed</u> ~~fixed your computer~~?
> **2** When was the last time you had <u>your eyes tested</u> ~~tested your eyes~~?
> **3** Do you ever <u>have</u> ~~had~~ your homework checked by your parents?/ Have ~~Do~~ you ever had your homework checked by your parents?

Homework Workbook page 88

COMPUTER UPDATE 10

Developing speaking p130
Comparing and contrasting photos

> **Warmer**
>
> Brainstorm language students can use to describe a photo. Elicit:
> - General phrases, e.g. *This is a photo of ..., In this photo, I can see ..., The photo shows ..., There is/are ...*
> - Prepositional phrases, e.g. *at the top/bottom (of the photo), on the left/right (of the photo), in the background/foreground, in the middle of the photo, Behind/In front of/Between/Next to the ... we can see ...*
> - Phrases for personal reactions, e.g. *I think ..., I imagine ..., It seems to me that ..., If you ask me ...*
> - Fillers, e.g. *Well, Umm, Let me see,* etc.
>
> Remind students of the work they did in Unit 4 on describing photos. Also elicit the key questions students should try to answer: *Who can you see? What are they doing? What do they look like? Where are they? When was the photo taken? How are the people feeling and why?*
> Tell students they should always move from the general to the specific, starting with a general description of the situation before giving more precise details.

1 SPEAKING
- With less confident classes, make sure students understand that the focus is on finding similarities and differences between the photos, not simply on describing picture a and then picture b. Collate ideas from this preparation stage on the board.

2 79
- Ask students if they thought the student did the exam well and to explain why or why not.

3 79
- With less confident classes, make sure they have placed the two expressions correctly before they listen to the recording again to identify which expressions the student used.

> **Answers**
> **Comparing: 2** Both of the photos show ...
> **Contrasting: 1** In the first photo ... but/whereas in the second photo ...
> The student used the following expressions:
> Both of the photos show ...; in the first photo ..., whereas in the second photo ...; In [the first photo] ... However, in [the second photo] ...; one similarity between the photos is ...; Another important difference between the photos is ...

4 **Answers**
> 1 f 2 b 3 e 4 c 5 a 6 d

5 SPEAKING
- Before students do the task, check they have understood that – unlike the work they did in Unit 4 – the emphasis here is not simply on describing the two photos but on comparing and contrasting. This is a common exam-type activity.

Mixed ability
To simplify the activity, less confident students use the photos in exercise 1 instead of the new photos at the back of the book. Tell them to use their preparation time to review the expressions in the Speaking bank and the sentence halves in exercise 4. Remind them that they won't be allowed to look at these expressions when they do the task.
Alternatively, with less confident classes, give students time to practise with the photos in exercise 1 before moving on and repeating the task with the new photos at the back of the book.

Practice makes perfect
6a SPEAKING
- Remind students that if they cannot think of things to say, they can use the questions *What? Who? Where? Why? When?* etc. to give them ideas. They should also think of possible questions that the examiner will ask them about the photo.
- Tell students not to worry if they don't know a word. They should think of similar words, more basic or general words or explain the word.
- Remind students to use words and expressions like *Both of the photos show ..., One similarity is that ..., One thing they have in common is ...* to say things that are similar in the two photos; words and expressions like *but, whereas, however, One difference between the photos is that ...* to say things that are different in the two photos and fillers like *Well, Hmm* or *Let me think* to give themselves time to think of what they are going to say next.
- ✓ **Exam tip** To answer the question in the Exam tip box, remind students that if they are not 100% sure of what they can see, they should speculate using expressions like *It may/might be, I'm not sure but I think, It looks like, It seems that,* etc. Students should not be afraid of saying simple, obvious things. The important thing is for them to say something because the examiner basically wants to hear them speaking English.

Homework Workbook page 89

113

10 COMPUTER UPDATE

Developing writing p131
Messaging

> **Warmer**
> Books closed. Write the following features of mobile phones on the board: *taking photos, making calls, playing games, listening to music, watching videos, using social networks, using the Internet, paying for things*. Discuss as a class which features students think are most important, and elicit any other key features students can think of. Elicit and discuss how important *messaging* is to students and which apps or services they currently use to communicate.

1 After checking answers, ask students what other abbreviations they can remember from page 53. Elicit them to the board and ask students to explain what they mean. (*PS* = here is some additional information to my letter or note; *e.g.* = for example; *i.e.* = that is, this is exactly what I mean; *etc.* = and other things of the same type) Ask students what these four expressions have in common. (They are all from Latin.)

> **Answers**
> 1 In my opinion 2 as soon as possible 3 for your information
> 4 by the way

2a SPEAKING

> **Answers**
> 1 please 2 weekend 3 at 4 later 5 before 6 are
> 7 thanks 8 be right back

2b Follow up by asking: *Do you have lots of abbreviations in your language? When do you use them? When shouldn't you use them? Do you make them in similar ways, for example, by taking away vowels or by replacing parts of words with numbers or symbols?*

- Make sure students understand that we usually only use abbreviations in English in informal contexts. The only exceptions to this are *e.g., i.e.* and *etc.* which are acceptable even in formal contexts.

3 When checking answers, check the spelling of each word carefully.

> **Answers**
> 1 tonight 2 your 3 what 4 see you 5 great 6 homework
> 7 message 8 speak

4 Follow up by asking: *Do you have conversations with friends that look like this? Which of your friends uses the most abbreviations? Who uses the least? What about emoticons and emojis? Are you a fan?*

> **Answers**
> 1 By the way, I can help you with your homework later.
> 2 Thanks. See you at your house at seven o'clock?
> 3 OK! Joe is coming.
> 4 Bring your laptop.
> 5 OK. See you later.
> 6 Not if I see you first. Just kidding.

🌐 Culture notes

Emoticons, e.g. :-) for 'happy', :-(for 'sad', :-o for shocked, first became popular on Japanese phones in the 1990s. They rapidly gained popularity as they added a friendly, informal feel to what could have been seen as a cold form of text-based communication.

At the end of the 1990s, Japanese artist Shigetaka Kurita designed the first set of 176 simple coloured icons to replace the original punctuation-based emoticons. These have had a major impact on modern design and are now on display in MoMA, New York.

Over time, these icons evolved into much more detailed **emojis**, e.g. 😀 😐 😟. The popularity of these has spread to such an extent that in 2015 the Oxford Dictionaries 'Word of the year' was simply 😂. Today all major IT and phone companies are adding an ever-increasing number of icons to their emoji dictionaries, and many now also allow users to customise emojis with their own faces.

5
> **Answers**
> 2 Thx 4 helping me with my hmwk.
> 3 Can U come 2moro 2 fix my computer?
> 4 IMO, U shd B happy bcz yr exam results R xcellent.
> 5 BTW, don't 4get 2 send me a msg L8R 2nite.
> 6 I want 2 C U n Jo b4 I spk 2 the teacher 2moro.

➕ Extra activity

Write the following abbreviated message on the board, and ask students to write the complete message:
Hi Jo. wot R U doing? yr hmwk? R U bzy 2day? C U L8R? Meet @ the cinema 2nite? Let's have food b4 a film. If not, 2moro is OK 2 bcz it's a holiday! LOL 🙂 TTYL bestie!
When checking answers, check/teach: *bzy* = busy, *2day* = today, *LOL* = laughing out loud, *bestie* = best friend

> **Answer**
> Hi Jo. What are you doing? Your homework? Are you busy today? See you later? Meet at the cinema tonight? Let's have (some) food before a film. If not, tomorrow is OK too because it's a holiday! Laughing out loud! Talk to you later best friend!

Homework Workbook page 90

COMPUTER UPDATE 10

Test yourself p133

Grammar test

1 Answers
1 Computers are used everywhere.
2 A lot of chocolate is eaten in the UK.
3 Long coats aren't worn in summer.
4 Portuguese is spoken in Brazil.
5 Fish isn't sold here.
6 Cars are made by robots in this factory.
7 This programme is watched by thousands of people.
8 Chinese New Year is celebrated at the end of January or the start of February.

2 Answers
1 A biography of Steve Jobs was <u>written</u> ~~wrote~~ by Walter Isaacson in 2011.
2 The 2016 Nobel Prize® in Literature <u>was</u> ~~is~~ won by Bob Dylan.
3 London is visited <u>by</u> ~~for~~ thousands of people every day.
4 The radio <u>was</u> invented <u>by</u> Marconi.
5 Many smartphones <u>are</u> made in Vietnam nowadays.
6 Yesterday the eclipse was <u>seen</u> ~~saw~~ by many people around the world.
7 Oh no! His car has <u>been</u> stolen.
8 My phone was ~~been~~ stolen last week.

3 Answers
1 They had/got the house painted.
2 He has/gets it washed.
3 We had/got it built.
4 I had/got it corrected.
5 She has/gets it done.

Vocabulary test

1 Answers
1 c 2 b 3 a 4 f 5 e 6 d

2 Answers
1 download 2 software 3 update 4 delete 5 subscribe
6 crash 7 log in (*log on* is also possible)

3 Answers
1 forward 2 attachment 3 bounce 4 copy and paste
5 save 6 address

115

Exam success Units 9–10 p134

Reading

1

> **Answers**
> 1 A 2; *The second of these two books*, Mr. Stink *was ...*
>   B 3; *He has also ... swum ... the length of the River Thames.*
>   C 1; *His voice has also appeared in animated films such as Missing Link.*

2

> **Answers**
> 1 E <u>This</u> showed that he could <u>act in serious plays and films</u> (= Walliams appearing *in a range of different roles on TV*), not just comedies.
> 2 B <u>It</u> (= *The second of these two books*, Mr. Stink, ...) was so popular that he decided to produce another <u>one</u> (= children's book).
> 3 G <u>Today</u> (moves us to the present for the paragraph talking about his professional life now), he is considered to be one of the most successful children's <u>writers</u> (contrasts with the reference in the next sentence to *his busy acting schedule*).
> 4 C Due to their (= his books') popularity, they have been translated into <u>over 50 languages</u> (links with *so many young people around the world* in the next sentence).
> 5 A For example (= an example of an *extreme challenge*), he swam for ten hours across the English Channel (links with *He did <u>this</u> to ...* in the next sentence).

- If you wish, go to page 148 to continue working through the Exam success section for these two units.
- See the Exam trainer, Workbook page 97, for more information and practice on this Preliminary for Schools task.

Collaborative project 5 p135
A famous writer from your country

1 SPEAKING

- As a class, brainstorm all the famous writers from their country students can think of and collate these on the board.
- Students work in groups of 3–4. On this project, if you wish, allow students to organise themselves into the groups they most enjoyed working in, and found most productive, from Collaborative projects 1–4.
- Write: *male/female? century? region? language? genre?* on the board. In their groups, students select five writers from the ones on the board, including as much variety as possible. They then discuss the questions.

2 SPEAKING

- Students continue to work in their groups from exercise 1.
- Negotiate as a class which author each group will research, aiming for variety (*male/female*, *century*, *region*, *language* and *genre*). If you have a very large class, then two groups may work on the same author independently.
- If you feel your class has worked on a fair range of project types in Collaborative projects 1–4, then allow them to choose the one they enjoyed most and repeat that type for this project. Point out that, in return for this 'freedom of choice', there will be an extra step in the *Evaluation* section, where the class will vote on the winner in each category.

3 Ask individuals to read aloud the tips and discuss them with the class.

- After reading the *Digital skills* section, ask students for the common URL endings used in their country and what these mean. Point out that *.edu*, *.ac.uk* and *.gov* (and their equivalents in the students' country) can generally be considered reliable sources of information.
- After reading the *Academic skills* section, highlight the importance of crediting sources. If students take a specific quote word for word from a site, this should be in quotation marks and credited; and if they use another person's idea, even indirectly, they should also credit this.

4 SPEAKING

- Remember to establish a clear plan for the project (interim dates/deadline; stages to be done at home/ in class). Remind students that as much discussion as possible should be in English, both in and out of class.

5 After marking the projects, students vote for their 'class awards'. In their groups, they agree on the best project in the class for each category, i.e. *Content*, *Presentation*, *Design* and *Language*, and which one they would award the *Best project* title to. They write their votes on a piece of paper and hand these to you. Check groups don't vote for themselves.

- Collate the results and announce the winners in the five categories.

- Connect with teachers and students in other countries and encourage students to present their projects to each other.

Reach higher

UNIT 1 p136

Answers
Vocabulary in context (page 6)
Possible answers
D – daughter, E – extended family, F – father, G – grandchild, grandparent, H – husband, M – mother, N – niece, O – only child, P – parent, partner, R – relative, S – son, T – twin, U – uncle, W – wife

Reading (page 7)
2 The age of a boy who is legally forcing his mother to stop sharing images of him online.
3 The fine the boy is asking his mother to pay if she doesn't stop sharing images of him online.
4 How much parents in France may have to pay if they post photos of their children without their permission.
5 The age when children should start being consulted about having their photos posted, according to the University of Michigan.

Grammar in context 1 (page 8)
1 am/'m helping 2 are, shouting 3 works 4 don't understand
5 Do, need 6 is lying

Developing vocabulary (page 9)
1 confidence 2 adolescence 3 argument 4 solution
5 independence 6 explanation

UNIT 2 p136

Answers
Vocabulary in context (page 18)
1 robbery/theft 2 burglary 3 vandalism 4 murder 5 shoplifting
6 cybercrime 7 mugging 8 kidnapping 9 smuggling 10 arson

Reading (page 19)
Text A
1 In a pizza restaurant in Washington DC
2 On Wednesday night
3 A woman
4 Theft
5 The officer arrested her and charged her with the theft of his chips.

Text B
1 In an old building in Surrey
2 Last Friday
3 Two men
4 Burglary
5 The police charged them with suspected burglary.

Text C
1 In a museum in Nuremberg, Germany
2 Last week
3 A 91-year-old woman
4 She destroyed a work of art/vandalism
5 Nothing

Grammar in context 1 (page 20)
Possible answers
D – did, E – enjoyed, F – fell, G – grew, H – had, I – ignored, J – jailed, K – knew, L – left, M – met, N – named, O – observed, P – paid, Q – questioned, R – read, S – saw, T – took, U – understood, V – vanished, W – wrote, X – x-rayed, Z – zigzagged

Developing vocabulary (page 21)
2 The CIA began to look into the case.
3 They came across the ring in the garden.
4 I lost my jumper and it turned up two days later in the library!
5 It was a difficult maths problem, but Tom worked it out with a calculator.
6 Mia found out that she was the school football captain this morning.

Grammar in context 2 (page 24)
Possible answers
1 My parents were/weren't working.
2 The sun was/wasn't shining.
3 I was/wasn't studying.
4 I was/wasn't listening to music.
5 It was/wasn't raining.
6 My family and I were/weren't wearing pyjamas.

Reach higher

UNIT 3 p136

Answers
Reading (page 33)
1 False, Paragraph 2   2 True, Paragraph 2   3 True, Paragraph 3
4 False, Paragraph 2   5 True, Paragraph 4
Grammar in context 1 (page 34)
a some   b some   c any   d any   e some
Grammar in context 2 (page 38)
Possible answers
1 A girl whose mother is your sister/sister-in-law or whose father is your brother/brother-in-law.
2 Someone that/who commits the crime of arson.
3 When someone breaks into a building in order to steal things.
4 A police station is a building where police officers work.
5 Portuguese is the language that/which people speak in Brazil.
6 The period of life when you change from being a child to being a young adult.

UNIT 4 p137

Answers
Vocabulary in context (page 44)
Possible answers
thum<u>b</u> – <u>b</u>ack – <u>k</u>nee – <u>e</u>lbow – <u>wr</u>ist – <u>t</u>hroat – <u>t</u>oe – <u>e</u>ar
thum<u>b</u> – <u>b</u>ack – <u>k</u>nee – <u>e</u>lbow – <u>wr</u>ist – <u>t</u>high – <u>h</u>eel – <u>l</u>eg
Reading (page 45)
Text A
1 sore neck, pains in your back, headaches
2 looking down at a screen for a long time
3 EyeForcer Smart Glasses
Text B
1 colds and flu
2 touching your phone
3 washing your hands frequently, trying not to use other people's phones, keeping your phone clean, not taking your phone to the bathroom
Text C
1 hurting yourself, breaking your arm or leg
2 walking while looking down at your smartphone
3 apps that lock your phone or send an error message when you use your phone on the move, traffic lights on the pavement
Grammar in context 1 (page 46)
1 Have you ever had a very high temperature?
2 Have you ever slept in a hospital?
3 Have you ever made soup?
4 Have you ever taken medicine that tastes really bad?
5 Have you ever visited a friend in hospital?
6 Have you ever broken your arm?
Developing vocabulary (page 47)
1 health centre   2 food poisoning   3 first-aid kit   4 painkiller
5 black eye   6 Sunburn
Grammar in context 2 (page 51)
a Have, broken   b have   c went   d broke   e 've, broken
f 've had   g 've crashed   h Have, fallen   i haven't   j fell

UNIT 5 p137

Answers
Reading (page 59)
Possible answers
1 To give an example of an unusual reality show.
2 Some shows use actors, the situations are carefully planned, it's easy to edit what people say to make them say something different.
3 Because producers need contestants that attract more viewers.
4 Some documentaries say they are in one place when in fact they are filming in a different location, in some shows they 'surprise' contestants with things they knew about already, and most shows give a false idea of time.
5 It can give us unrealistic ideas about what we can do, it can confuse us, it can make us stop believing everything we see on TV.
Grammar in context 1 (page 61)
1 are not as violent as/less violent than American series.
2 are as interesting as talent shows.
3 are not as popular as/less popular than video games with teenagers.
4 are as exciting as crime series.
5 is not as scary as/less scary than watching them in the cinema.
6 are not as informative as/less informative than books.

UNIT 6 p138

Answers
Vocabulary in context (page 70)
1 glacier   2 drought   3 flood   4 global warming   5 waste
Reading (page 71)
1 The NOAA is the source of the information in Paragraph A.
2 The Eiffel Tower appears as a comparison to show how big the sea gate that protects Rotterdam is.
3 275 million is the number of people living in areas which are going to be at risk from rising sea levels.
4 The Netherlands are an example of a place where flooding has always been a problem but also where architects and engineers are always coming up with different solutions for the flooding problem.
5 2025 is the year in which the tenth anniversary of the Paris Agreement will be.
6 82 mm is how much higher the global sea level was in 2016 than the 1983 annual average.
Developing vocabulary (page 73)
1 red, become   2 sure, receive   3 worst, understand
4 consume, obtain or buy   5 sunny, bring   6 late, arrive
Grammar in context 2 (page 77)
1 If I pass all my exams this year, I'll have a special holiday in the summer.
2 Mark will help you with your homework if you ask him.
3 The world will be in trouble if we don't do something about climate change.
4 If you climb that mountain, you'll need special equipment.
5 If we don't leave now, we'll be late for school.
6 Some towns on the coast will be underwater if sea levels rise much more.

Reach higher

UNIT 7 p138

Answers
Reading (page 85)
1 AV 2 B 3 AV 4 AV 5 B 6 AG

Developing vocabulary (page 87)
1 part-time 2 blue-eyed 3 well-off 4 easy-going
5 badly-paid 6 well-known

Grammar in context 2 (page 90)
2 If my mum didn't work late during the week, she could come to the school show.
3 If they spoke to people, they'd have some friends.
4 If Ava knew the answer, she would tell us.
5 If I had a Saturday job, I'd have some money.
6 Matt would be coming to the party tomorrow if you had invited him.

UNIT 8 p139

Answers
Vocabulary in context (page 96)
1 get on well (with) 2 fall out (with) 3 make up 4 see eye-to-eye (with) 5 have in common (with) 6 close

Reading (page 97)
1 Paragraph 1 (Possible answer: People have started seeing robots as toys instead of as machines.)
2 Paragraph 6 (Possible answer: People hesitated before switching a robot off when the robot begged them not to do it.)
3 Paragraph 5 (Possible answer: PARO is a robot that helps people with dementia.)
4 Paragraph 3 (Possible answer: WALL-E and R2-D2 are robots that only exist in fiction.)
5 Paragraph 2 (Possible answer: In the story 'Robbie', the child's mother changes her mind when the robot saves her son.)
6 Paragraph 4 (Possible answer: Some robot toys can show sadness, disappointment or are designed to get upset.)

Grammar in context 1 (page 98)
a had learnt/learned b had passed c had given d had met
e had not/hadn't seen f had taken

Developing vocabulary (page 99)
1 madness 2 Leadership 3 weakness 4 freedom 5 wisdom
6 boredom

Grammar in context 2 (page 102)
creating ~~create~~ (line 2) playing ~~play~~ (line 4) thinking ~~think~~ (line 5) walking ~~walk~~ (line 6) being ~~to be~~ (line 7) to relax ~~relaxing~~ (line 8) Eating ~~Eat~~ (line 8) to make ~~making~~ (line 9)

UNIT 9 p140

Answers
Vocabulary in context (page 110)
autobiography – a book about your life that you write yourself
cookbook – a book that contains recipes and instructions for preparing food
fairy tale – a traditional children's story in which magic things happen
main character – the central/most important person in a book
masterpiece – an excellent book
newspaper – a set of sheets containing news, articles, etc.
young adult – a (book for a) person in their teens or early twenties

Reading (page 111)
Possible answers
1 It took her an hour to get to work and she had time to read on the Underground.
2 She finished reading a book and decided to leave it on the train for someone to read.
3 They offer free stickers to show the books are part of the scheme. They would like people to share a photo of the book on social media when they leave it on the train.
4 To get publicity. They leave lots of copies of a new book in different stations and they take photos or make videos of them and post them on social media.
5 You need permission from the local transport system.

Grammar in context 1 (page 112)
1 said, I sometimes wear glasses. 2 told, I'm from another planet.
3 told, I can fly. 4 said, I'm working as a journalist. 5 said, I don't like kryptonite. 6 said, I have an 'S' on my costume.
'He' is Superman.

Developing vocabulary (page 113)
1 read out 2 cross out 3 fill in 4 scroll down/up 5 flick through 6 make up

UNIT 10 p140

Answers
Vocabulary in context (page 122)
1 pad, screen 2 cam 3 load 4 drive 5 cable, port
6 set, phones 7 up 8 virus

Reading (page 123)
Possible answers
1 This is the number of search queries on Google® every minute.
2 This is a country that had an Internet blackout from morning until evening on exam days.
3 This is an airport that is closed to celebrate 'Nyepi', the Balinese New Year.
4 This is how much Internet blackouts cost countries in 2015–16.
5 This is the number of Internet users in Indonesia.
6 This is the amount of money spent every minute by online shoppers.

Developing vocabulary (page 125)
1 inbox (N) 2 forward (V) 3 attach (V) 4 bounce back (V)
5 save (V) 6 address (N) 7 account (N) 8 paste (V)

Grammar in context 2 (page 128)
1 Traditional encyclopaedias have been transformed by Wikipedia.
2 Wikipedia wasn't started by Sir Tim Berners-Lee.
3 Wikipedia articles are being changed at the moment.
4 Wikipedia articles have been written by ordinary people.
5 Some Wikipedia articles have been ruined by 'vandals'.
6 A Wikipedia was being created for children.

Exam success Units 1–2 p144

Listening

3

> **Answers**
> a Egypt (... *after she finished school she and her mother travelled to Egypt, where ...*)
> b army (*He was a member of the army and ...*)
> c nurse (*During the war, Agatha became a nurse.*)
> d 1920 (*Agatha didn't get it published until 1920, after ...*)
> e ship (*... she and her husband went on a ten-month world tour on a ship.*)
> f play (*... the longest-running play in history ...*)

Speaking

5 SPEAKING

- Before students do the task, highlight the sentence 'The examiner wants to hear what you have to say.' in the Speaking exam tip box. Explain this also means trying to use interesting vocabulary wherever possible.
- Look at the second question together and say to students *Don't think about just your mother and father or brothers and sisters. Who else in your family can you talk about?* Elicit any more distant/complex family relationships, e.g. *aunt/uncle, cousin, great-grandmother/father, stepbrother/sister, half-brother/sister*. Tell students that if they can talk about someone like this, they can show the examiner they know more complicated vocabulary.
- Look at the third question together and elicit any unusual free-time activities students do. Again, encourage students to talk about something unusual if possible.
- Tell students not to invent, though – a Speaking exam can be stressful enough without having to improvise. A useful rule is for students to tell the truth, but to choose things to talk about which allow them to show they know more than the 'minimum'.

Writing

6 Before students do the task, write or project on the board:

What is the purpose of this notice?
a to find new, regular reporters for the website
b to learn how popular crime programmes are with teenagers
c to share young people's ideas and opinions on the website

Ask students to read the notice and choose the correct answer (**c**).

- Explain that this is an example of an exam-type question for Writing, and that students will see more of these later on in the course.

Exam success Units 3–4 p145

Reading

3

> **Answers**
> **1 B** (*challenge* [B] is used for something hard to do, but it is more positive than *difficulty* [A], which could suggest the person failed. The word 'extra' before the gap is not a common collocation with *trouble* [C]. The verb usually used with *effort* [D] is 'make', not 'have'.)
> **2 D** (*exist* [D] is the most common collocation with *language*, not *live* [C]. *Last* [A] implies duration and *happen* [B] implies a single event.)
> **3 A** (*Invent* [A] here has the meaning of 'create something new'. *Think* [B] would be a possible answer if there was the preposition 'of' after the gap, but it also doesn't suggest the amount of work required in creating a language. *Offer* [C] would imply that Peterson had already invented a language that the producers wanted to use. *Achieve* [D] is usually used for more abstract goals, not for creating specific things.)
> **4 C** (*End* [C] up is a phrasal verb meaning 'do something after a long period'. The other phrasal verbs exist, but have different meanings and none make sense in this context: *show* [B] up can mean 'appear in a place by surprise'; *look* [C] up can mean 'try to find information in a book or online'; and *turn* [D] up can mean 'increase the volume/temperature/etc' or 'appear in a place by surprise'.)
> **5 A** (*Particularly* [A] is used here to emphasise how hard the work was for Clarke. It's the opposite of *slightly* [D], which would not make sense here. *Clearly* [B] is used to state something which is fairly obvious; and *sincerely* [C] is used to talk about how deep a feeling is.)
> **6 B** (*Lines* [B] are the specific words an actor needs to learn. *Roles* [A] refer to the characters an actor plays. *Intervals* [C] refer to periods of time, or – in an entertainment context – the break in a concert/play/musical/etc. *Comments* [D] are small things you say or write.)

Speaking

4

> **Possible answers**
> breathe slowly and deeply
> use any preparation time to think about what you can say, and use filler words/phrases (like *Well* and *Let me think, ...*) if you run out of things to say while speaking
> 'show what you know', i.e. say something that's true, but choose things to talk about which show you know more than the 'minimum'

Writing

6 Before students do the task, highlight the importance of the word limit. Explain that to get maximum marks in a writing exam, candidates need to include all the information in the question. In this case, that means using all four notes (in orange boxes) on the email.

- Remind students that they should write close to the suggested number of words. They should be aware that if writing responses are too long, they may contain irrelevant content and have a negative effect on the reader, and this could affect the final mark.

Exam success Units 5–6 p146

Reading

7

> **Answers**
> a every/each (used before a singular countable noun ('minute') to mean 'all the things in the group/period/event', in this case 'the adventure')
> b than (comparative construction)
> c if (first conditional)
> d much (part of the phrase *too much* used before an uncountable noun to mean 'more than is necessary')
> e of (part of the phrase *loads of* used before plural countable nouns and uncountable nouns to mean 'a lot of')
> f most (superlative construction)

Writing

8 If your class is less confident, give students time to discuss the statement in groups and then as a class. Collate students' ideas on the board and tell students to note them down.

9 Read through the plan with the class and tell them that each point should be in a separate paragraph.

- If your class is less confident, tell them to choose from the ideas they shared in the previous exercise and to concentrate on expressing the ideas correctly and organising them according to the plan.

Exam success Units 7–8 p147

Speaking

4 SPEAKING

- Before students do the task, remind them of the Speaking exam tip from page 144, i.e. don't give very long answers, but try not to give one-word answers.
- Demonstrate this by writing: *too short, a good answer* and *too long* on the board. Nominate students to ask you the questions and give an answer to each one, e.g. *Where do you live?* 'Barcelona'. Then ask students to decide if it was a good answer or not, e.g. *too short*. Make sure you include examples of answers of all three types, i.e. also include some which are good models, and some which are long and unclear.
- Also exemplify some of the fillers from the Speaking exam tip box in your answers, i.e. *Hmm*, *Well*, *That's a very good question* and *Let me think*.

Writing

6 Read the Writing exam tip box with students and make sure they understand that to get maximum marks, they need to include <u>all</u> the information in the question. In this case, that means all four notes (in orange boxes) on the email. They also need to follow the <u>same order</u> as the question.

- Before students do the task, remind them of the Writing exam tip from p145, i.e. check the number of words you have to write and don't forget to use the correct formal or informal style. Check students have understood the task by asking: *How many words do you have to write?* (about 100) and *Should your email be formal or informal?* (informal).

Exam success Units 9–10 p148

Reading
3
> **Answers**
> a by (passive construction with *by* introducing the agent)
> b to (preposition at the end of a sentence as part of the construction: *add* + something + *to* [+ something])
> c to (preposition as part of the construction: *allow* + someone + *to do* + something)
> d of (preposition used after *source*)
> e the (superlative construction)
> f more (used before a number to say the actual number is higher)

Speaking
6

- Before students do the task, remind them of the Speaking exam tip from p145, i.e. look at the photo carefully and include as many details as possible. Elicit some examples of details that students could include in their answers, e.g. colours, time of day, weather, clothes, what people are doing. Also remind them that they can speculate and talk about why they think the people are in the places and who they think they are.

Listening
7

> **Answers**
> a Wales (*… she's from Wales.*)
> b laptop (*… she found out that she loves writing stories – right after she was given her own laptop.*)
> c 15 (*When Beth was 15, her life changed forever. That's when she started writing her first novel …*)
> d problems (*It's about friendship, typical teenage problems and the romantic relationship …*)
> e blog (*… read each new chapter of her book by uploading notes for her audience to read online … Readers could also post their own comments about her book, …*)
> f film (*Beth sold her story so that it could be made into a film for Netflix.*)

CLASS AUDIO SCRIPT

UNIT 1

Vocabulary in context, p6
1

Ages and stages of life
baby
child
middle-aged man
middle-aged woman
senior citizen
teenager
toddler
young adult

2

The family
aunt
brother-in-law
sister-in-law
cousin
daughter
father-in-law
mother-in-law
grandchild
grandfather
grandmother
grandparent
grandson
granddaughter
great-grandfather
great-grandmother
husband
nephew
niece
son
son-in-law
daughter-in-law
stepfather
stepmother
uncle
wife

3b

A legendary family!
Chrissy Teigen is a famous model and food writer who is married to another celebrity. Her husband is the Oscar-winning singer John Legend. They have two children, a daughter called Luna and a son called Miles.
In the photo, John has got Luna in his arms. Chrissy has got one sister, Tina. She is Luna and Miles' aunt. John's brothers, Vaughn and Ronald, are Luna and Miles' uncles. Tina is John's sister-in-law, and Vaughn and Ronald are Chrissy's brothers-in-law. They aren't in the photo. They're a very happy family!

4

Words connected with the family
divorced
extended
immediate
one-parent
only child
partner
relative
single
twin

Listening, p12
2, 3 and 4 06

Presenter: So, remember, here on Teen Talk Time this week, we asked you to call us and tell us about some of the typical arguments you have with your parents. Here are just some of the things you told us.

Oliver: Hi, my name's Oliver. I don't really have many arguments with my parents. They give me quite a lot of independence, which is great. The only thing we really argue about is video games. My dad hates it when I play them; he says they're a waste of time, even games like Minecraft!® I don't think it's fair because I only play them when I finish all my homework. And they help me to relax. The funny thing is that my mum doesn't usually say anything because she likes playing them, too!

Emma: Hi there. I'm Emma. Erm, my problem is my little sister. You can probably hear her now. She's playing music really loudly. And singing … really badly! We always have arguments about it. The thing is, I get angry with her, and then she goes and tells my mum. And my mum always protects my sister because she's only ten. I tell my mum that I can't concentrate on my homework but my mum just tells me to be nice to my sister!

Harry: Hey … I'm Harry. I'm in a bit of an unusual situation. My dad is a teacher … well, no, in fact, he's the headmaster at the school that I go to. That's not a big problem at school. But at home it's really strange. When I'm not studying or doing homework, for example, if I'm playing a video game, my dad says 'Hey, why aren't you working? Haven't you got anything to do?' But then at other times, when I'm doing homework or revising at home, my dad says 'Hey, why are you spending all your time studying?! You need to relax and enjoy yourself!'. I never win!

Charlotte: Charlotte here. You were asking about typical arguments with parents. I have a problem, and I don't know if it's just me. My mum's a doctor and, well, she really wants me to study medicine at university and become a doctor like her. The thing is, that just doesn't interest me. I hate biology for a start. She doesn't realise that it's *my* life and I need to decide for *myself* what I study and do afterwards.

Poppy: Oh, hi, I'm Poppy. I think arguments with your parents are just a normal part of being a teenager. Adolescents and parents see things differently. For example, the arguments I have with my parents are nearly always about my bedroom! They tell me to make my bed in the morning, put my clothes away, keep my desk tidy … I mean, I know my bedroom is a mess, but I just don't care. I have other things to do. But when I'm middle aged, I can imagine having arguments with my daughter about her bedroom!

Developing speaking, p14
2 and 3 07

Holly: So, Dylan … Have you got any brothers or sisters?
Dylan: Yes, I've got a sister. She's 14. She studies at my school. What about you?
Holly: I've got one brother and one sister.
Dylan: How old are they? Do they live at home?
Holly: Yes, they do. My brother is 15 and my sister is 12. They're both studying at my school.

CLASS AUDIO SCRIPT

Dylan: Cool. So ... What do you do at the weekend?
Holly: I play basketball on Saturdays.
Dylan: Really? How often do you play?
Holly: I play in a team, so we train twice a week. I love watching basketball too. My favourite team is the Golden State Warriors. What about you? Do you like basketball?
Dylan: Hmm ... Not really ... I don't really like sport. I prefer playing video games. On Saturdays my friends come to my house and we play together. *Spider-Man* is our favourite.
Holly: Oh, I hate video games!
Dylan: What about school? What's your favourite school subject?
Holly: That's easy – biology!
Dylan: Really? That's my favourite too!

4a and 4b
1 Have you got any brothers or sisters?
2 What about you?
3 What do you do at the weekend?
4 How often do you play?
5 Do you like basketball?
6 What's your favourite school subject?

UNIT 2

Vocabulary in context, p18
2
Crimes
arson
burglary
cybercrime
kidnapping
mugging
murder
robbery/theft
shoplifting
smuggling
vandalism

3b
1 arsonist
2 burglar
3 cybercriminal/hacker
4 kidnapper
5 mugger
6 murderer
7 robber/thief
8 shoplifter
9 smuggler
10 vandal

4
Detective work
accuse a suspect
analyse evidence
arrest a suspect
charge a suspect
investigate a case
prove something
question a witness
search for evidence

5b
A police detective's job – the basics
After a crime, the first thing detectives need to do is investigate the case. Firstly, they search for evidence, i.e. anything that can help to show that somebody in particular did the crime. When they find the evidence, they need to analyse it, studying it in detail. Of course, it's not so difficult to solve a crime when somebody actually saw what happened. In that case, the police need to question the witness. When the police have specific evidence, they can prove that the suspect committed the crime. When that happens, they can accuse the suspect and say they did it. They then arrest the suspect, taking them to a police station and keeping them there because they think they committed the crime. They need to charge the suspect, making an official statement that says the suspect actually committed the crime.

Grammar in context 1, p20
2b
finished   liked   passed   watched
arrived   discovered   planned   stayed
needed   painted   started   wanted

Listening, p24
2 and 3
Ava: Hi, Tom. How are you today?
Tom: Good. And you, Ava? Did you do anything last night?
Ava: Not much. I studied for an hour or two and then I watched TV.
Tom: Oh. Did you watch anything interesting?
Ava: Yeah, a new series of *Sherlock* started last night. I mean, detective series aren't my favourite. I used to watch them when I was small but then I stopped. But Benedict Cumberbatch is a great actor, he's a favourite of mine, especially when he plays Sherlock Holmes.
Tom: Benedict Cumberbatch? That reminds me! Did you read about what he did?!
Ava: What? You mean the *Avengers* film?
Tom: No. He was in the newspapers because he was actually at a real crime scene.
Ava: Really? What happened?
Tom: Well, while he was travelling in a taxi, he saw a crime. There were four muggers. They were attacking a cyclist ... he was young ... about 20. Cumberbatch saw them and told the taxi driver to stop. He ran out of the taxi and tried to stop them.
Ava: And?
Tom: The muggers hit the cyclist with a bottle. They were trying to steal his bike, I think. And the poor man on the bike was shouting at them to stop. That's when Cumberbatch came and started to pull the muggers away from the cyclist with his own hands. That's what the taxi driver said.
Ava: Did they actually fight?
Tom: No, I don't think so. But the taxi driver called him a 'superhero'. He said he really knew what he was doing.
Ava: I suppose actors learn to defend themselves, don't they? When they're preparing for adventure films.
Tom: That's true. Anyway, when the muggers realised who he was, they decided to run away!
Ava: Maybe they were thinking it really *was* Sherlock Holmes, not Benedict Cumberbatch!
Tom: Ha! Maybe. Anyway, thanks to him, they didn't steal anything.
Ava: And the cyclist? Did he go to hospital in the end?
Tom: No, he was lucky.
Ava: Very lucky. Where did this happen? New York?

CLASS AUDIO SCRIPT

Tom: No, that's the funny thing. It was in London, really close to Baker Street!
Ava: Wait! Didn't Sherlock Holmes use to live in Baker Street?!
Tom: Yes, exactly! I'm sure things like that didn't use to happen in those days.
Ava: Are you sure this wasn't publicity for the new series or something? Maybe he was just acting …
Tom: I don't think so. The police confirmed there was an attack on a cyclist. But Cumberbatch didn't appear in the police report. The cyclist was quiet about it too, even though he was very grateful for the help. The only one who spoke to the newspapers about it really was the taxi driver.
Ava: Did the taxi driver help?
Tom: Well, Cumberbatch's wife, Sophie Hunter, was riding in the taxi too. But yes, he got out and helped. It's just a pity they didn't arrest the criminals though.
Ava: Wow, can you imagine that? Sherlock Holmes arriving at a police station with four muggers!

Developing speaking, p26
3b
Saying sorry
People in the UK say 'sorry' a lot! A YouGov survey found that they say it around eight times a day. One in eight British people say 'sorry' up to 20 times a day!
According to the same survey, British people say 'sorry' more than Americans. For example, if they're five minutes late, 84% of British people say sorry, compared with 73% of Americans. The survey didn't include Canadians, but Canadians also have a reputation for saying 'sorry' a lot!
People in the UK often say 'sorry' for things they are not responsible for. For example, 36% say sorry when another person hits them accidentally! Only 24% of Americans do this.
In general, in the UK, saying 'sorry' is simply a way of being polite, especially with people we don't know very well.

4 and 5
1
Speaker 1: Hey, where's my water? I left a bottle here on my desk just a moment ago.
Speaker 2: Oh no. I'm sorry. Was it yours?
Speaker 1: Yes. Did you take it?
Speaker 2: Yes. I'm so sorry. I was really thirsty and I just saw it there.
Speaker 1: Oh well. It doesn't matter. It's only water.
Speaker 2: Let me get you a new bottle in the break.
Speaker 1: Don't worry about it.

2
Speaker 3: Hi Elliott. Did you bring my book?
Speaker 4: Which book?
Speaker 3: The book we have to read for English. The one I lent you yesterday.
Speaker 4: Oh no! I left it at home. Sorry!
Speaker 3: But I need it for my class now. The teacher's going to be really angry!
Speaker 4: I'll make it up to you.
Speaker 3: How?
Speaker 4: Erm …
Speaker 3: Elliott, that's the last time I lend you anything.
Speaker 4: I'm really, really sorry. I feel terrible.

UNIT 3

Vocabulary in context, p32
1b
Languages
Arabic
Bulgarian
French
German
Italian
Japanese
Polish
Portuguese
Russian
Spanish
Thai
Turkish

2
Countries
Argentina
Austria
Brazil
Bulgaria
Egypt
Japan
Mexico
Poland
Russia
Switzerland
Thailand
Turkey

5a
Learning languages
accuracy
accurate
essay
exam
exercise
fluency
fluent
homework
memorisation
memorise
mistake
practice
practise
revise
revision
study
translate
translation

5b
Advice for learning English
When you learn English, remember that making mistakes is natural – the important thing is to learn from the things you do wrong. It's also important to practise as much as possible – use the language in lots of different situations. Frequent revision is essential, too – look back at new language regularly. This will help you to memorise the new vocabulary and grammar and store it in your brain. Translation can be useful sometimes, but remember that grammar and vocabulary don't usually work in exactly the same way in different languages. And, finally, when we talk about speaking, there are two main goals: accuracy is good

CLASS AUDIO SCRIPT

because it means what you are saying is correct and being fluent means that you can keep talking without frequently stopping.

Developing vocabulary, p35
2a, 2b and 2c

uncomfortable
incorrect
informal
unhappy
illegal
illogical
unofficial
impolite
impossible
irregular
irresponsible
unusual
invisible

Listening, p38
3

Presenter: Welcome to another podcast in our series, 'A world of languages'. Today we're talking about a language that not many people know about ... yet. It's called Toki Pona, and here to tell us about it is language specialist Marta Davis. Marta, tell us a bit about Toki Pona.
Marta: Well, the first thing to say is that Toki Pona is an artificial language. That means it's a language that somebody created. It isn't a language that grew naturally over a long period of time.
Presenter: So it's similar to Klingon in *Star Trek*.
Marta: Yes, but Toki Pona doesn't appear in any series or films.
Presenter: OK, so who created it and why?
Marta: Sonja Lang is the person who created it. Sonja, who's from Toronto, is a translator of French, English and Esperanto, which is another artificial language, of course. Above all, her idea was to create a language to communicate good and positive feelings. It's all in the name. 'Toki' means language and 'pona' means good or simple!
Presenter: What makes Toki Pona special?
Marta: Well, the unusual thing about Toki Pona, which only began in 2001, is that it's a very small language. Small because it only uses 14 letters and has about 120 words. Sonja wanted to create a language that was simple, a language where you could express a *lot* but using *few* words.
Presenter: Can you give me an example?
Marta: Yes, take colours. In Toki Pona there are only five words for colours. But, of course, you can make new colours by combining words. So, 'laso' is blue in Toki Pona, and 'jelo' is yellow. So 'laso jelo' is green.
Presenter: What about numbers? Are they similar to English numbers, for example?
Marta: No! At first there were only words for one, two and many! Now they also have the numbers five and ten. But the idea is to only have words that are completely necessary. So there are no words for 'please' or 'thank you'. You just smile or use body language.
Presenter: So is it an easy language to learn?
Marta: Some people say that Toki Pona is a language which you can learn to speak in just 30 hours. That was another of the objectives that Sonja had when she created it. The idea was to make it easy to bring people together from all around the world.
Presenter: How many people actually speak the language then?
Marta: I'm not sure about speaking. But hundreds of people are using the language online on social media. And it is quite international, too. Japan, Belgium, New Zealand and Argentina are just some of the countries where people are using it.
Presenter: Thanks, Marta. I must say it's the idea of being able to learn a new language in just two days that I like the most!
Marta: Yes, I agree!

Developing speaking, p40
2 and 3

Receptionist: Good morning. This is the Toronto Easy English Centre. How can I help you?
Student: Good morning. I'd like some information about your summer courses.
Receptionist: Yes, of course. We have a course for students aged between 14 and 17. It begins on the 2nd July.
Student: Sorry, did you say the 2nd July?
Receptionist: Yes, that's right. The course lasts two weeks.
Student: Do you organise accommodation?
Receptionist: Yes, we do.
Student: How much is the course?
Receptionist: The price of a two-week course is 1,400 Canadian dollars.
Student: I'm not sure I understood what you said.
Receptionist: I said the price is 1,400 Canadian dollars.
Student: How many hours of classes are there each day?
Receptionist: Four hours a day.
Student: Does the price include other activities?
Receptionist: Yes, it does.
Student: What other activities are there?
Receptionist: There are excursions and lots of sports activities, including tennis and hockey.
Student: Where can I find more information?
Receptionist: On our website. There's a registration form there, too.

UNIT 4

Vocabulary in context, p44
1

Basic parts of the body
arm
ear
face
finger
foot
hand
head
leg
mouth
neck
nose
stomach
toe

CLASS AUDIO SCRIPT

2
More parts of the body
ankle
back
calf
cheek
chest
chin
elbow
forehead
heel
hip
jaw
knee
shoulder
thigh
throat
thumb
wrist

3
1 heel
2 ankle
3 calf
4 knee
5 thigh
6 elbow
7 thumb
8 chest
9 chin
10 cheek
11 forehead
12 jaw
13 throat
14 shoulder
15 back
16 wrist
17 hip

Grammar in context 1, p46
3c
Has anybody ever really done that?
1 False.
In 1972 23-year-old Vesna Vulović fell 10, 160 metres from a plane without a parachute and survived.
2 Yes.
In 2016, Aleix Segura Vendrell stopped breathing for 24 min 3.45 seconds. Aleix is a professional diver from just outside Barcelona.
3 False.
Herbert Nitsch is from Austria. He's dived more than 200 metres underwater without oxygen twice. Once he dived 253.2 metres!
4 No.
Nobody has ever run a marathon in under two hours. In 2019 the world record was 2 hours 1 minute 39 seconds.
5 False.
In 2007, Martin Strel, from Slovenia, became the first person to swim the whole of the Amazon River. That's about 6,400 kilometres!
6 Yes.
The American Evel Knievel broke at least 433 bones in his lifetime. He was famous for doing very dangerous motorbike jumps.

Grammar in context 1, p47
6c
1 People have used the main active ingredient in aspirin since at least 400 BC.
2 The International Red Cross and Red Crescent Movement has existed since 1863.
3 Doctors have known how to do heart transplants for about 50 years.
4 People have studied things with microscopes since about 1600.
5 It has been possible to X-ray the body for approximately 120 years.

Listening, p50
2 and 3

Presenter: Now, Mike, you're a BASE jumper. Can you just remind us what the word BASE means when we talk about BASE jumping?

Mike: Yes, BASE actually comes from the letters B, A, S, E. B is for building; A is for antenna; S is for span, that is, the main part of a bridge; and E is for earth, mountains, for example. We jump from those different places. It's important to ask for permission, of course. My friends and I never do illegal jumps.

Presenter: I've just seen some of the videos you've made. They look incredibly dangerous to make! How dangerous is BASE jumping?

Mike: Very! I mean, jumping from a high place with a parachute is always a risk. And obviously you can never do a jump without planning, training and the right professional equipment.

Presenter: Have you ever hurt yourself?

Mike: Yes. I've already sprained my right ankle and had a few cuts and bruises.

Presenter: So is it the danger that attracts you?

Mike: I'm actually very careful in my day-to-day life. And when I jump, it's more about controlling and beating your fears. But you can have really bad accidents … like the Norwegian BASE-jumper Karina Hollekim.

Presenter: Karina Hollekim … I think I've heard that name. Has she ever been in the news?

Mike: Yes, she has.

Presenter: Why? What did she do?

Mike: It was in 2006. She was in Switzerland. In theory it was an easy dive, a skydive, not a BASE jump. But her parachute didn't open correctly. She actually hit the ground at over 100 kilometres per hour!

Presenter: But … how did she survive?

Mike: She couldn't control her position because of her speed. But when she touched the ground she wasn't in a terrible position. It sounds strange but she was really lucky!

Presenter: How bad were her injuries?

Mike: Well, she broke both her knees and injured her legs in lots of different places. The doctors told her it was impossible for her to walk again. But after spending some time in a wheelchair, she did it! But it took her two years! And about 20 operations!

Presenter: That's amazing. Has she started BASE jumping again yet?

Mike: No, she hasn't done that yet but she's already begun skiing again, which is something she's always loved.

Presenter: Wow, well, she's certainly a great example of fighting against adversity.

Mike: Yes. She's made a film about her experiences and also written a book. And now she gives talks to motivate others.

CLASS AUDIO SCRIPT

Presenter: That's great ... Now what about you, Mike? What's your next goal?
Mike: Well, if everything goes well ...

Developing speaking, p52
2a, 2b and 3

Speaker: Well, in this photo I can see four people, erm, four football players. You can only see the legs of one of the players, you can't see his face. And you can't see the ball or anything ... The players are all wearing blue shirts, black shorts and white socks. And football boots, of course. They aren't playing at the moment. I think they've just stopped because in the middle of the photo there's a player on the floor, on the ground. The player is touching his knee. He's holding it. Errm ... I think he's just injured himself, or maybe somebody has just kicked him or something. His knee is obviously very sore and he's in pain. I'm not sure but maybe he's broken his leg because the other three players are concerned. They look very serious. I think they're probably his friends and I imagine they're very worried about him ... Personally, I enjoy playing football but I don't play in a team. So I've never hurt myself like this player. I mean, once I had some scratches and bruises when I played with my friends in the park last year. But I've never had a bad injury like this, or broken my leg or anything like that ... I like watching football but I don't like the photo much because they aren't playing. In fact, one of the problems is that in real football matches, the players spend a lot of time on the floor ... like here. The thing is that sometimes you don't know if they're really in pain or not ... Hmmm ... Maybe in this photo, the players are just acting and he hasn't really hurt himself! I'm not sure now!

UNIT 5

Vocabulary in context, p58
1

TV programmes and series
cartoon
chat show
comedy
crime series
documentary
drama
fantasy series
film
food programme
game show
reality show
science-fiction series
sports programme
talent show
the news

2a

Words connected with TV and online video
binge-watching
channel
contestant
episode
mobile device
screen
season
spoiler
streaming service
viewer

2b

True or false?
1 Hulu was the first TV streaming service. It began before Netflix.
2 It's possible to watch video content made exclusively for mobile devices such as smartphones.
3 A television produced in 1982 had a screen that was just 5 cm.
4 In 2016, Alejandro Fragoso watched TV continuously for 94 hours and so broke the world record for binge-watching.
5 BBC Two was the first TV channel in the UK to transmit programmes in colour.
6 The US sitcom *The Big Bang Theory* stopped after 12 seasons.
7 There haven't been over 1,000 episodes of *The Simpsons*.
8 In 1969, about 600 million TV viewers around the world watched a live programme showing the first astronauts to walk on the Moon.
9 The first ever contestant to win the talent show *America's Got Talent* was only 11 years old.
10 They filmed different endings for the very final episode of *Game of Thrones* to stop the possibility of spoilers.

3 🔊 37

Adjectives describing TV programmes
annoying
awful
brilliant
dull
entertaining
funny
informative
inspiring
moving
original
scary
violent

Grammar in context 1, p60
6b 🔊 39

1 True
Jennifer Lawrence was born in 1990 and Emilia Clarke was born in 1986.
2 True
In the US, watching American football is much more popular than watching football.
3 False
Superman was created in 1938 and *Spider-Man* was created in 1962.
4 True
Going to the cinema is far more expensive than renting films online.
5 True
Avengers: Endgame cost $356 million to make and *Captain Marvel* cost $152 million.

Listening, p64
2 and 3 🔊 40

Presenter: Today we're talking about binge-watching, you know, when you start watching one episode of your favourite TV series, then you're having such a good time that you just can't stop. We want to know ... why is binge-watching so common nowadays? Can it become a serious problem, like an addiction? Or is it all just good, relaxing fun? Here's what different listeners told us.
Holly: Hi, my name's Holly. I never binge-watch. In fact, I think binge-watching is such a problem!

I saw some statistics this week that are really frightening. Did you know that 55% of young people say that binge-watching is their favourite hobby?! Twenty-six percent say they eat lots of unhealthy food while they binge-watch! And 28% say they sleep less because of binge-watching! ... The thing is, I'm a teacher. Sometimes my students are soooo tired in the morning and often it's because they watch TV until late at night. They sleep six hours or less and that isn't long enough to rest. Parents need to be careful with the number of hours kids watch TV.

Noah: Hi, I'm Noah. I don't think it's a good idea to watch so much TV, obviously. But I do binge-watch sometimes. What happens to me is that a friend tells me about a great series that I've never heard about, then I watch one episode and I discover that I like it. I watch the next episode and I find that it's so good that I feel I need to watch every single episode ... of every different season that I missed! ... And sometimes I binge-watch because I don't want to have problems with spoilers. It's so annoying when somebody tells you about an important moment in a series before you actually see it!

Jenna: My name's Jenna. I'm old enough to remember when we just had three or four channels and no streaming services. You needed to wait a week between each episode of your favourite series and you could only watch episodes live. Now, with a lot of series you can watch the complete season on the same day. So, I think there's more binge-watching because of streaming services ... I also reckon that series are much better now. The episodes have such surprising endings that you're too excited to switch off and go to bed. So, you watch the next episode, and the next ... That's what I do, at least.

Lee: I'm Lee and I'm in my last year at school. I'm calling because one day I realised that I was spending too much time watching TV. Some mornings I didn't have enough energy to study much! It was awful. So now I've stopped. I give myself a time limit before I start watching. I say I'm going to watch until nine, for example, and then I switch off at exactly nine o'clock. Or I decide how many episodes I can watch that evening. And then I switch off after that number of episodes, not *one* more! You need to decide before you start. After all, there are better and more important things to do than just sit and watch TV for hours, aren't there?

Developing speaking, p66
2, 3a and 4 🔊 41

Teacher: I'm going to describe a situation to you. A young girl studies very hard and needs to find an activity to help her relax. Here are some activities that could help her to relax. Talk together about the different activities she could do and say which would be the most relaxing. All right? Now, talk together.

Student A: OK. What do you think about reading?
Student B: Reading is a great activity. But I think it's a bit tiring for somebody who studies all day. What about you?
Student A: Yes, I agree. In my opinion, watching TV is much more relaxing than reading because you don't have to think much.
Student B: Yes, you're right. There are lots of comedies that make you feel happy. What about running?
Student A: Well, it's tiring for your body. But doing sport can really help you to rest your mind.
Student B: Yes, but it can be a bit boring when you run on your own. I reckon playing video games with friends is better because it's really gripping but you can talk to your friends at the same time.
Student A: Maybe, but playing video games can be bad for your eyes. Especially when you spend a lot of time studying in front of a computer screen.
Student B: That's true. What about cooking with friends?
Student A: It's interesting because you're doing something together. And you're making something!
Student B: Yes, and you can eat what you make when you finish. But it isn't very easy to cook well.
Student A: What about the last one – playing a musical instrument?
Student B: Well, it's brilliant if you know how to do it. But learning a new instrument is probably quite difficult, especially when you don't have much free time.
Student A: Yes, I agree. So, let's decide which one is the best. Personally, I think that watching TV, running or cooking with friends are the three best activities for a busy student. What about you?
Student B: Yes, I reckon they're all good activities. But I think the most relaxing for this girl is watching TV because she needs an activity that's really easy to do.
Student A: OK, why don't we choose TV then?
Student B: OK.

UNIT 6

Vocabulary in context, p70
1

Geographical features
beach
cave
cliff
coast
desert
forest
glacier
hill
island
jungle
rainforest
lake
mountain
mountain range
ocean
sea
river
stream
valley
waterfall

CLASS AUDIO SCRIPT

3a
Verbs connected with the environment
consume
recycle
reduce
reuse
save
throw away
waste

3b
Some simple tips for protecting the environment
Because of global warming, the temperature of the planet is rising at the moment. To help with this problem, we need to reduce greenhouse gases – the UK government promised to do this by 80% by 2050. To reach this goal, we need to use less energy. You can save energy by doing simple things like switching off the lights when you leave the room. And don't forget that we waste energy when we leave computers or TVs on all night. When we recycle plastic, glass or paper to make new products, we are also helping to protect the environment. But it's also good to reuse things instead of using them just once. In general, it's sensible to consume less – we buy lots of things that we don't really need and then quickly throw away all these useless items.

4
The environment
carbon emissions
climate change
drought
flood
fossil fuels
global warming
melting ice caps
air pollution
sea pollution
non-renewable energy
renewable energy
sea level rise
toxic waste

Listening, p76
2, 3 and 4

Presenter: Here on Green World, we're really excited to have Carol Hasper with us, who's going to tell us all about a great idea called PLOGGING. Carol, hi! What exactly is plogging?

Carol: Hi James. It's a very simple idea which combines running and picking up the rubbish you find on your way. Then you throw it away carefully, or recycle it, of course.

Presenter: Where does the strange word come from?

Carol: It's a blend of the words 'plocka upp', which is Swedish for 'pick up', and 'jogging'. If you combine these words, you get 'plogging'!

Presenter: Is the idea originally from Sweden?

Carol: Yes, it seems it was the idea of a Swedish man called Erik Ahlström. He started a community of ploggers in Stockholm. But, actually, before that, and completely separately, there used to be a thing in the US called trash running, which was similar.

Presenter: What do you need to be able to do it?

Carol: Your usual running equipment. And then most people wear gloves and carry a bag of course.

Presenter: Why did you start?

Carol: I've always loved running. I began because I wanted to get fit. But when I was running I started seeing so much litter and I got angry about it.

Presenter: Not surprising! Did you know 81% of people in Britain are angry about litter in streets? And each year it costs a billion pounds to clear up litter in the UK!

Carol: Right … So, one day I heard about plogging on social media and thought 'what a great idea!'.

Presenter: How much rubbish do you usually collect in one run?

Carol: I normally fill one big bag on a five-kilometre run!

Presenter: Doesn't that get heavy?

Carol: I don't pick up very heavy items. But yes, it does! That's the thing, though. With 'plogging', not like jogging, you bend down, stretch, get up again and then carry the rubbish. And we all know that you use up more calories if you move more. That's another reason why I do it, to get a better work-out.

Presenter: Some people might say that just picking up a bag or two of rubbish doesn't really make a big difference to the environment. Or they may think people will drop more litter in the street if they know that people like you will pick it up. What do you think?

Carol: Look, if I don't pick up this rubbish, maybe a bird or some other animal will eat it. It may get ill or die. So, perhaps it is a small step but it can make a real difference. And it will make a massive difference if lots of people do it. The plogging community is growing fast all around the world. I think that's because when you finish running, you feel good because you feel healthier. But ploggers feel even better because they know they're also doing something good for their neighbourhood, and for the planet.

Presenter: Maybe plogging isn't the most beautiful word in the world, but the idea certainly is! Get your running shoes and your gloves on and get out there! Thanks Carol!

Developing speaking, p78
2, 3 and 5a

Jamie: Are you up to anything this weekend?

Danny: Not really. What about you?

Jamie: If the weather's good, Alex and I are going to go to the beach. Do you fancy coming?

Danny: Sure. What time shall we meet?

Jamie: How about 11 o'clock?

Danny: OK. Why don't we meet at the station?

Jamie: Fine. I know. I'll bring some sandwiches and we can have lunch on the beach.

Danny: What will we do if it rains?

Jamie: I'll give you a ring and we'll go somewhere else.

Danny: OK. Listen. I'll ring Liz too and see if she wants to come.

Jamie: Good idea. See you tomorrow at 11.

Danny: See you.

CLASS AUDIO SCRIPT

UNIT 7

Vocabulary in context, p84
2
Jobs
architect
au pair
chef
company director
construction worker
economist
fashion designer
firefighter
journalist
lawyer
mechanic
nurse
photographer
plumber
police officer
receptionist
shop assistant
vet

4a 🔊 50
Personal qualities
ambitious
calm
caring
clever/bright
confident
creative
determined
fit
flexible
hard-working
patient
reliable
responsible
sensitive
sociable/friendly
strong
well-organised

4b 🔊 51
Essential qualities in the world of work
There are jobs where you need to have a specific skill or personal quality. But there are many personal qualities that are useful in almost any job. For example, it's always important to be well-organised, i.e. to plan things carefully and know exactly what you're doing. It's also important to be flexible so that you adapt to changing situations. Being creative isn't just a quality that artists and writers need – it's essential in any job where you need imagination to think of new ideas or solutions to problems. Working in teams is always important, so it's good if you are sociable and friendly and like working with other people. It's vital that you are reliable and responsible, too, so that people know they can depend on you. It also helps if you're calm and patient so that you don't panic or get angry when things start to go wrong. And, finally, it's OK to be ambitious and to want to be a big success in your job!

Grammar in context 1, p86
2b
1 should
2 firefighter
3 scientist
4 mustn't
5 discipline
6 designer
7 plumber
8 calm
9 sight
10 listen
11 hours
12 talk
13 know
14 scene
15 column
16 wrist
17 thumb
18 wrap

Developing vocabulary, p87
2a and **2b** 🔊 54
badly-paid
badly-behaved
blue-eyed
brown-eyed
green-eyed
easy-going
full-time
part-time
good-looking
long-haired
short-haired
right-handed
left-handed
well-paid
well-behaved
well-known

Listening, p90
2 and **3**
Layla: Wow! Harry, have you seen this?
I didn't know this job really existed!
Harry: Which job?
Layla: Being a professional ice cream taster! Can you imagine?
Harry: Yes, Layla, I can! I can imagine that if I ate ice cream every day, I'd put on weight really fast! Actually, I wonder how much ice cream you have to eat.
Layla: Err … Wait, it says it here … Louise Bamber, she's in charge of tasting ice cream for a big UK supermarket … She says that sometimes she tastes up to 250 ice creams a day!
Harry: Really? I like having an ice cream or two in the summer but if I did that job I'd get tired of it. Unless you really loved ice cream, you wouldn't want to eat it all through the winter.
Layla: But wait! You don't actually eat all that ice cream, you just taste it. It's not the same. Nobody could eat all that sugar! And you do other things too. For example, Louise travels a lot. She's always looking for new flavours and ideas and that's the part that sounds the most interesting to me. If I had that job, I'd really enjoy inventing new flavours. Tomato ketchup or blue cheese!
Harry: Yuck … Seriously, though, I reckon if you did that job, you'd need to visit the dentist regularly!
Layla: True! But what about you, what would your dream job be?
Harry: I've just finished a great book called *Ravenmaster*. The man who looks after the ravens at the Tower of London wrote it. His name is Christopher Skaife. That's probably my dream job!
Layla: Wait, isn't there a legend about the ravens? If the six ravens at the Tower of London fly away, the Kingdom and the Tower of London will fall?

CLASS AUDIO SCRIPT

Harry: Yeah, that's why it's so special. You're responsible for the future of the country!
Layla: Hmm. So, what qualifications do you need for a job like that?
Harry: You must have at least 22 years of military experience. I suppose you have to like birds too … What I'd love about the job is that you live inside the Tower of London!
Layla: Pff! I would be really frightened if I lived inside the Tower of London! Didn't prisoners die there?
Harry: A long time ago.
Layla: Actually, I find ravens quite scary too.
Harry: Christopher says the birds are usually friendly with visitors but it isn't a good idea to get too close to them. He has lots of marks on his arms where the ravens have attacked him. He also says visitors should be careful because the ravens sometimes steal things, especially crisps and biscuits!
Layla: Is he responsible for feeding the ravens?
Harry: Yes, he has to give them chicken … and mice … and rats!
Layla: Oh!
Harry: Yes, but at least he doesn't have to catch them!
Layla: If I were you, I'd choose a different dream job … For example, one where there's ice cream, not mice or rats!

Developing speaking, p92

2, 3 and 4

Interviewer: What do you like doing in your free time?
Amelia: Err … I love playing basketball and I've always played in the school team. We're in the Dynamik National Schools League. This year the school asked me to help train our youngest girls' team. The girls are 10 and 11.
Interviewer: What skills have you learned from that? And what qualities do you think you have that help you?
Amelia: Well, I think I've learned to motivate others. For example, we only had seven girls in the team when I started training them. Now we have a full team of 12. That's because they enjoy playing and training more this year so they asked their friends to join the team. Another thing to say is that I think it's important that I'm friendly and caring. For instance, the team can see that I have a good relationship with them and that means they try harder for me. Also, to train a team, you have to be good at organising people, and I think I'm good at that. Let me give you an example … Last year the team didn't know exactly when they were going to train. I've made a timetable, you see, so they know exactly what day and time we have training sessions and matches. That really helps!

UNIT 8

Vocabulary in context, p96

1

Feelings
afraid
anger
angry
bored
boredom
confused
confusion
delight
delighted
disappointed
disappointment
embarrassed
embarrassment
excited
excitement
fear
happiness
happy
loneliness
lonely
pride
proud
relief
relieved
sad
sadness
upset

4a

Friendships
circle of friends
classmate
close
fall out
get on well
hang out
have arguments
have in common
make up
see eye to eye
through thick and thin
ups and downs

4b 🔊 59
Best friends forever
I have a great circle of friends – there are about eight of us. I'm very good friends with a few of my classmates. I often hang out with them at my house after school, or at the park or shopping centre. Apart from my classmates, I have one really close friend called Leo, who I spend a lot of time with. Leo's also a friend of my cousin. In fact, I met him at my cousin's house. The first time I chatted to Leo, we found that we have similar opinions and see eye to eye on lots of things. There are many things that we have in common, for example, we like the same sports, school subjects and TV series … Maybe that's no surprise, because I have a good relationship with my cousin too – I've always got on well with him. Leo and I have our good moments and bad moments, our ups and downs. But we rarely get angry with each other or have arguments. We've never seriously fallen out, you know, stopped being friends. But if we had a serious argument one day, I know we would make up very quickly and become friends again. That's what true friendship is about, staying together through thick and thin, in even the most difficult situations.

Listening, p102

2 and 3 🔊 61

Presenter: In this week's Student Life podcast, we're looking at friendships. There are certain myths about friendships, things that people always say about them but that aren't perhaps true. We went out onto the street and asked what you thought – are they myths or is there some truth in them?

CLASS AUDIO SCRIPT

Myth number 1 – To be really good friends, you have to have the same interests and like doing the same things. Sally Smith.

Sally Smith: Well, up to a point, yes, I agree. Imagine that you and your friend have nothing in common and you enjoy doing completely different things in your free time. You'll never want to spend time together! That doesn't mean you have to have exactly the same tastes or spend all your time together. In the end, that might even be bad ... One of my closest friends usually goes shopping on Saturday morning, you know, looking for clothes in Uniqlo. But I often go running because I want to get some exercise. But when we meet up afterwards, we have lots to talk about. Anyway, the strongest friendships always have a bit of give and take. Some Saturdays we both go shopping and others we both go running!

Presenter: Myth number 2 – Having a few close friends is more important than having a large circle of friends. Mark Price.

Mark Price: I've never really thought about that, to be honest. I mean, I'm not interested in counting my friends. What *is* a friend, anyway? How close do you have to be? I'm in a football team, actually, I'm at the Chelsea Football Academy, and I get on with everybody but I'm not sure I'd call them all my friends. And I spend time chatting with classmates, but I don't hang out with them all after class ... But I do agree that it's really important to have one or two close friends, people you can talk to about problems and depend on. Thinking about it, the number of friends you have isn't important, the only important thing is feeling comfortable and happy with the person or people that you spend your free time with.

Presenter: Myth number 3 – Social media is bad for friendships and causes loneliness. Maya Shaw.

Maya Shaw: There's definitely a problem with social media. I have a lot of friends who've fallen out because of misunderstandings on social media, or because they said inappropriate things about a friend in a post. I think if you say anything on social media, you should also be prepared to say it to a person's face ... Some people get lonely too because they see other people having fun together but they aren't invited or part of it. I think it's a bad idea to spend too much time looking at all that stuff. It's better to spend more time face to face with people. I mainly use social media to stay in touch with friends who I can't see very often. Without social media, it would be difficult to keep those relationships alive. So, it isn't all bad!

Developing speaking, p104

2

Jayden: Hi, Emma. How's things? Did you have a good weekend?
Emma: Hey, Jayden. Yes, my weekend was brilliant.
Jayden: Where did you go?
Emma: I went to a pop music festival, the Fusion Festival. Have you heard of it?
Jayden: Yes, I have. What was it like?
Emma: Amazing!
Jayden: Who did you go with?
Emma: With my mum and dad, and Lily and Ryan came with us, too.
Jayden: How many people were there? Was it big?
Emma: Yeah, it was massive. That was the only bad part, getting in, because there were so many people. It was a relief when we were finally there. In fact, my dad was lucky to get tickets. He'd heard about the festival ages ago so he bought them back in December.
Jayden: Who played at the festival? Anybody famous?
Emma: Yeah, Shawn Mendes! He was brilliant.
Jayden: Oh, I used to listen to him all the time. But I haven't heard any of his new songs for a while ... Did you meet anybody there?
Emma: Yes. When we were getting something to eat, we saw Jack and Claire. It was really funny because Claire and I were wearing exactly the same T-shirt!
Jayden: Ha! ... What was the food like?
Emma: Oh, you know, it was the typical stuff, burgers, salads, pizza ... It was good, but a bit expensive.
Jayden: What time did it end?
Emma: I think it was about 10 pm. But we don't live too far away from there so it wasn't too bad. Anyway, the music was so good that I'm really glad I went. Next year you should come with us!
Jayden: Yeah, that sounds good!

UNIT 9

Vocabulary in context, p110

1

Things we read
blog
comic/graphic novel
cookbook
encyclopaedia
guidebook
magazine
manual
newspaper
novel
play
poetry
short story
textbook

2

Genres
autobiography
biography
crime/detective/spy fiction
fairy tale
fantasy
historical fiction
horror
mystery
romance
science fiction
thriller
YA (young adult)

4a

Book reviews
adaptation
award
to be set in
to take place in
bestseller

CLASS AUDIO SCRIPT

ending
main character
masterpiece
plot
style
theme
twist

4b

A modern classic
You may know *Mortal Engines* already as it has been a bestseller since it appeared in 2001, with hundreds of thousands of copies sold. It has won awards, too, such as the Blue Peter Book of the Year. There is also a 2018 film adaptation by the famous *Lord of the Rings* director, Peter Jackson.
But in case you don't know, *Mortal Engines* is a brilliant adventure story which is set in the future, a future where cities move from one place to another on giant wheels. The main characters are Tom Natsworthy and Hester Shaw. The plot of the story is very original and totally gripping.
There are lots of sudden twists as situations change unexpectedly. And when the book finishes, it is not the typical happy ending that you often get in YA books.
The style of the book is very dynamic and easy to follow, and it examines interesting themes such as the need to protect the environment and the horrors of war.
I believe *Mortal Engines* is a YA masterpiece, one of the best books of its kind. Don't miss it!

Developing vocabulary, p113
1

Phrasal verbs connected with reading
flick through
read on
read out
scroll down
scroll up
turn over

3

Phrasal verbs connected with writing
cross out
fill in
look over
make up
write down

Listening, p116
2 and 3 🔊 70

Presenter: On today's Literature Podcast, we're looking at literary pseudonyms. University professor Paula Jones is with us to tell us about some famous cases. Paula, why do writers choose to write under a different name?
Paula: There can be lots of different reasons. One simple reason is the author wants to remain anonymous. They don't want any public attention. One famous example is the Italian writer Elena Ferrante, the author of international bestsellers such as *My Brilliant Friend* or *The Story of the Lost Child*.
Presenter: So, who is Elena Ferrante?
Paula: That's it. Nobody knows … yet. There are different theories. One theory is that it's actually a man, not a woman. But nobody knows for sure. Ferrante once said that when a book is finished, it has no need for an author. She said it was important for her to stay anonymous.
Presenter: What other reasons are there for using a pen name?
Paula: Sometimes it's because writers don't want people to know if they're men or women. Look at J.K. Rowling, the author of the *Harry Potter* books. J.K. Rowling isn't really a pseudonym, but it was important to her that the name could be a man's or a woman's name. At first, nobody knew the identity of Rowling. But she appeared on TV a few months after her first book became famous, so soon everybody knew Rowling was a woman.
Presenter: What is J.K. Rowling's full name?
Paula: Joanne Rowling.
Presenter: And the K?
Paula: It's K for Kathleen. *But* that's not her name. It was her grandmother's name. The publishers wanted two letters, to sound more interesting … J.K. Rowling has also written other books under a pen name, Robert Galbraith.
Presenter: Are they fantasy novels?
Paula: No, they're crime, not like *Harry Potter*. That's a third reason why writers sometimes use pen names – they use a different name when they write a different type of fiction. If you usually write romance and then you write a YA novel, you might use a different name. In the case of J.K. Rowling, she probably didn't want people to compare these new books with the *Harry Potter* novels. And, maybe, like Elena Ferrante, she didn't want people to have any idea it was her, she just wanted people to read the books without any previous ideas.
Presenter: Did many people buy the first book? If they didn't know it was written by her?
Paula: It seems that, at first, they only sold about 500 copies. But then somebody discovered the secret and once it was in the newspapers, thousands of people bought it.
Presenter: Personally, I can understand why authors sometimes want to remain anonymous. The important thing is the book, not the private life of the person who wrote it.
Paula: Hmm. But knowing about the author's life can also help you to understand more about the book.
Presenter: True … It's a fascinating area to explore. Thanks, Paula.

Developing speaking, p118
2 and 3 🔊 71

Speaker: I'm going to talk about a series of books called *A Series of Unfortunate Events*. They're written by Lemony Snicket, but I don't think that's his real name. I've read all 13 books in the series so you can see that I really like it! The books are young adult fiction and they're all bestsellers. Let me tell you why I like this series so much.
First of all, the plot is really complex. At first, it seems like the books are for younger children but then you realise how clever the story is. There are lots of unusual twists. It always seems there's going to be a bad ending but it's still gripping.

CLASS AUDIO SCRIPT

What's more, the style of the books is brilliant. The narrator is part of the story and the way he tells it is really funny, even though what is happening is quite tragic at times. I think you can learn a lot about how to tell a story by reading these books.

It's also true that I like the books because of the characters, even though some of them can be a bit annoying at times. But you're always interested in finding out what's going to happen to them. That's why you want to read on.

Last but not least, the books and chapters are all quite short. That makes it easy and fast to read, especially because of all the humour.

To sum up, I think *A Series of Unfortunate Events* is the best series of books I've ever read because it's a great story, it's funny, and, above all, it's well-written. They've made film and TV adaptations which are entertaining, but I think the books are much better.

UNIT 10

Vocabulary in context, p122
1

Computers and accessories
desktop
(external) hard drive
flash drive
headset (headphones/microphone)
keyboard
monitor/screen
mouse
printer
scanner
speaker
touchpad
touchscreen
USB cable
USB port
webcam

3b
1a I want to <u>download</u> this song.
1b The <u>down</u>load didn't work.
2a I always make regular <u>backups</u> of my documents.
2b Did you remember to *back* <u>up</u> the computer?
3a The <u>set</u>-*up* is taking forever.
3b It takes time to *set up* a new computer.
4a My antivirus software has automatic <u>updates</u>.
4b I need to <u>update</u> my operating system.
5a You need to remember to *log* <u>in</u> each time.
5b I can remember my <u>login</u>, but not my password.

Grammar in context 1, p124
2c

All in sixty seconds!
1 375,000 apps are downloaded.
2 The Earth is hit by lightning about 6,000 times.
3 About 21,000 slices of pizza are eaten in the US.
4 25,000 GIFs are sent via Messenger.
5 14,896 cups of tea are drunk in London.
6 More than 190 sharks are killed by humans.
7 4.3 million videos are watched on YouTube.
8 One million plastic bottles are bought.
9 3,472 journeys are taken on the London Tube.

Developing vocabulary, p125
1 🔊 76

Collocations with *email*
account
address
attachment
bounce
check
forward
inbox
junk
reply to
send

2 🔊 77
Collocations with *document*
attach
copy and paste
create
cut
open
save

Listening, p128
2 and 3 🔊 78

James: Today we continue our series on the world's most unusual museums. In Helsingborg, Sweden, there is a Museum of Failure! It's being talked about a lot at the moment, and Holly has just come back from visiting it. Holly, what was it like?

Holly: Hi James. It was brilliant. The museum was opened just a few years ago, in 2017, by 44-year-old psychologist Dr Samuel West, and one of the surprising things is that after visiting the museum, you come out feeling really positive and inspired! You see that even the most successful people or the biggest companies fail sometimes. The important thing is to learn and bounce back from failure. There's a great example of that in the museum. The Apple Newton was invented in 1993. It was one of the first handheld devices. You wrote on the touchscreen using a type of pen and you could get your handwriting automatically made into a document. You could connect the device to a printer easily, or use it to send emails. The real problem was that the handwriting recognition didn't always work very well. You wrote one thing by hand but the Apple Newton sometimes wrote something quite different. So in 1998 it was cancelled. But, later, when the first smartphones and tablets were being invented, they looked at some of the technology from the Apple Newton. So it was a very important and useful step on the way to creating the handheld devices that we know today.

James: What else did you see there?

Holly: There was an invention from Sweden, a TeleGuide. It was sold for the first time in Sweden in 1991. It was a bit like a basic form of the Internet before the Internet existed. It had a telephone, a basic computer screen and a keyboard, all built together. You could use it to make phone calls, find out information, for example, about taxis or banking. You could even use it to do shopping.

135

CLASS AUDIO SCRIPT

James: So what was the problem?
Holly: The price! It was too low. Every time somebody bought one, the company didn't make money, it lost money! After just six months they stopped making them!
James: Why didn't they have the price checked by an expert first?
Holly: Exactly! … Oh, there's also a video game there, the Atari ET, which some people say is the worst in the world. Basically, ET falls into holes and then he can't get out! They say it's hard to find a game that's more boring! Maybe they forgot to get the game tested by players before selling it.
James: Is the museum only for technology?
Holly: No, there are over 60 products there and they include food and drink. Some very unusual food products have been created over the years. For example, green or even blue, orange or purple tomato ketchup! At first kids loved the green ketchup and lots of it was sold. But then suddenly kids and parents became tired of it.
James: Personally, I'm not surprised! … Well, it sounds like a great museum! And it's good to know that failure is just a step on the way to success!

Developing speaking, p130
2 and 3 🔊 79

Speaker: OK, so, both of the photos show people using computers. But in the first photo, I think they're using them to play video games, whereas in the second photo they're using them for work. In the first photo, you can see that some of the people are using headphones or headsets. However, in the second photo, they're all wearing headsets. I'm not sure but maybe they're talking and listening to people all the time, maybe it's part of their job. I think it's probably hard work because it seems they're all quite serious. But I suppose one similarity between the photos is that they're all concentrating hard, even the people playing the video games. You know, they aren't laughing or smiling. I don't know, but maybe the games are really difficult to play … Another important difference between the photos is that in the first photo they're wearing quite informal clothes but in the second photo they're wearing more formal work clothes. Erm, personally I wouldn't like to be in either of these places because I don't really like video games much, and I wouldn't like to work in the office in the second photo because it looks really dull. I think the problem with the people in both photos is that nobody's speaking … or smiling!

Exam success Units 1–2, p144
3 🔊 ES1

Speaker: My presentation is about the life of the famous British author Agatha Christie. She's one of the most successful crime writers of all time.
Agatha was born in 1890 and died in 1976 at the age of 85. From an early age she always loved to read. For her high school education, Agatha studied in Paris and after she finished school she and her mother travelled to Egypt, where she first had several ideas for future writing projects.
When Agatha was 25, she fell in love with a British man called Archibald Christie. They got married in 1914, just after the beginning of World War I. He was a member of the army and he often travelled for work. During the war, Agatha became a nurse. She helped the doctors and looked after many injured soldiers.
It was Agatha's sister who encouraged her to write her first novel. So, in 1916, she wrote about the now famous Belgian detective called Hercule Poirot. However, Agatha didn't get it published until 1920, after she changed the ending of the story.
Agatha's second book was published in 1922 which was also the year she and her husband went on a ten-month world tour on a ship. Then in 1928, her first marriage ended. After that, Agatha decided to go on an adventure of her own and in 1930, she went on a train journey on the Orient Express from France to the Middle East. While she was there she met Max Mallowan, an archaeologist, who became her second husband. They were happily married for 45 years.
In July 1951, Agatha wrote a play called *The Mousetrap*. It's the longest-running play in history and you can still see it in a theatre in London. By the end of her career, she had written 82 detective novels, 19 plays, 6 romance novels and an autobiography.

Exam success Units 5–6, p82
2 🔊 ES2

1

Speaker 1: Did you like any of the photos at the exhibition?
Speaker 2: Well, the photo of the small island was cool, but I also liked the one of the really high cliffs by the coast. Umm … I'm not sure which I liked best.
Speaker 1: I noticed those too, but I couldn't stop looking at the one of the big cave.
Speaker 2: The one that has a beach in it?
Speaker 1: That's right. There was something about the cave. I couldn't stop looking at it, though I wouldn't want to go inside it.
Speaker 2: Oh really?

2

Speaker 3: It looks like it might rain soon.
Speaker 4: Yeah, the clouds are pretty grey! That's annoying, because I'm bored of binge-watching TV. Aren't you?
Speaker 3: No, this series is totally gripping! But I'd like to take a break for a while. How about we go skateboarding?
Speaker 4: Even though it isn't very nice outside?
Speaker 3: Yeah, for a bit. I haven't had enough fresh air. After all, we've been inside all day.
Speaker 4: Why not? Let me just finish my sandwich. We can watch the rest of this series later.
Speaker 3: Sure.

CLASS AUDIO SCRIPT

3

Speaker 5: How was your weekend?
Speaker 6: It was great!
Speaker 5: What did you do? Did you go with your family to that new restaurant in town?
Speaker 6: No, I went hiking with my parents. We were going to see an art exhibition in the city, but the weather was too nice to be inside a museum all day. I'm glad my parents changed their minds. What about you?
Speaker 5: I actually spent the weekend drawing. That was fun. I just love it.
Speaker 6: I'd love to see your drawings sometime! Here, I'll show you a photo I took of a waterfall. This is where we hiked and had our picnic.
Speaker 5: Wow!

3

1

Speaker 1: Did you watch the historical drama series *Victoria*?
Speaker 2: Yeah, but I don't usually watch shows like that. They're usually too slow and serious for me. All I want to do is relax and have a laugh when I watch TV. But this one's not what I expected. It's entertaining because the actors who play the main characters – Queen Victoria and her husband – play their roles so well. But since you're interested in history, , you probably won't like the show – the stories in the series aren't the same as the historical facts.
Speaker 1: Yeah, that was the one thing I didn't like about it.

2

Speaker 3: I think there are some great programmes and some awful ones on TV – that's just how it's always been.
Speaker 4: Well, there are certain programmes I like more than others – you know, like game shows, where you can actually learn something from them. Sure, some of the facts the competitors need to know aren't common knowledge. But I also discover stuff that can help me in my everyday life.
Speaker 3: I always switch off the TV when there isn't anything good on – which is most of the time!

3

Speaker 5: I don't know about you, but I'll do almost anything to avoid watching TV – I'll even practise the piano for hours, that always makes my mum happy.
Speaker 6: Well, I know I spend too much time watching TV and should do more things with my friends. But when everybody's talking about a new reality show, I want to see if it's any good, too.
Speaker 5: But they never are any good! I'd rather see my friends waste my time watching stuff that doesn't mean anything to me.

Exam success Units 7–8, p108

3 ES4

Evan: Hey Sarah. Are you still taking acting lessons?
Sarah: Hi Evan! Yeah, and they've helped me to improve a lot. Hey, guess what. My cousin who designs websites for movies told me about a production company that needed more actors for a film that they're about to start filming. And when I contacted them, they hired me. *[she sounds anxious when she says this last line]*
Evan: That's great! Then why do you look so worried?
Sarah: Well, for this job I'm going to be an extra, which is a role where I won't have to remember any lines. This won't be the first time I've been an extra, so I know that I'll be doing really normal things like walking down a busy street or sitting in a park. But I haven't been told if I'm in one or loads of scenes, so I'm a bit anxious about that. I'm not sure I want to do it if it's just one scene.
Evan: What kind of film are you going to be in? Is it one of those scary films – I love those!
Sarah: That would be nice, but no it isn't. And it isn't one of those cool action movies either – where people are jumping out of planes and driving expensive cars. It's about a really famous composer who was a celebrity in the 18th century and how he became deaf towards the end of his career.
Evan: Will you be working with any famous stars?
Sarah: Probably. Everyone wants to take photos with them, but I don't. They're there to do their job well, so I take any opportunity that I can to see how they act. I get acting tips just from watching them. Of course, I'd love to chat with movie stars, but I want to be as professional as possible.
Evan: I see. How was your last acting job?
Sarah: I was an extra for that film too, and I earned quite a lot from it. So, I can't complain that I had to arrive at work when most people were still sleeping! I guess doing the same scene over and over again is what I found most difficult. But not all directors do that.
Evan: What should I do if I want to try acting?
Sarah: Well, don't expect to get the lead role in your first film! It takes a lot of hard work to even get small jobs – like being an extra in both good and bad films. So, don't get upset if you're only getting those kinds of jobs at first, because maybe one day you will end up being a star.

Exam success Units 9–10, p148

7 ES5

Speaker: For my presentation, I'm going to talk about my favourite author. Her name's Beth Reekles and she's from Wales. She's also a blogger and a physics graduate.
When I researched this author, I learnt that she was only 11 when she found out that she loves writing stories – right after she was given her own laptop. Before then, she was just like most people her age.
When Beth was 15, her life changed forever. That's when she started writing her first novel and began posting it online onto a story-sharing online platform. Now more than 19 million people have read it, which is an incredible achievement!

137

CLASS AUDIO SCRIPT

Beth came up with her idea for her story because she was tired of reading books that she didn't like very much. So, she decided to write a novel that she would want to read. It's about friendship, typical teenage problems and the romantic relationship between two high school students. Maybe you're thinking: What's new about that? Well, the way she interacted with her readers was totally new and made a big difference.

Beth was great at encouraging people to read each new chapter of her book by uploading notes for her audience to read online. She did this so that people could see what she was thinking when she wrote new parts to the story. Readers could also post their own comments about her book, and she got many fans from this.

Another way that Beth was able to help promote her online book was to write regular posts about it. She put them online every few days to keep people interested in what was happening with her story.

Most recently, Beth sold her story so that it could be made into a film for Netflix. It's been a huge success for Netflix – and for Beth.

CLASS VIDEO SCRIPT

UNIT 1

Great Learners, Great Thinkers, p10
2 and 3 VIDEO

Narrator: Scientists know that our mental attitude can really help us as we grow old.

Chris is a middle-aged doctor. He wants to know how it feels to be old and to see how other people treat him as a senior citizen.

In just a couple of hours, he goes from being 36 to being over 80, all thanks to Hollywood-style make-up. Is this how he's really going to look one day?

Chris is interested in seeing how other people react to him, now that he looks old.

Chris: Yay!

Chris: Have we met?

Chris's dad: We might have …

Narrator: This is Chris' dad. He doesn't recognize him.

Chris: And what's it like being old?

Chris's dad: I quite like it.

Chris: Do you?

Chris's dad: Yeah.

Narrator: Finally, Chris's dad recognises his son. Chris's dad likes being old. The great news is that recent studies show that being positive can add up to seven years to your life.

But often the way we feel depends on the way other people treat us. Chris wants to see how people in the street react to him, now that he's a senior citizen!

People are happy to move away and let him go up the stairs easily.

Chris: Sorry!

Pedestrian 1: Sorry!

Narrator: Bus drivers let him cross the street. They don't get angry or shout at him. But not everybody pays attention to him! On public transport, middle-aged Chris can't always find a seat. But old Chris can! At the end of the day, Chris feels quite positive about getting old!

UNIT 2

Great Learners, Great Thinkers, p22
2 and 3 VIDEO

Narrator: Keyboards. They can be very dangerous. Hackers can use them to steal our money, our identities and our secrets.

Meet Mat Honan. Mat is a journalist who writes about new technology. He thought he was safe on the Internet. But last year he discovered he was wrong!

One day he tried to charge his phone, when suddenly he saw an unusual icon.

He connected his phone to his computer. But the screen went blue and asked for a PIN.

He knew he didn't have a PIN. He took out his tablet and the tablet asked for a password.

But his password didn't work! That's when he knew it was hackers. But what did they want? It was terrifying. In just 45 minutes, they stole his complete digital life! Mat wrote online about what happened. The hackers did something unusual. They contacted him. They wanted to tell him how they did it. How did Matt feel about that?

Mat: I was angry, I was scared, I mean I was … I was concerned, I was … I was a lot of things like that, but I also realised pretty quickly that this was an interesting story.

Narrator: So how did they do it? Easily! Mat used an online shopping service and a credit card for that service. The hackers just had to take control of his password. And that's what they did!

And that gave them access to the last four numbers of Mat's credit card number. With this information, they took control of his other accounts, even his social media.

The hackers knew about different mistakes in online security. With this knowledge, they stole someone's digital life – and they were just teenagers.

UNIT 3

Great Learners, Great Thinkers, p36
2a, 2b and 3 VIDEO

Narrator: How do animals communicate? And is animal communication the same as language?

At Port Lympne Reserve in the UK, we can observe many different types of animal communication.

In the animal world, we have birds singing, meerkats making whistling sounds when there's danger, elephants using their trunks to call each other, dolphins clicking to indicate food.

And primates? Their communication seems a little more complex.

They can make different sounds to express fear, joy, even love. But it's still a long way from human communication.

Presenter: They're so closely related and yet so completely different. And I think it is language that's the thing that's most different about us.

Narrator: Professor Michael Tomasello studies animals and their ability to communicate. Like many people, he agrees that language is what separates humans from other animals.

But is it possible that primates can learn a language? Professor Tomasello thinks the key difference between us and primates is that they only communicate the emotions they feel at that moment. If they're frightened, they make one sound, if they're excited, they make another. In contrast with humans, their communication is quite limited and inflexible.

And another problem for primates is they don't have all the necessary muscles in their faces to make sounds like we do.

But they can make signs – very successfully, in fact! If only they could say a few words too!

CLASS VIDEO SCRIPT

UNIT 4

Great Learners, Great Thinkers, p48
2a and 2b VIDEO ▶

Narrator: Have you ever wondered why so many people have allergies today?
Professor Syed Hassan Arshad has studied allergies in Britain for many years.
He has discovered that the number of people with allergic diseases is going up. Asthma affected about 1% of children in the 1950s. But now it affects between 10 and 12%.
Nowadays, between 25 and 30% of people in the UK suffer from some type of allergy, including asthma, hay fever and food allergies.
Statistics show that the risk of allergies is higher in more developed countries such as the UK, Australia, Italy and America. And people like Professor Syed Hassan Arshad are looking for the reasons why.
Maybe it's because of city life or perhaps our lifestyle in general, but one in three of us are becoming allergic.
Professor Graham Rook believes that microorganisms like bacteria and fungi could explain why allergies are increasing.
Even when we think we are alone in our environment, we never are because microorganisms are absolutely everywhere. You can't see them, of course, but the air is full of bacteria – particularly when there are animals nearby. And these bacteria are healthy and part of the natural world.
The problem is that modern life is separating us from these microorganisms and bacteria. We live in a world of metal, and glass, and air-conditioning – and this kind of world doesn't give our bodies a chance to live with natural bacteria.
Is it possible that this separation from the natural world is the reason why the number of people with allergies is going up?

UNIT 5

Great Learners, Great Thinkers, p62
2 VIDEO ▶

Narrator: Today 13- to 24 -year-olds spend more time online than watching TV. YouTube videos have become more and more popular and have changed the way that people watch TV.
Many famous YouTubers like Charlie McDonnell started off by filming themselves in their bedrooms.
Charlie: No, I don't think I'm number one YouTube person at all. I mean there was a point in my life where I was the most watched person in the UK. It's a bit mad.
Narrator: YouTubers like Charlie know exactly who their audience is because YouTube provides them with extremely detailed information.
Charlie: 72.6% of my viewers are female. Forty-five percent of those girls fit into the 13- to 17-year-old category.
Narrator: One interesting thing about online video is that it is a dialogue. People who watch the videos communicate directly with the people who make the videos. They tell them what they like and what they don't like.
YouTube created a big new studio in London to help young YouTubers to take their videos to the next level ... instead of just filming in their bedrooms.
But the space doesn't look like a traditional TV studio. It's more like a playground for these YouTubers to hang out together and have fun.
So why has YouTube created a place like this?
Chris(YouTuber): This place has been really good to get everyone to come together and make bigger stuff 'cos I think everybody knows, like, animators and musicians and stuff ...
Narrator: But what about the quality of online video?
When TV began it was about educating and informing, not just entertaining. Now, with online video, you don't have to follow those rules. You can watch what you want, when you want. But is what you want always good for you?

UNIT 6

Great Learners, Great Thinkers, p74
2 and 3 VIDEO ▶

Narrator: The south eastern coast of Spain. It's a beautiful place, but very dry. In fact, it's the driest area in Europe and home to its only desert.
There are few people or buildings in this region.
The temperatures can get up to 50 degrees Celsius, and there is little rain.
Presenter: You would think nothing could grow here, but you'd be wrong.
Narrator: Let's go up in the air now and find out how exactly it's possible to grow anything in such a difficult environment.
Presenter: Ah, it's wonderful!
Narrator: From high up here, you can't see any fruit or vegetables ... In fact, there's plastic everywhere you look!
Presenter: Right out to the base of the mountains, almost, almost touching the Mediterranean down at the coast, right out as far over there as I can see in the distance. This is Europe's market garden.
Narrator: But what is the impact of these plastic greenhouses on the environment?
It's easy to see that the beauty of this area is in danger. And here, as we get closer to the sea, we can see how big the problem of plastic really is. These men are examining plastic – plastic that is now part of the earth and the ground.
And where does this plastic come from? The greenhouses, the market garden.
From here, it's just a small step to the sea. And when this plastic breaks into small parts, it will end up in the ocean and inside fish and other sea life.

The Mediterranean holds 7% of the world's plastic waste. And this gets into our food and into our drinking water.

These plastic gardens offer Europe cheap fruit and vegetables. But at what cost? Will the price be too high for the environment?

UNIT 7

Great Learners, Great Thinkers, p88
2 and 3 VIDEO

Narrator: Meet Jess Wheeler. She's 25. She's an illustrator, and she lives right here, next to a river, in Suffolk.

She sleeps in one tent and lives and works in the other. It's very different from her old life in London! With little space indoors, she has to live with only the things she really needs.

Eighteen-year-old Zeki Basan also lives with very little. The Highlands of Scotland are his playground and his office. He teaches survival courses where he shows we don't need as much as we think.

He can live for days, weeks, even months with just the things he carries in his backpack. This too is a very different life from the nine to five of working in the city.

Take food, for example. He doesn't have to spend any money because he eats what he catches and finds. And he cooks it by making fire in the old traditional way.

Back by the river, a new day is beginning for Jess. After preparing and eating a simple breakfast, it's time for work. Without the distractions of the Internet or other people, she has more time to be creative. She draws illustrations for magazines, menus and invitations, plus animal portraits.

Like Jess, Zeki is happy to be without the Internet or screens. He believes people are addicted to them. But is that what life is really about?

You mustn't forget what is really beautiful, what you really should enjoy.

In fact, Zeki is happier without modern gadgets and without modern materials.

He uses the bark from trees and the skins of animals to produce soft, natural leather. And with this leather, he makes different types of objects and products and then he sells them.

So, live and work in the city or in the great outdoors like Zeki and Jess?

UNIT 8

Great Learners, Great Thinkers, p100
2 and 3 VIDEO

Narrator: Playgrounds can, at times, be very lonely places. But these buddy benches, also known as friendship benches, can help children to find a friend.

Boy 1: For people like ... who [um] are alone and if you go over to them and say hi.

Boy 2: You can sit down on it and wait for someone to ask you if they wanna play with you.

Narrator: Benches like this are not new in schools. But in Ireland they are trying to do something different with them.

This is the 247th school to receive a bench. But the important thing is not just the bench.

The school uses the bench to start important conversations about well-being. They discuss the importance of students being aware of their own feelings and the feelings of others. And they practise helping others.

School principal: The children need to understand what the bench is about.

Narrator: The bench is a symbol of friendship, inclusion, listening to each other and, above all, the importance of expressing feelings.

Independent expert: We found that 40% of the children told us that they had actually used the benches at the time of the study. And over 90% said that they would talk to a child if that child was sitting on the bench. So, certainly there doesn't appear to be any issues around stigma.

Narrator: Nowadays, many countries are paying special attention to student well-being at school.

Who knows? Perhaps this simple idea of having buddy benches in playgrounds will help to stop loneliness and also give future generations the confidence to open up and express their feelings. That's something that will certainly help them as adults too.

UNIT 9

Great Learners, Great Thinkers, p114
2 and 3 VIDEO

Narrator: William Golding's *Lord of the Flies* is a classic novel. Since it first appeared in the 1950s, the book has had many different covers. Many designs have been colourful, some more basic and others quite scary, to reflect the book's plot.

Now, William Golding's daughter, Judy, is a judge in an exciting new competition for teenagers.

The aim of the competition is to create a new cover for the book. They need to show the main themes of the story, which is about a group of children living alone on a desert island.

Looking at the teenagers' work, Judy thinks that they have really understood the message of the novel.

Real books in a real bookshop. Today many people are buying ebooks instead. But real books have something that ebooks don't – covers.

And in this bookshop, most customers prefer buying traditional books with attractive, well-designed covers.

Bookshop customer: I like the tactile feel of a book and the whole, I don't know, magic of a book. So, I can't make that ... that emotional step to ebooks.

Narrator: Neil Gower is a professional artist and designer of book covers. He's working on a new cover now.

CLASS VIDEO SCRIPT

Neil Gower: I cannot imagine a world without physical books.
Narrator: He thinks covers in the future may turn books into beautiful art objects.
Neil hopes that physical books with their beautifully illustrated covers will be with us for many years to come!

UNIT 10

Great Learners, Great Thinkers, p126
2 and 3 [VIDEO ▶]

Narrator: At Cambridge University they are working on something quite extraordinary. They're teaching computers to read human feelings!
To do this, the computer needs to learn how to analyse our body movements, because this can give it clues about how we feel.
Speaker: You can decode this kind of body language 'cause you've learnt over years and years and years to read people but computers haven't. They have no idea about this stuff.
Narrator: To teach the machines how to decode our feelings, they concentrate on the most expressive part of our body – the face.
Speaker: The computer is literally trying to read my mind, telling me what I'm feeling just from my expressions!
Narrator: It produces a graph to show our mental state. It concentrates on the person's mouth, eyes and eyebrows. It learns that nodding your head and smiling at the same time usually means the person is agreeing with something.
Speaker: And I'm getting … yeah! I'm getting good agreement scores.
Narrator: The computer also identifies interest. Psychologists have identified 412 emotions for the computer to learn. But even then, some of our expressions can seem ambiguous. For example, opening your mouth could express surprise or happiness. The difference is the colour inside your mouth.
Speaker: I can see machines are becoming a bit more human. Wouldn't it be great if they really knew when you were angry with them? Or shocked?
Narrator: And what if computers could show human emotions? The presenter is going to try to understand what Charles the robot is feeling.
So what is he feeling here? Pain or frustration? Perhaps a combination of both.
But the next emotion is more complex. Disgust? No, the robot was actually demonstrating arrogance. It just shows how difficult the interaction between humans and computers really is.

Macmillan Education Limited
4 Crinan Street
London N1 9XW

Companies and representatives throughout the world

Gateway to the World B1 Teacher's Book
ISBN 978-1-380-04273-6
Gateway to the World B1 Teacher's Book with Teacher's App ISBN 978-1-380-04271-2

Text, design and illustration © Macmillan Education Limited 2021
Written by Tim Foster

The author has asserted their right to be identified as the author of this work in accordance with the Copyright, Designs and Patents Act 1988.

This edition published 2021
First edition entitled "Gateway" published 2011 by Macmillan Education Limited

All rights reserved. No part of this publication may be reproduced, stored in a retrieval system, or transmitted in any form or by any means, electronic, mechanical, photocopying, recording, or otherwise, without the prior written permission of the publishers.

Original design by EMC Design Ltd
Page make-up by SPi Global
Cover design by Designers Educational
Picture research by EMC Design Ltd

The author and publishers would like to thank the following for permission to reproduce their photographs:
Alamy/Dimitar Gorgev p3 (classroom); **Getty Images**/Barcroft Media/ Contributor p10 (9), Getty Images/d3sign p3, (br), p4 (tr), Getty Images/DenisTangneyJr p10 (2), Getty Images/Gary Hershorn/Contributor p10 (7), Getty Images/hudiemm p5 (tablet), Getty Images/George Karbus Photography p2 (cr), Getty Images/KTSDESIGN/SCIENCE PHOTO LIBRARY p10 (3), Getty Images/matejmo p10 (10) Getty Images Ian McKinnell p10 (5), Getty Images/mgkaya p4-5 (laptop), Getty Images/MOIRENC Camille/hemis. fr p10 (6), Getty Images/NurPhoto/Contributor p2 (br), Getty Images/reserved Light Photography p6 (b), Getty Images/Pete Rowbottom p10 (1), Getty Images/Vostok p10 (8), Getty Images/Wavebreakmedia p3 (classroom screen inset), Getty Images/Trevor Williams p10 (4); **Macmillan Education Limited**/p4 (B1 Gateway to the World Student's Book cover), Macmillan Education Limited/p4 (B1 Gateway to the World Workbook cover), Macmillan Education Limited/p4 (Secret Garden Reader cover), Macmillan Education Limited/asiseeit p6 (t)

Commissioned photograph by Pepe Sánchez Moreno p8

Video footage and stills supplied by Fortemus Films Ltd. p3 (tr), (cr), Red Hill Media Ltd. p3 (cl), Digeo Productions Ltd. (vloggers video still) p3 (bl)

The author and publishers are grateful for permission to reprint the following copyright material:
p65: Rebecca Lindsey, 'Climate Change: Global Sea Level', NOAA (2019), Climate.gov
p98: Isaac Asimov, Letters to the Children of Troy, Troy Public Library (2017)

Additional sources:
p59, p129: Sarah Goodyear 'The Binge-watching Life', OnePoll (March, 2019), https://www.onepoll.com
p69, p130: 'Public Anger over Government's Lack of Action on Britain's Litter Epidemic', Blue & Green Tomorrow (December, 2015), http://blueandgreentomorrow.com
p86: Aike C. Horstmann, Nikolai Bock, Eva Linhuber, Jessica M. Szczuka, Carolin Straßmann, Nicole C. Krämer, 'Do a Robot's Social Skills And Its Objection Discourage Interactants from Switching the Robot Off?', PLoS ONE, 13.7 (July 2018), https://doi.org/10.1371/journal.pone.0201581
p108 (act 2c, items 1, 4 and 7), p134 (audio 75): Jeff Desjardins, 'What Happens in an Internet Minute in 2018?', Visual Capitalist (May 2018), https://www.visualcapitalist.com
p108 (act 2c, item 2), p134 (audio 75): 'Lightning', National Geographic, https://www.nationalgeographic.com
p108 (act 2c, item 3), p134 (audio 75):

Jennifer Hussein, '50 Mouthwatering Facts About Pizza', *Eat This, Not That!* (October 2019), https://www.eatthis.com

p108 (act 2c, items 5 and 9), p134 (audio 75): 'A London Minute', *Barratt London*, https://www.barratthomes.co.uk

p108 (act 2c, item 6), 134 (audio 75): Phil Haigh, 'How Many Sharks Are Killed Each Year And How Many Humans Are Killed by Sharks?', *Metro* (7 August 2018)

p108 (act 2c, item 8), p134 (audio 75): Sandra Laville & Matthew Taylor, 'A Million Bottles a Minute: World's Plastic Binge ''as Dangerous as Climate Change''', *The Guardian* (28 June 2017)

p125: YouGov, Apology Survey © YouGov plc. (2015), yougov.co.uk

Alexa is a trademark of Amazon which does not sponsor, authorize or endorse this publication.

BBC, DOCTOR WHO, DALEK and TARDIS (word marks, logos & devices) are trademarks of the British Broadcasting Corporation which does not sponsor, authorize or endorse this publication.

Cortana is a trademark of Microsoft which does not sponsor, authorize or endorse this publication.

Disney/Pixar, Disneyland and Marvel are all trademarks of Disney which does not sponsor, authorize or endorse this publication.

Eyeforcer is a trademark of Medical Wearable Solutions which does not sponsor, authorise or endorse this publication.

Facebook is a trademark of Facebook which does not sponsor, authorize or endorse this publication.

Frida Kahlo is a trademark of the Frida Kahlo Corporation which does not sponsor, authorize or endorse this publication.

Google Assistant and Google are trademarks of Google which does not sponsor, authorize or endorse this publication.

Hulu is a trademark of Hulu, LLC which does not sponsor, authorise or endorse this publication.

Kahoot! and the K! logo are trademarks of Kahoot! AS.

Messenger is a trademark of Facebook which does not sponsor, authorize or endorse this publication.

Minecraft is a trademark of Mojang Synergies AB which does not sponsor, authorize or endorse this publication.

Nintendo is a trademark of Nintendo which does not sponsor, authorise or endorse this publication.

Nobel Prize is a trademark of the Nobel Foundation which does not sponsor, authorize or endorse this publication.

Persil is a trademark of Unilever which does not sponsor, authorise or endorse this publication.

Siri is a trademark of Apple Inc. which does not sponsor, authorize or endorse this publication.

Spotify is a trademark of Spotify which does not sponsor, authorize or endorse this publication.

Sony is a trademark of Sony Corporation, Japan, which does not sponsor, authorise or endorse this publication.

STAR TREK is a trademark of CBS Studios Inc. which does not sponsor, authorize or endorse this publication.

Star Wars is a trademark of Lucasfilm Ltd which does not sponsor, authorize or endorse this publication.

The Olympic Games are a trademark of The International Olympic Committee which does not sponsor, authorize or endorse this publication.

TM DOLMIO, UNCLE BEN'S MARS are Trademarks of Mars, Incorporated and its affiliates which do not sponsor, authorize or endorse this publication.

Twitter is a trademark of Twitter Inc. which does not sponsor, authorize or endorse this publication.

YouTube is a trademark of Google which does not sponsor, authorize or endorse this publication.

Full acknowledgements for illustrations and photographs in the facsimile pages can be found in the Student's Book ISBN 978-1-380-03097-9 and in the Workbook ISBN 978-1-380-04272-9.

These materials may contain links for third party websites. We have no control over, and are not responsible for, the contents of such third party websites. Please use care when accessing them.

The inclusion of any specific companies, commercial products, trade names or otherwise does not constitute or imply its endorsement or recommendation by Macmillan Education Limited.

Printed and bound in Spain

2027 2026 2025 2024 2023
32 31 30 29 28 27 26